MW01489486

AUTHORITY IN SEARCH OF LIBERTY

The series SCRINIUM,
Monographs on history, archaeology, and art history,
is published under the auspices of
The Dutch Institute in Rome
and
*The Foundation of Friends of the
Dutch Institute in Rome*

Editorial Board: Joh.S. Boersma, F.W.N. Hugenholtz,
Th.J. Meijer, R.W. Scheller

SCRINIUM VII

AUTHORITY IN SEARCH OF LIBERTY

The Prefects in Liberal Italy

Nico Randeraad

THESIS PUBLISHERS
AMSTERDAM 1993

The publication of this book was made possible by the funds from
the Dutch Institute in Rome and the European University Institute in Florence

CIP-DATA KONINKLIJKE BIBLIOTHEEK, DEN HAAG

Randeraad, Nico

Authority in Search of Liberty : the Prefects in Liberal
Italy / Nico Randeraad. - Amsterdam : Thesis Publishers.
- Tab. - (Scrinium ; 7)
With ref.
ISBN 90-5170-218-3 bound
NUGI 641
Subject headings: municipal government ; Italy ; history /
Italy ; political history.

© Nico Randeraad 1993

All rights reserved. Save exceptions stated by the law no part of this publication may
be reproduced, stored in a retrieval system of any nature, or transmitted in any form
or by means, electronic, mechanical, photocopying, recording or otherwise, included
a complete or partial transcription, without the prior written permission of the
publisher (copyright holder), application for which should be adressed to the
publisher. Thesis Publishers, P.O.Box 14791, 1001 LG Amsterdam, the Netherlands.

In so far as it is permitted to make copies from this publication under the provisions
of article 16B and 17 of the Autuerswet 1912 (Copyright Act), you are obliged to
make the payments required by the law to the Stichting Reprorecht (Repro Law
Founadation) P.O.Box 882, 1180 AW Amstelveen, the Netherlands. To use part of this
publication in anthologies, readers and other compilations (article 16 Auteurswet
1912) your are obliged to contact to the publisher.

ISBN   90-5170-218-3 bound
ISSN   0929-6980
NUGI 641

Parentibus

Table of contents

List of tables

List of abbreviations

ACS	Archivio Centrale dello Stato
all.	allegato
AP	Atti parlamentari
Arch. Gen.	Archivio Generale
ASB	Archivio di Stato di Bologna
ASRC	Archivio di Stato di Reggio Calabria
ASV	Archivio di Stato di Venezia
b.	busta
cat.	categoria
f.	fascicolo
Gab.	Gabinetto
legisl.	legislatura
MAIC	Ministeri di Agricoltura, Industria e Commercio
Min. Int.	Ministero dell'Interno
Pref.	Prefettura
RAR	Rivista Amministrativa del Regno
R.D.	Regio Decreto
RTDP	Rivista Trimestrale di Diritto Pubblico
sc.	scatola
Sen.	Senato
sess.	sessione
s.f.	sottofascicolo

Preface

Administration is a slow-moving river, filled with relics of its past. Yet these often remain invisible to the spectator by the waterside. While on the surface curious objects sometimes attract his attention, the unstoppable undercurrents smooth the pebblestones that slowly roll along the bottom. As the river flows on, it gathers strength and volume from a thousand tributaries. Some of them are large enough to speed up the flow, but not for long. The river gradually broadens out, which once again slows down its flow. The public administration that came with the Unification of Italy in 1861 was not a new phenomenon. Neither its centralized organization nor its intervention in society were complete novelties. In many parts of Europe the Napoleonic period had given administrative modernization a decisive spur. Although some Italian states of the Restoration claimed to have revived their prerevolutionary administrative traditions, the results corresponded remarkably with the French innovations. Therefore, one of the biggest challenges facing the new state, unified in name but torn by internal contrasts, was not so much the choice of administrative system but rather its implementation in an unresponsive society. It is the conflict-ridden confrontation between the old and the new – like a large tributary suddenly reaching the main stream – that constitutes the underlying problem of this study.

This book is a somewhat enlarged version of my doctoral thesis defended in May 1992 at the European University Institute in Florence. The revision chiefly entailed the addition of a chapter on the European context of my theme. The central problem, the treatment of the sources and the conclusions have remained the same.

The sources used for this research are varied. As always in historiography, the research was considerably influenced by the availability of material. The Italian public administration has been a rather careless custodian of its own history. There are large lacunae in the central archives of the Ministry of the Interior. For instance, most material belonging to the ministerial cabinet and the directorate of civil administration have not survived war and random destruction. The archives of the selected prefectures, therefore, form the main body of sources. But these archives have shortcomings too. Only the prefectural papers preserved in the state archive of Reggio Calabria have a systematic inventory. Those preserved in Bologna are arranged according to the original filing system (which in its turn, as I found, was not very strictly followed). Rearrangement has begun but proceeds very slowly. The prefectural archives of Venice are spread over two depots. The most important papers – those belonging to the cabinet – cover only the period up to 1887, and are practically inaccessible, since their arrangement follows nineteenth-century filing methods which changed every five years. Moreover the list of available dossiers mentions only the category numbers according to which the material is arranged. Their actual contents had to be reconstructed by consulting several dossiers of each category. For these reasons the archival references in the footnotes are different for each prefecture and seem to lack consistency.

One objection to the use of such sources could be that reports and letters of prefects and their staff present a rather one-sided view of the world that surrounded them. The prefectural archives, however, contain much more than the written products of the prefectural offices. Apart from documents of all administrative levels many dossiers include letters of private citizens, books and copies of newspapers and journals. Whereas the prefects may have used this material solely from their point of view, I have tried to take a more detached view of it. I hope that this study contributes to a greater awareness, among historians and archivists, of the richness and importance of the prefectural archives.

I have been helped by more people than I can name here. In 1985 Guido Melis introduced me to the world of administration – a world that I have continued to explore ever since. Stuart Woolf, my supervisor at the European University Institute, gave me the opportunity to modify a research project already in progress, urging me not to be afraid of 'broad questions'. At a later stage he generously offered me his assistance in practical matters, sometimes down to the smallest detail. From the start Sabino Cassese has followed my research with true interest. I am greatly indebted to Enrico Gustapane, who furnished me with many details of the inner workings of public administration in Italy today and in the past. I want to thank Raffaele Romanelli who in a few conversations managed to put my research on the right track. Jaap van Osta, Gjalt Zondergeld and Henk van Dijk kindly read the manuscript and made valuable suggestions. The remaining mistakes are, of course, entirely mine. Sander Kollaard never turned me down, when I wanted to make use of his computer facilities. I am grateful to the staff of the Italian archives and libraries I visited during my research. I particularly thank the European University Institute, the Dutch Ministry of Education and the Dutch Institute in Rome, which funded my research at various stages. The Dutch Institute and European University Institute also subsidized this publication. Throughout this study my wife Patricia Lulof continued to encourage me, despite the many mountains that were between us during too many periods of separation. Our daughter Sarah was born, when the first chapter of the thesis had barely been written. Her presence made it easy to write the other chapters and finish it before her first birthday. I am proud to say, now that our second child Daniel is born, that the thesis has turned into a real book.

Chapter 1

Administration between state and society in post-Napoleonic Europe

1 THE PRIMACY OF THE STATE

This study is a comparison of the workings of three Italian prefectures (Venice, Bologna and Reggio Calabria) in the liberal period, confined here to the years 1861-1895. Its main focus is on the prefect's control of municipal government, local finance and parliamentary elections – basic aspects of modern public administration. To find a certain balance between control and local selfgovernment was the underlying challenge to the process of administrative modernization in continental Europe, set in motion by the offensive of French armies, officials and ideas during the revolutionary and Napoleonic period. In the first half of the nineteenth century, under the influence of the revolutionary-Napoleonic model, administrative control acquired both an educational and an authoritarian connotation. The state allowed local government a sphere of its own and helped to expand it, but at the same time tied local government down to uniform rules and regulations. This duality – the twin faces of 'good administration' – developed out of the constant sense of the need for a strong link between state and society that characterized the desires of most ruling elites in continental Europe. It is my purpose to show that the notion of 'good administration' made itself felt in the wide array of activities of the Italian prefects after Unification.

Historians have often conceptualized the long-term impact of the French Revolution and Napoleon's reign over Europe in terms of a lasting division between state and civil society. The king lost his divine aura and became first servant in a more abstract state; society was no longer dominated by corporate associations and estates, but consisted of free individuals. Napoleon himself strongly believed that, if the appropriate administrative structures were created, the state would be able to remodel society. He thereby elaborated on the idea of French civilization, which had gained much ground before and during the revolutionary years in Europe.[1] First, a new relationship between state and society was to be established, based on the growing participation of citizens; second, a new concept of political nation was to arise, eliminating local and popular practices; and third, the way would be cleared for a

---

1   S.J. Woolf, 'French Civilization and Ethnicity in the Napoleonic Empire', *Past and Present* (1989), n. 124, 96-120.

new social and economic order, built on the development of the individual and the free market.[2] Put in such wide terms, the division of state and society, one could argue, had already been prepared by political theory since the middle of the eighteenth century, and to some extent it emerged in the practices of government under the Old Regime. Nevertheless, the watershed clearly lay in the years arond 1800. The antagonism of state and society has been a major theme in German historiography, but one finds echoes in many European countries, not least in Italy, where the dichotomy between *paese legale* and *paese reale* is still widely debated. The changing relationship between state and society is thus a logical starting-point for a social history of administrative change in the nineteenth century.

My purpose is not to offer yet another contribution to the major theoretical and historical debate about state-society relations, but to use the divergence of state and society in the nineteenth-century (continental) European context as the broader and longer-term context of the role of the prefects in postunitary Italy. The social and economic backwardness of Italy, which lasted throughout the century, and the moderate political aims of the Italian ruling class after Unification, make it necessary to go back to the first half of the century in order to find comparable practices in government and administration.

Few historians would deny that the state played an important role in the political and economic modernization of continental Europe in the first half of the nineteenth century. As representative bodies (with the exception of England) were still in a weak position, reforms were largely dependent on state bureaucracies, not only for their implementation but also for their design. Even if most absolute regimes had a more or less well-developed administrative apparatus, the major thrust towards a centrally led, hierarchically organized bureaucracy came with the Revolution and Napoleon. This was acknowledged by most contemporaries, including Tocqueville in one of his perspicacious but lesser known writings: 'The French Revolution, which has introduced so many novelties in the world, has not created anything newer than that part of political law that is concerned with administration in the strict sense of the word. Here, nothing is like what came before; almost everything is of recent date: functions as well as officials, obligations as well as guarantees. But newer than anything else is the systematic order which underlies this vast organization, and the rigorous and logical chain of command which makes one body out of all its parts'.[3]

After the collapse of the Empire, the Napoleonic project left a lasting imprint on the administrative structure of the Restoration monarchies.[4] This structure made rapid and efficient action possible. Through administration the state could and did actively intervene in such divergent fields as poor relief, education, agriculture, industry,

---

2   S.J. Woolf, *Napoleon's Integration of Europe* (London, 1991), 10-12.
3   A. de Tocqueville, 'Rapport fait à l'Académie des Sciences Morales et Politiques (1846) sur le livre de M. Macarel, intitulé: *Cours de droit administratif*, in: Id., *Oeuvres complètes*, XVI, *Mélanges* (Paris, 1989), 186.
4   S.J. Woolf, *Napoleon's Integration*, especially chapter 6, 'The Heritage', 238-245.

commerce and even constitutional legislation. However, as much as under Napoleon, there were obvious social constraints upon the unbridled exertion of state power. On the one hand, the social organization that had existed in feudal or patrimonial areas of Europe with its numerous centres and peripheries was difficult to reconcile with the hierarchical structure of the Napoleonic model, which imposed an executive chain linking the centre alone with a multiplicity of subordinate and – administratively speaking – uniform peripheries. On the other hand, the demands of the emerging middle classes often went futher than the administrative monarchies of the Restoration were prepared to go, which eventually led to the revolutions of 1830 and 1848. What were the main cleavages between state and society that arose in the Restoration states? Our understanding of the development in Germany has long been dominated by the thesis of the partial or defensive modernization of Prussia in the first half of the nineteenth century. R. Koselleck's interpretation (reduced to its bare essence) is that the Prussian bureaucracy, initially keen on bringing about massive social and economic reforms, soon retired into its shell, and after 1815, rather than furthering a constitution and parliamentary institutions, set itself against a more general modernization.[5] Instead of allowing the rising liberal bourgeoisie to participate in political life, the state officials set themselves up as the representatives of society. As early as 1819 the Prussian minister Beyme asserted that the administration 'was ordered in such a way, that it brought about the same results as were ascribed to representative bodies in other states'.[6] In short, administrative reform came before constitutional reform.

The economic achievements of Prussian bureaucratic rule are well-known. They were, contrary to the assertions of an older historiography, less visible in industrialization, which in the first decades of the nineteenth century was still in an infant stage and limited to the western provinces. Agrarian reforms, including the abolition of serfdom, the division of common lands, the end of collective cultivation, etc., were more drastic and encroached deeply upon rural society. It is commonly held that the Prussian bureaucracy played a leading role in these reforms, which created the legal framework for the promotion of capitalist agriculture.

The role of the bureaucracy was different in the south German states. It has been shown that state building in Prussia, where social and economic reforms were preferred to constitutional concessions, sharply contrasted with that in south German states, such as Bavaria, Baden and Württemberg, where constitutionalism gained the upper hand over social and economic policies.[7] In a first phase the reforms in Southern Germany, strongly guided by the Napoleonic model, were carried through

---

5 R. Koselleck, *Preußen zwischen Reform und Revolution: Allgemeines Landrecht, Verwaltung und soziale Bewegung von 1791 bis 1848* (Stuttgart, 1967, 3rd ed. 1981).

6 Cited by B. Vogel, 'Beamtenliberalismus in der Napoleonischen Ära', in: D. Langewiesche (ed.), *Liberalismus im 19. Jahrhundert. Deutschland im europäischen Vergleich* (Göttingen, 1988), 50.

7 J. Breuilly, 'State-Building, Modernization and Liberalism from the Late Eighteenth Century to Unification; German Peculiarities', *European History Quarterly* 22 (1992), 257-284, with many references.

by a strongly state-orientated bureaucracy.[8] The emphasis was on the installation of a small number of professional ministries and a centrally led administration penetrating the intermediate and local level. But much more than in Prussia – and this became all the more clear after the collapse of the Napoleonic empire – the political reforms in Bavaria, Württemberg and Baden went beyond a mere reorganization of the state. Abolishing the existing administrative entities and the powers of the old corporations, reformers like Montgelas in Bavaria and Reitzenstein in Baden paved the way for a new relationship between state and society. Once the old order had been erased, the state allowed itself to recede slowly and granted the gradual introduction of participation and representation. The south German states, therefore, did not fall back on some sort of 'state absolutism', but entered the Restoration era with a genuine constitution (or promulgated one shortly after 1815).[9]

Although Baden's political importance among the Restoration states should not be overrated, its constitutional development in the *Vormärz* period is in many ways exemplary of the opportunities and limits of liberals in action. Taking their cue from the reforms and reform plans of the years 1806-08, the constitutionalists in Baden first sought to consolidate the state as it had emerged from the Napoleonic era. Claims of the aristocracy to restore old privileges were resolutely turned down. The state bureaucracy, imbued with a strong liberal spirit, continued to play a leading role. The constitution of 1818 was the work of a group of non-noble officials led by Nebenius and Winter. Throughout the first half of the nineteenth century on average 50% of Baden's parliament, the *Landtag*, consisted of officials.[10] Liberalism in Baden, thus, originated from the heart of the state.[11] The fundamental political problem was not, as in Prussia, the promulgation of a constitution, but the further development of constitutional principles. Winter and Nebenius were well aware of the need to change the old agrarian legislation, to open up the ranks of the bureaucratic hierarchy, to settle the relations between church and state, and so on. However, the capacity of this civil service liberalism to adapt to social change and to put its ideas into practice was limited. The only real reform that was carried through was, perhaps not surprisingly, the communal law of 1831 – again an organizational administrative innovation, not a major economic reform.[12] Equality of citizenship within and between communities,

---

8   In this paragraph I follow the acute analysis of P. Nolte, *Staatsbildung als Gesellschaftsreform. Politische Reformen in Preußen und den süddeutschen Staaten 1800-1820* (Frankfurt/New York, 1990).

9   E. Fehrenbach, 'Verfassungs- und sozialpolitische Reformen und Reformprojekte in Deutschland unter dem Einfluß des napoleonischen Frankreich', in H. Berding & H.-P. Ullmann, *Deutschland zwischen Revolution und Restauration* (Düsseldorf, 1981), 65-90; E. Weis, *Deutschland und Frankreich um 1800: Aufklärung, Revolution, Reform* (Munich, 1990).

10   W. Fischer, 'Staat und Gesellschaft Badens in Vormärz', in: W. Conze (ed.), *Staat und Gesellschaft im deutschen Vormärz 1815-1848*, 2nd ed. (Stuttgart, 1970), 143-171, especially 146.

11   On this theme, L.E. Lee, *The Politics of Harmony. Civil Service, Liberalism, and Social Reform in Baden, 1800-1850* (Newark, 1980).

12   L. Gall, *Der Liberalismus als regierende Partei. Das Großherzogtum Baden zwischen Restauration und Reichsgründung* (Wiesbaden, 1968), 47-48.

a large electorate, a considerable degree of selfgovernment, and limited legal control by higher authorities were the main elements of this law. At the time it was widely acknowledged that in all Europe Baden had the most liberal organization of munici-pal government.[13]

France, as it was left by Napoleon, was just as afraid of a return of the Old Regime as of the chaos and despotism of the Revolutionary period. The constitutional monarchy, therefore, maintained Napoleon's centralized administrative organization in order to consolidate the new regime. A political justification and adaptation was offered by the doctrinaire liberals, a loose but influential group led by Royer-Collard, Guizot and others. They saw the atomization of society as the most important outcome of the Revolution. It was their conviction that traditional associations and the local or regional centres of aristocratic society had disappeared in order to make way for, on the one hand, free citizens within a single society and on the other, a strengthened central government. They accepted the irreversibility of social change, which had come to light so dramatically in the foregoing years, and adopted centrali-zation as their means of guiding society to progress. The political problem to be solved was how to reach a certain balance between local autonomy and state power, between the periphery and the centre. The liberals in power did not want the state to withdraw but, on the contrary, approved of a strong state in order to win over the notables to their rule. That is why they saw no contradiction in the liberties granted by the Charter of 1814, including limited suffrage, and administrative centrali-zation.[14]

Recent French historical research has emphasized the central importance of Guizot *cum suis* in Restoration politics.[15] He saw representative government as the most effective weapon against the excesses of both revolution and counter-revolution. It was, together with a uniformly organized administrative structure, the most direct link between state and society: 'It is characteristic of the representative system – and that is also its greatest advantage – that it incessantly reveals society to its govern-ment and to itself, and government to itself and to society'.[16] Political capacity, in Guizot's definition 'the ability to act according to reason', was the cornerstone of this notion of representative government. Although strictly speaking capacity entailed

---

13 It is in this respect quite telling that the law was extensively discussed in an authoritative international review of the period: see Moerdes, 'Loi sur l'organisation et l'administration des communes dans le grand duché de Bade, en date du 31 décembre 1831', *Revue étrangère et française de législation et d'économie politique*, 2 (1835), 1-31.

14 L. Siedentop, 'Two Liberal Traditions', in A. Ryan (ed.), *The Idea of Freedom. Essays in Honour of Isaiah Berlin* (Oxford, 1979), 153-174, especially 160-168. P. Rosanvallon, 'Etat et société (du XIXe siècle à nos jours)', in: *L'Etat et les pouvoirs*, edited by J. Le Goff (Paris, 1989), 491-617, especially 505.

15 Cf. P. Rosanvallon, *Le moment Guizot* (Paris, 1985); G. de Broglie, *Guizot* (Paris, 1990); *François Guizot et la culture politique de son temps*, Colloque de la Fondation Guizot-Val Richter, edited by M. Valensise (Paris, 1991).

16 Cited by P. Rosanvallon, 'Guizot et la question du suffrage universel au XIXe siècle', in: *François Guizot et la culture politique de son temps*, 136.

more than the right to vote, the connection was evident: only those who had certain property qualifications or could prove a certain educational level were entitled to vote. This electoral principle had lasting consequences, outside France as well. Even if universal suffrage was introduced in 1848 in France, the heyday of the *régime censitaire* was still to come in the Netherlands, Belgium, Piedmont and later Italy, and other countries.

2 THE ORGANIZATION OF LOCAL ADMINISTRATION

So far state and society have been treated as rather abstract concepts, almost detached from reality. I have discussed the change in their relationship after the fall of the absolute monarchy in order to create a context for the analysis of the concrete workings of public administration, which in the course of the nineteenth century acquired such a crucial position between state and society. On the one hand, in most European nation-states centralization and uniformity were accentuated, giving continued impetus to the growth of bureaucracy. On the other hand, the liberal ruling classes sought ways to increase participation. Tocqueville was one of the first to emphasize the delicate relationship between politics and administration: 'What should one do (...) to reconcile modern administrative institutions with representative monarchy, which is the form political liberty has assumed in our time? (...) Those who write on politics and those who write on administration have so far worked apart; nobody has presented himself, standing high enough to see these two related but distinct worlds in a single glance, and to find out what could harmonize them'.[17]

The difficulties posed by the *marriage à raison* between centralized administration and representation, so acutely noted by Tocqueville, run through the political history of continental Europe. To avoid confusion, we are concerned here not with a political history of great events and distinguished statesmen, but one of administration in action and its social constraints.

The similarities in the administrative systems of the post-Napoleonic European states can be taken as the starting-point for a comparative study of the ways in which different stages of social and economic development influenced the intricate workings of administration and representation. A discussion, however brief, of the most salient characteristics of centralized administrative organization, in terms of the links of the executive chain with the periphery, provides the appropriate context for the study of the Italian case after 1861. It is at the local level, where state and society were most clearly in collision, that the workings of administration are best analyzed.

---

17 Tocqueville, 'Rapport', 196-197. He also wrote a separate article on this topic, see A. de Tocqueville, 'La centralisation administrative et le système représentatif' (1844), in: Id., *Oeuvres complètes*, III, *Ecrits et discours politiques*, vol. 2 (Paris, 1985), 129-132.

It is hardly possible to ignore Napoleon's law of 28 Pluviôse Year VIII (1800), if one wants to get to the heart of centralized administration. Admittedly, a major change towards uniformity in local administration had already taken place in the years between 1789 and 1791, and it may even be claimed that the roots of professional bureaucracy lay in the period of the Old Regime. But the straightforward principles of the Napoleonic system proved to be the most direct reference-point for many administrative laws to come: local autonomy was sacrified to centralization, single-headed bodies substituted collegial organs, nomination was preferred to election, and departmental agencies were executive rather than decision-making institutions. The law placed a prefect, to be appointed by the government, in charge of the depart-ment. He was responsible for transmitting the government's laws and regulations, and for supervising their execution. 'Your powers', said a ministerial circular explaining the law, 'embrace everything that relates to the public fortune, national prosperity, and tranquillity of the people over whom you are charged with the administration'.[18] Not only the prefects but all local agents, such as subprefects, mayors, and provincial and communal councillors, were nominated by the govern-ment or its representatives.

The prefectural system was maintained in the Restoration. Alongside it, however, came elected bodies. The seminal importance of this novelty has somewhat over-shadowed the prefect's figure. The historiography has tended to reduce his role to a political one and has overlooked his activities as administrative mediator and reformer *vis-à-vis* the traditional elites.[19] Such a view has lately been challenged. Reliance on and cooperation with the local elites have been put forward as necessary conditions for 'good administration' by the prefects. In many backward regions of France municipal government was firmly in the hands of traditional elites. Under the Napoleonic laws, which remained valid in the first period of the Restoration, the head of state or, for smaller municipalities, the prefect appointed mayors, aldermen and municipal councillors. The restricted local franchise introduced in 1831 changed the system of appointment from above, but still left the power in the communes with a closed group of notables. Their interests were not always identical with those of the state. On many occasions the prefect's interference, aimed at serving the general interest in public health, schools, road building and the like, met with tenacious opposition. The prefects used to complain about this. In 1833 the prefect Romieu bitterly noted that 'if you leave the communes to their own affairs, you will erect a feudal structure, not in its great forms but in its most vicious ones'.[20] Some ten years later, still according to Romieu, the situation had not changed much: 'In drafting the

    18   Cited, in R.R. Palmer's English translation, by L. Bergeron, *France under Napoleon* (Princeton, 1981), 27.

    19   See, for a 'political' view on the French Restoration prefects, N. Richardson, *The French Prefectoral Corps 1814-1830* (Cambridge, 1966).

    20   Cited by E.N. Anderson & P.R. Anderson, *Political Institutions and Social Change in Continental Europe in the Nineteenth Century* (Berkeley and Los Angeles, 1967), 102.

municipal law the legislator has assumed that election was the surest means of bringing into the communal council the inhabitants most capable and most honored, those whom the general will was accustomed to call upon to direct affairs. But this supposition, plausible in theory, and even clear to a deaf-mute who has had contact only with books, does not take into account any of the usual circumstances of a communal election. It leaves out the apathy of some, the forced service of others, the ignorance of all. It ignores the jealousies and envious hatred, the family conspiracies, so aristocratic in the hamlets; the physical violence without protection, the tyrannies of usury, which everything assists'.[21]

Such observations, which, as we shall see, returned with almost the same wording in the reports of the Italian prefects after 1861, were indicative of the prefect's difficulties in dealing with a backward social structure that to a large extent was kept intact by the *régime censitaire*. It was this kind of evasiveness on the part of local elites that led Guizot to his fundamental belief in administrative uniformity, which could only be attained by centralization. As he said in a parliamentary speech: 'Local administration has to be one, homogeneous, and inspired by the same principles, so that the same influences that guide the government centrally, guide administration locally'.[22] In his view centralization and political liberties were two sides of the same medal.

The burgeoning science of administrative law, still narrowly connected to the practices of administration, developed the idea of civilization and administration going hand in hand. Without exception French juridical thinkers of the first half of the nineteenth century presupposed a fundamental harmony between general and private interests. This harmony could be guaranteed by good organization and efficient control. Even profound supporters of decentralization – understood as local government exercising control over local interests – were convinced of the benefits of uniformity in legislation. F. Béchard, proposing a form of decentralization based on associations, did not hesitate to write at the same time: 'We do not only want unity in our laws and courts, in our government, in our military and diplomatic service; we also want unity in our general administration: that from the height of his throne, from which he rules over the entire social order, the king may impose a rapid and uniform movement upon the entire administrative organization'.[23]

Taking this line of reasoning one step further, others were positive about the need for control of lower administrations. E.V. Foucart, author of a widely used manual of administrative and public law, had serious doubts about the capacities of municipalities to administer themselves properly. He pointed to possible fraud, ignorance, and illiteracy among local administrators. He concluded: 'It is thus in the general interest, in the interest of the communes themselves, that they be subjected to controlling

---

21 *Ibidem*.
22 P. Rosanvallon, *Le moment Guizot*, 63.
23 F. Béchard, *Essai sur la centralisation administrative*, II (Paris/Marseille, 1837), 491.

agencies, to supervise the administration of their property, the use of their revenue, to authorize, direct and check their expenditure: such control should be entrusted to the superior administration, which sees things from a higher position, is generally surrounded by more knowledge, and is less prone to error than the municipal administration'.[24]

The French notion of control returned in the administrative laws and juridical literature of, for example, Belgium, Spain, the Netherlands, Piedmont and, in its footsteps, Italy.[25] Again it was Tocqueville, with his keen eye for such matters, recognized the potential purport of French administrative law: 'One may rest assured that wherever a similar revolution will take place – and it will take place all over Europe – here begun by the people, there by the kings, sometimes with the help of political laws, more often under the cover of civil laws, one will see the birth of something analogous to our administrative law, because this law is in itself nothing less than one of the forms of the new state in the world: we call it the *French* system, but one ought to say the *modern* system'.[26]

The continuity of control from above in the laws regulating local administration is at least as significant, though less acknowledged, as the introduction of local elections. The Belgian communal law of 1836, clearly marked by the principles of its French predecessor of 1831 but more elaborate, has often been cited as a model.[27] The Piedmontese legislators in particular admitted to the influence of the Belgian reforms.[28] Even the Dutch, who at the time of the promulgation of the new communal and provincial laws (1850-51) had the separation of Belgium still fresh in their minds, openly referred to the Belgian legislative example.

---

24 E.V. Foucart, *Eléments de droit public et adminstratif, ou exposition méthodique des principes du droit public positif, avec l'indication des lois à l'appui, suivis d'un appendice contenant le texte des principales lois de droit public*, II, *Droit administratif* (Paris/Poitiers, 1835), 376-377.

25 The similarities between the various nineteenth-century municipal laws in Europe were emphasized by A. Shaw, *Municipal Government in Continental Europe* (London, 1895).

26 Tocqueville, 'Rapport', 196.

27 The Belgian communal law of 30 March 1836 had 157 articles, whereas the French communal law of 21 March 1831 had only 55 articles. The former dealt in great detail with the powers of the communal council, the mayor, the aldermen and municipal administrators, whereas the latter merely stated that 'every deliberation of a communal council having to do with subjects outside its powers is legally declared null and void' (art. 28), and did not mention the extent of these powers nor those of other agencies of local government (these were regulated in the subsequent law of 18 July 1837).

28 The Belgian roots of the Italian communal and provincial law were discussed, article by article, by P.C. Boggio & A. Caucino, *Legge provinciale e comunale. Commento* (Turin, 1860), also published as 'Commentario della legge sull'amministrazione comunale e provinciale del 23 ottobre 1859' in *RAR*, 11 (1860), which has been used here. The Belgian political and administrative sytem had had great influence on the post-1848 legislation of the Kingdom of Sardinia, and hence lived through after Unification, see A. Taradel, 'Il modello cavouriano di amministrazione centrale', in: *L'educazione giuridica*, IV, *Il pubblico funzionario: modelli storici e comparativi*, II, *L'età moderna* (Perugia, 1981), 368-371.

3 ITALY BEFORE UNIFICATION

The political and administrative history of postunitary Italy has been heavily influenced by two perspectives. The first, widespread among the 'makers' of Unification, sees 1861 as a clean break with the preunitary period. In the second the political and administrative system of the new state is anachronistically measured against full democracy and participation of all citizens, and is consequently regarded as extremely backward. By stressing both the importance of the preunitary experience and the peculiarities of the relationship between politics and administration in Italy, I hope to avert the shortcomings of the traditional perspectives.

The sphere of French power on the Italian peninsula, primarily through the first Republic and Kingdom of Italy (1802-1814), was not only an important experience of unity, but also left the various states confirmed at the Congress of Vienna with an administrative blueprint, from which they could not easily extricate themselves. As one observer pointedly said: 'The Restoration regime shrewdly used in favour of royal absolutism what the Revolution had tried to gain in favour of liberty'.[29] All preunitary states preserved essential characteristics of the French organizational model: a hierarchical state bureaucracy, controlled by the Ministry of the Interior, with prefect-like administrators in the periphery (*commissari distrettuali* in Parma, *cardinali legati* in the Papal States, *intendenti* in the Neapolitan Kingdom and in the Kingdom of Sardinia, etc.). Of course, the precise organization of local administration (composition of the communal council, appointment of the mayor, extension of controls from above) varied from state to state, but the administrative systems in their broadest outline were fairly similar.[30] Accordingly, the thinking on administration in the various parts of Italy during the Restoration produced analogous lines of reasoning.[31] First and foremost, the discussion was concerned with the gradual detachment of the sphere of public administration from the other powers, notably from the judiciary but also from the sovereign (insofar as it related to executive tasks). The notion of administration in the first half of the nineteenth century, though not necessarily applicable to administrative practices after Unification (but we shall come to that problem later), had some characteristics that were to live on until the end of the century. 'Good administration', on the one hand, was meant to have constructive or emancipatory effects, and – in the long term – to achieve the participation of all citizens; on the other hand, it never lost a strongly authoritarian func-

---

29 A. De Sterlich, *Annotazioni alla legge sull'amministrazione comunale e provinciale del 20 marzo 1865* (Naples, 1865), 25. De Sterlich was at the time a senior official of the Ministry of the Interior.

30 M.S. Giannini, 'I comuni', in: *Atti del congresso celebrativo del centenario delle leggi amministrative di unificazione. L'ordinamento comunale e provinciale*, vol. 1, *I comuni*, edited by M.S. Giannini (Vicenza, 1967), 16-22.

31 A succinct introduction to the development of the science of administrative law in the nineteenth century remains M.S. Giannini, 'Profili storici della scienza del diritto amministrativo' (1940), now in: *Quaderni Fiorentini per la storia del pensiero giuridico*, 2 (1973), 179-274.

tion, in that it was meant to affirm the presence of a central authority in the farthest corners of the country. In other words, identification with the administered, but equally identification with the central government. The juxtaposition of general and local interests, going back to the French administrative writers of the early nineteenth century, formed the pivot of the theorizing about the administrative structure of the liberal state.[32] The conciliation of the two ends was simple in theory: the nation was to be organized in such a way that national and local interests were equally protected by laws and institutions. Hence the active role of administration: administrative control was needed to harmonize the various interests.[33] The dual role imposed on administration was markedly present in the peripheral administrative representatives of the state in most European countries, and can also be found in the functions of the Italian prefect after Unification, representative of the state and advocate of local interests at the same time.

The notion of a double-faced administration was clearly formulated by Giovanni Manna (Naples, 1813-1865), halfway between the Napoleonic period and Unification. Almost throughout his professional life Manna taught political economy and administrative law at the University of Naples. In addition to this he held various important administrative posts in the Kingdom of the Two Sicilies as well as in the Kingdom of Italy.[34] In his major work, *Il diritto amministrativo del Regno delle Due Sicilie*, first published between 1839 and 1842, he insisted that the modern state had a regulating function in concentrating and distributing public wealth (the famous *doppio movimento*), for the ultimate purpose of guaranteeing private property and individual rights (the *sine qua non* of liberal thinking). The state, preferably in the person of a single agent, Manna argued, could exercise this function by means of a hierarchically organized administration. The administration in its turn should be divided, first, into the so-called state administration (*amministrazione di stato*), whose function was to concentrate public wealth; second, into the civil administration (*amministrazione civile*), entrusted with the distribution of public wealth; and third, into the contentious consequences of administration (*contenzioso*), which had merely a secondary function. Consequently, Manna never had any doubts as to the executive function of administration in controlling the municipalities: 'Control over municipalities requires two different actions. First, the central authorities have to help and sustain the municipalities, so that they become stronger and reach the goal they are aiming at (...). Second, the central authorities have to contribute indirectly, by completely moral means, to the increase and acceleration of the internal development of municipal society, that

---

32 See, among many others, J.Ch. Bonnin, *Principii di amministrazione pubblica*, Italian translation of the third French edition, edited by A. De Crescenzi & M. Saffioti, I (Naples, 1824), 104; J.M. de Gérando, *Institutes du droit administratif français ou éléments du code administratif*, 4 vols (Paris, 1829-30), II, 362-363.

33 The problem was treated by the prefect Luigi Tegas, *Interesse generale e interessi locali. Studi* (Brescia, 1871), who underlined its continuity into the unitary state.

34 On Manna, see G. Rebuffa, *La formazione del diritto amministrativo in Italia. Profili di amministrativisti preorlandiani* (Bologna, 1981), 33-71.

is by letting, so to speak, the idea of the common origin and goal of humanity, and the idea of a society superior to that of the municipalities sparkle in the eyes of their inhabitants and administrators'.[35]
Whereas Manna was sincerely liberal in his wish to get rid of traditional juridical relations, his ideas on the goals of administration were still firmly embedded in an authoritarian context. His stance reflects more or less the attitude of many jurists of the Restoration, not only in the Neapolitan Kingdom.[36] In the North the young Angelo Messedaglia (Villafranca di Verona, 1820-1901) proposed, in 1851, a political and administrative academic curriculum independent from that of law. Inspired by the German jurist Von Mohl he defended his proposal by pointing to the specific tasks of the administrator: 'The special qualities of the administrator, in contrast to those of a judge, are his activity, practical tact, profound knowledge of men and their interests, unfailing judgement, strong character and a broad view of society'.[37] This underlined once again the important place administration had assumed by the middle of the century, gaining impetus from the expansion and rationalization of state intervention in society. The objective of public administration, according to Messedaglia, was twofold: first, it had a controlling function in the removal of material obstacles; second, it had an active, educational function in setting aside moral obstacles.[38] Other barriers, essentially unwillingness or hostility, had to be levelled out by prevention or repression, which were described as tasks of the police (in its modern, more restricted sense). In short, Messedaglia, like Manna, tried to elaborate a notion of an active administration, but both writers were doing so from a non- or pre-constitutional vantagepoint: control was superior to participation. Whether guided by caution or fully convinced of their solutions, they saw in good administration a substitute for a liberal constitution. In other words, administrative science was practiced in order to develop constitutional ideas without a constitution. Administrative thinking in the Kingdom of Sardinia before 1848, though far from recognizing any indebtedness to French rule, was equally concerned with the specificity of public administration, both as science and as executive power. The Piedmontese were extremely proud of their own tradition of civil administration,

---

35 Cited from the second edition, in which he published only the first part of his major work, G. Manna, *Partizioni teoretiche del diritto amministrativo ossia introduzione alla scienza ed alle leggi dell'amministrazione pubblica* (Naples, 1860), 261.

36 On the development of the science of administrative law in the Kingdom of the Two Sicilies, L. Martone, 'La scienza amministrativa nel Regno delle due Sicilie (1815-1848). Diritto e politica', now in: Id., *Potere e amministrazione prima e dopo l'Unità* (Naples, 1989), 19-46.

37 A. Messedaglia, *Della necessità di un insegnamento speciale politico-amministrativo e del suo ordinamento scientifico* (Milan, 1851), 21. In the preface Messedaglia claimed that he had already written his book two years earlier. On Messedaglia, see C. Mozzarelli & S. Nespor, *Giuristi e scienze sociali nell'Italia liberale* (Venice, 1981), particularly 29-34; and P. Beneduce, '"Punto di vista amministrativo" e Stato di diritto: aspetti del germanesimo dei giuristi italiani alla fine dell'Ottocento', *Annali dell'Istituto storico italo-germanico in Trento*, 10 (1984), 119-194, particularly 147-149.

38 Messedaglia, 95.

which they traced back to the eighteenth century. In the introduction to their administrative dictionary, published in six volumes between 1840 and 1857, Vigna and Aliberti defined the relative autonomy of administration by describing its wide range: 'Administration is subject to many eventualities, and the cases which require an administrative decision are subject to endless changes which arise from unforeseen circumstances, awkward situations, the need for provisions, and the intricacies of public and private interests; that is why administration has to be studied separately from civil law'.[39] Interestingly enough, the editors of the dictionary reverted to the prerevolutionary Piedmontese laws, pointing out that the kings of Sardinia were the first to adapt the administrative laws to 'modern times'. The reforms had started in 1723, long before the French Revolution, with the Royal Constitutions and culminated in 1775 with a *regolamento dei pubblici* 'that was considered a true model of communal administration'.[40] After the Revolution and Napoleonic domination, Vigna and Aliberti argued, the Kingdom of Sardinia tried to reimpose its own idea of uniformity on administrative organization. But it was clear that it did so in order to adopt new principles under the veil of a return to history. In 1842 and 1843 *regie lettere patenti* were promulgated, offering among other things an updated regulation for the office of the general intendant, the head of the provincial administration. Although a very slender form of representation was introduced (the richest citizens gained access to the communal and provincial councils), simultaneously the juridical and controlling tasks of the intendant were reinforced. It has repeatedly been demonstrated that a clear line of continuity ran from the Piedmontese general intendant of 1842, to the governor of 1859, and finally to the Italian prefect (who acquired this name by the royal decree of 9 October 1861, n. 250).[41]

The conception of the intendant's tasks – centred around the possibility of intervening in the lower levels of administration – followed naturally from the notion of administration that circulated in the Restoration. It did not radically change with the Piedmontese constitution of 1848 and the attendant communal and provincial law. The promulgation of the Albertine Statute carried with it a flood of educational literature, which confirmed the ruling elite's intention of creating from above a solid foundation for the constitutional state. This is the context in which one may safely place the *Rivista Amministrativa del Regno*, founded in 1850 by Vincenzo Aliberti.[42] The official credo of the review was laid down in the opening sentences of the first

39 *Dizionario di diritto amministrativo*, edited by L. Vigna & V. Aliberti, vol. 1 (Turin, 1840), 15.

40 *Ibidem*, 14.

41 A. Petracchi, *Le origini dell'ordinamento comunale e provinciale italiano*, vol. 1 (Venice, 1962); C. Ghisalberti, 'Dall'intendente al prefetto', in: Id., *Contributi alla storia delle amministrazioni preunitarie* (Milan, 1963), 3-35; A. Porro, *Il prefetto e l'amministrazione periferica in Italia. Dall'intendente subalpino al prefetto italiano (1842-1871)* (Milan, 1972).

42 Vincenzo Aliberti (1811-1880), editor with Luigi Vigna of the previously cited *Dizionario di diritto amministrativo*, directed the *Rivista Amministrativa* until 1872. He resumed this job in 1878, when his son Agostino (who had taken over in 1872) died at the age of 34. After Vincenzo's death another of his sons, Paolo, took over as editor.

issue: 'The public nature of its acts is among the first guarantees of good administra-tion and among the most efficient incentives to promote progress'.[43] Sticking to this principle, the review published laws, official decrees, sentences of administrative jurisdiction, abstracts of parliamentary discussions, news from the day-to-day routine of administration (promotions, transfers, etc.) and background articles with a certain theoretical depth. The objective of this varied programme was twofold: to provide those who were professionally or otherwise seriously interested in public administra-tion with background knowledge and to help administrators to translate the laws into administrative practice.[44]

Going through the first ten volumes (1850-1859) of the *Rivista Amministrativa del Regno*, one is struck by the multitude of issues that were dealt with. In fact, it was during this decade that most of the major postunitary problems had already been reviewed, such as the question of decentralization, electoral reforms and administra-tive jurisdiction. The central interest of the various contributions in the section *Materie generali* was the quest for administrative emancipation. This proved to be not only a task facing the local administrative representatives of the government – that is, to guide the municipalities through the difficulties and the benefits of the liberal state – but also a call for reforms of the existing legislation. For example in 1855, in an introduction to an address given in 1833 by the French minister Adolphe Thiers (it had once again become *bon ton* to cite French politicians and writers), the editors wholeheartedly supported the assertion that liberal principles and the practical needs of administration could only gradually be reconciled.[45] In this instance the editors applied the notion of 'capacity' (an important criterion for voting rights too) to the municipal administration. If the capacity – which in practice meant the experience – of self-government was lacking, then it made no sense to bestow extensive liberties on the mayors or the communal councils: 'And one should not forget that the communes, under age-long strict and distrustful control of absolute government, excluded from any initiative, rigorously subject, not least for reasons of mere local and secondary interest, to the fundamental prescriptions of a superior authority, totally lack practical experience in administration, and hence the capacity needed for

---

43 *RAR*, 1 (1850), 5.

44 The *Rivista Amministrativa del Regno* was not the only periodical aimed at the diffusion of administrative knowledge. After Unification at least a hundred of these periodicals saw the light, some for one year or less, others for a longer period, cf. R. Romanelli, *Sulle carte interminate. Un ceto di impiegati tra privato e pubblico: i segretari comunali in Italia, 1860-1915* (Bologna, 1989), 33-41, 319-321; G. Melis, 'La burocrazia e le riviste: per una storia della cultura dell'amministrazione', *Quaderni Fiorentini per la Storia del Pensiero Giuridico Moderno*, 16 (1987), 47-104.

45 References to French jurists were legion in the post-1848 Piedmontese administrative literature: the introduction to administrative law given by the *Rivista Amministrativa* in its first volume spoke highly of Vivien, De Gérando, Trolley, and others, *RAR*, 1 (1850), 193-202. Highly illustrative is the republication in 1854 of a memorandum of Napoleon I on the conditions of the communes and the ways to improve them, *RAR*, 5 (1854), 497-503. Fabio Accame, in his manual of communal law, based himself often on the Restoration commentators of French legislation, see his *Del diritto comunale*, 2nd ed. (Genoa, 1853).

that purpose'.[46] The obvious persons to educate the lower administrations were the intendants. In 1858 Cavour himself, not widely known for his commitment to the functioning of the administration of the Interior ministry, issued instructions to the general intendants, urging them to 'give directions, advice and instructions to the local administrations'; but the intendants 'have to induce them [local authorities] simultaneously to take a greater initiative, to make them respect their decisions, should the laws or the general interest of the state be in conflict with them, and to abstain from ordering *ex officio* expenditure, even obligatory expenditure, without first trying the course of persuasion, which always reaches its aim if followed carefully and intellegently'.[47] The execution of the liberal administrative project was certainly no sinecure. Administration inherited the enterprising connotation it had developed under the 'administrative monarchy'. Yet administrative modernization after 1848 meant greater responsibility for elected organs. Paradoxically this led to an increase of control from above. Many municipal councils were not immediately up to the exercise of their new powers, which forced the controlling authorities to intervene frequently.

The practices of administration under the various preunitary regimes have been poorly studied. It is therefore difficult to assess to what extent there were significant continuities in this respect. Insofaras secondary literature allows, we shall point to relevant developments. However, it is clear that at this point a great deal of research remains to be done.

With Unification and especially with the annexation of the *Mezzogiorno*, where modern administration had progressed least, the dilemma between centralization and modernization was even more deeply felt than in the Kingdom of Sardinia after the revolution of 1848. Those involved in or closely associated with the practice of administration were greatly influenced by the doctrinary creed of the Restoration, and gave the benefit of the doubt to a system of strict control, rather than opting for some form of political decentralization. In their comment on the communal and provincial law of 1859 Pier Carlo Boggio and Antonio Caucino, both ardent contributors of the *Rivista Amministrativa*, said they understood why 'the legislator was by no means inclined to diminish the action of central power in an epoch in which the need for a concordant and energetic course of public affairs was evident'.[48] Tommaso Arabia and Mariano Adorni, senior officials of the Ministry of the Interior in the 1860s, looked rather pessimistically back to Italy's past, characterized as it was by a 'long and shameful servitude'. According to them this tradition had not failed to have its bad effects: in Italy 'one distrusts everything; one almost fears to contaminate oneself getting near the men in power, and one is always ready to rebel'. Therefore, government had to exert rigid control and, by implication, teach the local administra-

---

46 *RAR*, 6 (1855), 91.

47 *Circolare del Ministero dell'Interno*, 18 April 1858, also published in the *RAR*, 9 (1858), 294-299 (the citation is from p. 298).

48 Boggio & Caucino, 42.

tions, even through the 'iron hand of liberty' the capacity to administer themselves.[49]

Many prefects used to ideologize their job in similar ways, as we shall see, but few brought their views into the open. A notable example was Giuseppe Alasia (Turin, 1820-1893), prefect of Bari, L'Aquila and Ravenna and briefly secretary-general of the Ministry of the Interior, who in a book written in 1871 vigorously opposed the 'prevailing fashion' of his days: the blunt call for decentralization without much reasoning to support it. He tried to unmask the proposals of the 'decentralizers', which he considered merely the offshoot of an uncritical 'anglomania'. Following in the footsteps of many political thinkers of the first half of the century he denied that decentralization as such was a liberal principle, pointing out that it was widespread under the Old Regimes and that feudalism 'was a great and real decentralization'. Furthermore, leaning on his administrative experience, he listed many instances in which the municipal authorities had to be coerced to erect schools, to construct and maintain streets and bridges, to keep their archives in order, to make the necessary provisions for public health, etc. He therefore called for a watchful eye to be kept on the municipalities with the sole intention of fostering their development. He invited his readers to look around in the Italian Kingdom: 'Make this journey with me, register all these facts, and you will get a precise idea of what our communes would be if in their present state we withdraw everything that directly or indirectly has been achieved by control'.[50]

The concept of administration engendered by the Restoration cannot simply be used as a mould to explain 'administrative behaviour' after Unification. Nevertheless, it has been shown that the watershed of Unification did not alter the basic components of the notion of administration, notably its role as 'prime mover' of society – even before politics. Moreover, until the last quarter of the century administrative science developed in continuous discussion with administrative practice. The careers of public officials and theorists of administration frequently overlapped (for example, Manna and Messedaglia). Furthermore, because of its 'exegetic' and derivative character, loathed by Orlando from the 1880s onwards, administrative theory was not so far from the concrete workings of administration as it would later be.[51] The closeness of theory and practice clearly appears from the comments on the communal and provincial law, often written by active public officials.[52] These guides usually

---

49   T. Arabia & M. Adorni, *La legge comunale e provinciale del Regno d'Italia commentata* (Florence, 1865), CXXXVIII.

50   G. Alasia, *Lettere sul decentramento* (Florence, 1871), 271.

51   For V.E. Orlando's criticism of his precursors in the field of public law, see G. Rebuffa, 'I lessici e il tempo delle prolusioni di Vittorio Emanuele Orlando', *RTDP*, 39 (1989), 922.

52   Cf. the comment already cited of Arabia and Adorni, senior officials of the Ministry of the Interior; the successful guides of Carlo Astengo, senior official of the Ministry and prefect, on the communal and provincial laws of 1859, 1865 and 1889; L. Riberi & F. Locatelli (officials in the peripheral administration at the time of publication), *Manuale pratico d'amministrazione comunale e provinciale, ossia commentario della nuova legge comunale 20 marzo 1865* (Florence, 1865); A. Scibona (senior official of the Ministry in the 1860s),

treated not only the bare text of the law but the underlying doctrines, thus growing into manuals of administrative law. The administrative 'mind' or ethos of many prefects of this study was imbued with the idea of mobilization inherent in the theory and practice of preunitary public administration.[53] It is not unusual to find senior officials in the field referrring to Romagnosi's concept of *incivilimento* as the guiding principle of their actions.[54]

The ideas discussed so far centred around the assumption that public administration could bridge the gap between state and society. Whereas theory departed from the fundamental harmony of state and society, reality proved to be radically different. The discrepancy emerged painfully after Unification, when the introduction of the representative system was thought to effect the hoped-for rapprochement. After the liberals had achieved their principal aim – national Unification – they were faced with a wide range of problems, which put a greater strain on administration than it could bear. The major rifts in the early decades of united Italy are known. First, centralization and uniformity were held to be the best antidotes to the possibly corroding effects of regional differences. Nevertheless, the provincial and communal law of 1865, taken over from the Kingdom of Sardinia (which in its turn had adopted the Belgian model), could not prevent different developments in the North and the South. Second, the economic and financial crisis that soon set in forced the central government to burden the provincial and municipal budgets: in practice, national interests clearly prevailed over local interests. Third, the limited suffrage clashed more and more with the demands of emerging social groups and opposition movements. These geographic, economic and social contradictions profoundly hampered the positive role of administration as it was idealistically propounded. It is this confrontation of hopes and expectations with reality that underlies the present study. It will not be much concerned with theory hereafter. The notion of administration mainly serves to understand the enterprising spirit of the first generation of prefects – the pillars of the administrative system.

La nuova legge comunale e provinciale del Regno d'Italia... (Turin, 1865); A. Serpieri & D. Silvagni (both prefects), *Legge sull'amministrazione comunale e provinciale annotata* (Turin, 1884).

53 The reciprocity between social and administrative history on the one hand, and *Begriffsgeschichte* on the other has been stressed by R. Koselleck, 'Begriffsgeschichte und Sozialgeschichte', in: *Historische Semantik und Begriffsgeschichte*, edited by R. Koselleck (Stuttgart, 1979): 'social and political conflicts of the past must be interpreted and opened up via the medium of their contemporary conceptual limits and in terms of the mutually understood, past linguistic usage of the participating agents' (p.24).

54 ASB, Pref., Gab., b. 124, report of the subprefect of Imola on the moral, economic and political conditions of his district in the first quarter of 1866, 4 April 1866; ASV, Pref., Gab. (1872-76), cat. 19, 1/1, report of the district commissioner of Mestre on public affairs in the first half year of 1874, 4 July 1874. The latter hoped that 'the population would proceed on the path of greater physical, intellectual and moral perfection, which according to Romagnosi's succinct concept constitutes civilization (*incivilimento*)'.

Chapter 2

The prefects as mediators between state and society

1 THE HISTORIOGRAPHY

To define the place the prefect occupied in the alleged no man's land between state and society in liberal Italy, is an arduous undertaking. To begin with, it requires not only the evaluation of many heated polemics of the past, from which the prefect often emerged as a highly corruptible figure, but also needs to take into account the divergent perspectives of academic disciplines such as administrative science, the science of administrative law and political science. Futhermore, one should realize that these secondary views, despite their one-sidedness, have gradually settled into contemporary Italian historiography and tend to monopolize our understanding of the prefect's role.

The criticism levelled at the workings of the Italian political system and, as an inseparable part of this, at the prefect, reached a first peak in the early 1880s. Contemporaneously, a few 'angry old men' (such as Silvio Spaventa, Marco Minghetti, Pasquale Turiello) and the young Gaetano Mosca, each with his particular outlook, put the prefect on par with the – in their eyes – degenerated government.[1] The observations of Turiello, an exponent of the *Destra storica* and hence regarded with suspicion by many political opponents, on the all-embracing clientele system, particularly in the South, and the concomitant decadence of the prefectural class perfectly illustrate this widespread criticism. He explained how the first generation of administrators – elected or appointed – were sincere liberals, who tried to respond to the demands coming from society: 'Here a contract for provincial roads was drawn up well; there the number of nursery and elementary schools increased; the overbearing influence of some families was repressed; charitable institutions were supervised and reformed. All this was achieved through effective cooperation between prefects and communal councils, or through good commissioners for dissolved municipalities;

---

1 The most relevant writings of Spaventa on the subject are in S. Spaventa, *La politica della Destra*, edited by B. Croce (Bari, 1910); M. Minghetti's main work is *I partiti politici e l'ingerenza loro nella giustizia e nell'amministrazione* (1881), now in: Id. *Scritti politici*, edited by R. Gherardi (Rome, 1986); P. Turiello, *Governo e governati in Italia* (Bologna, 1882); G. Mosca, *Sulla teorica dei governi e sul governo parlamentare. Studi storici e sociali* (Palermo, 1884), now in: *Scritti politici di Gaetano Mosca*, vol. I, edited by G. Sola (Turin, 1982). See on Turiello and Mosca's views on the prefect G. Aliberti, 'Prefetti e società locale nel periodo unitario', in: Id., *Potere e società locale nel Mezzogiorno dell'800* (Rome, 1987), 147-183.

in short, through the cooperation of the best citizens called on and incited by the authorities'.[2] Soon, however, in an unforeseen way the theories and practices of local autonomy resulted in the reinforcement of local clienteles, which instrumentalized or were instrumentalized by the political centre. Consequently, Turiello argued, the prefects became more and more helpless, caught between the Scylla of the government of the day and the Charybdis of local elites.

After the turn of the century the negative image of the prefect was further developed by Gaetano Salvemini from yet another, left-wing, vantage point. For example, his *Il ministero della mala vita* is a vitriolic attack on the instrumentalization of public administration under Giolitti's rule. He virulently railed against public officials in the periphery, especially in the *Mezzogiorno*, who were knowingly involved in electoral corruption and arbitrary rule.[3] Once again the prefect was placed in the middle of imbroglios. What these polemical works have further in common, besides taking their examples mostly from the South, is their focus on the political side of the prefect's work. This focus, however, tends to blur the diversity of his job. Moreover the encroachment of political interests upon the realm of prefectural administration was seen as the logical first step to manipulation and gerrymandering. In a climate in which government and parliament were loathed for their ineffectiveness, the prefects could hardly escape a harsh judgement.

The politicized perspective comes close to the 'idea-type' of the relationship between politics and administration, distilled from the discourse on the division of powers: the primacy of the process of politics (the 'origin, development, and maturing of social will') versus a subordinate position for administration (merely the 'use of the reservoir of social will').[4] A high degree of centralization helps to tighten up this unequal relationship. Translated to the case of liberal Italy, this interpretation of the politics-administration dichotomy leaves no doubt that the prefect depended on the political centre for all aspects of his job. The 'political' prefect was, in this view, an essential trait of the structure of the polity.[5] The weakness of this approach, however, is that it disregards the process of formation of the Italian political system, which clearly differed from other European experiences. Most parts of Unified Italy did not have a tradition of representative government and direct elections (only the Kingdom of Sardinia from 1848). Parliament and intermediate bodies remained barely representative until the eve of the First World War. Well-disciplined political parties did not exist

---

2 Turiello, 297-298.

3 G. Salvemini, *Il ministero della mala vita* (1910), now in: *Opere di Gaetano Salvemini*, IV, *Il Mezzogiorno e la democrazia italiana*, vol. 1 (Milan, 1966), 73-141.

4 The definitions are from H. Finer, *The Theory and Practice of Modern Government*, 4th ed. (London, 1965), 7.

5 The most outspoken exponent of this opinion and, at the same time, the only author treating the history of the Italian prefects comprehensively is R.C. Fried, *The Italian Prefects. A Study in Administrative Politics* (New Haven, 1963). But similar views are brought forward to the present day, see U. Allegretti, *Profilo di storia costituzionale italiana. Individualismo e assolutismo nello stato liberale* (Bologna, 1989).

or were excluded from the parliamentary scene. And the executive power of the Crown and the government was hardly comparable to that in, for example, the German Empire under Bismarck. All these aspects had, as we shall see, profound consequences for the place and role of public administration in general and of the prefects in particular.

In juridically oriented approaches the political functions of the prefect have always been acknowledged as intrinsic to the protection of state interests. In some ways this view is more realistic than that evolved from political science, but it tends to look at the state as the uncompromising rule of law.[6] From this follows a rather positivistic, normative perspective on the prefect, which misses the reciprocity between state and society, and has therefore limited validity for the historian.[7]

My aim is to start off by separating politics and administration; but subsequently, against a too sharp, abstract distinction, to put them together in the context of nineteenth-century Italy. The 'lateness' of Italy in many fields (unification, industrialization, parliamentary government) deeply affected the relationship between public administration and politics. To sum it up in a few words, my approach reverses the order in which politics and administration are normally discussed: it was administration, preserving its traditional role as moderator of civic society, that created, in the framework of a project of administrative modernization, the system of political representation. This point of view, highlighting administration before politics, allows a more balanced insight into the practices of the prefectural system in liberal Italy.

This is, despite what I might have suggested so far, not a completely pioneering idea. Many assumptions of this study stem from the acute observations of scholars like Ernesto Ragionieri, Alberto Aquarone, Roberto Ruffilli, Sabino Cassese and Raffaele Romanelli.[8] Surprisingly, however, their stimulating ideas on the prefect's figure have not resulted in systematic research based on the prefectural archives. Partly, this is due to the bad state of many of these archives (as explained in the preface); partly to the enduring predominance of politicized perspectives. I have tried to obviate these shortcomings by linking my interpretation of the workings of the prefecture to the fruits of extensive archival research.

---

6 M. Fioravanti, 'Costituzione, amministrazione e trasformazioni dello Stato', in: *Stato e cultura giuridica in Italia dall'Unità alla Repubblica*, edited by A. Schiavone (Bari, 1990), 21-27.

7 See, for example, the still valuable contributions of L. Frezzini, 'Prefetto e sottoprefetto', in: *Digesto Italiano*, XIX, parte 1ª (Turin, 1909-1912), 308-367, and T. Marchi, 'Gli uffici locali dell'amministrazione generale dello Stato', in: *Primo trattato completo di diritto amministrativo italiano*, edited by V.E. Orlando, II (Milan, 1907), in particular 150-272.

8 I cite here only the essays that have most inspired me: E. Ragionieri, 'Politica e amministrazione nello Stato unitario', now in: Id., *Politica e amministrazione nella storia dell'Italia unita*, 2nd ed. (Rome, 1979), 81-137; A. Aquarone, 'Accentramento e prefetti nei primi anni dell'Unità', now in: Id., *Alla ricerca dell'Italia liberale* (Naples, 1972), 157-191; S. Cassese, 'Il prefetto nella storia amministrativa', *RTDP*, 33 (1983), 1449-1457; R. Ruffilli, 'La questione del decentramento nell'Italia liberale', in: *L'organizzazione della politica. Cultura, istituzioni, partiti nell'Europa liberale*, edited by N. Matteucci & P. Pombeni (Bologna, 1988), 429-448; R. Romanelli, 'Tra autonomia e ingerenza: un'indagine del 1869', now in: Id., *Il comando impossibile. Stato e società nell'Italia liberale* (Bologna, 1988), 77-150.

2 THE PREFECTS

The state made its presence felt at many fronts in society: schools, the military, building, and certainly civil administration were outposts of a national ideology aimed at integration and progress. It seems therefore particularly promising to study the workings of the prefecture and the central figure of the prefect in order to assess the precarious balance between centralized power and local autonomy, between national and local interests, between control and initiative, between authority and liberty. The prefects, the Italian 'statesmen in disguise', occupied an extremely precarious position in the middle of the executive chain from the central authorities down to the municipal administrations and vice versa: on the one hand, they were required to implement state policy in an often ill-disposed environment; on the other, they were so deeply involved in the day-to-day administration of their provinces that they came to be the most obvious persons to defend local interests at the central level.

The communal and provincial law invested the prefect with 'the executive power in the entire province'. He watched over all public administrations, and in case of need he could take the steps he considered indispensable for the functioning of the offices. He could make use of the police, and could call in the armed forces (art. 3 of the 1865 law). The prefect was assisted by a few councillors, who formed the council of the prefecture (*consiglio di prefettura*).[9] In the liberal period the prefectures (69 after the annexation of Rome) had on average 30 employees, not including the lower servants. For example in 1877 the prefecture of Rome had the highest number of employees (57), directly followed by Turin (53), Milan and Alessandria (both 52); the prefectures of Bologna and Reggio Calabria then had 30 employees, that of Venice 26 (R.D. 25 June 1877, n. 3925). These numbers underwent only minor changes in the following decades. The general feeling, particularly among the prefectural corps, was that this staffing was absolutely insufficient to attend to all services, but for budgetary reasons the Ministry of the Interior could not substantially augment its personnel until the beginning of the new century.

The regulations accompanying the law divided the prefectures in four divisions: the first consisted of the secretariat and attended to the services for the prefectural council and the provincial deputation; the second took care of lower administrative bodies (municipalities, charitable institutions, etc.); the third dealt with affairs related to public security, the military, and public health; the fourth occupied itself with the state administrations in the province, with accounting, and with matters not

---

9 The communal and provincial law of 1865 did not mention the rank of *consigliere delegato*, the substitute prefect. Officials of this name, however, did occur on the staff rolls of the prefectures. The royal decree of 15 November 1871, n. 535 apportioned extra pay to *consiglieri delegati*. According to later commentators of the law the rank of *consigliere delegato*, with an attendant salary, was created by the royal decree of 25 June, 1877, n. 3925, see for example A. Santini, *Codice dei comuni e delle provincie...* (Rome, 1889), 58.

attributed elsewhere. In addition to these divisions the prefects had their own cabinet, which dealt with confidential matters and personnel. From 1874 onwards a separate accountant's office (*ragioneria*) came into being.[10]

Office hours for the prefectural employees ran from 9 am to 4 pm (in summer from 8 am to 3 pm) or to 5.30, if lunch was eaten outside. On Sundays and holidays the employees were required to work only in the morning. The prefects were themselves allowed to issue internal regulations for the prompt settlement of the affairs in hand. They used to establish precise rules for the forwarding, signature and filing of documents, all in strict observance of the bureaucratic hierarchy. Severe penalties were decreed for breaking the confidentiality of official matters. The prefect of Reggio Calabria, for example, ordered fixed times for outsiders to visit the offices (from 10 am to 12), but only the prefect himself and the councillors had the right to receive visitors. Senators, deputies and public officials were given preferential treatment: they could pay their calls from the third to the penultimate office hour, and were received before any other waiting visitors.[11]

The social backgrounds of the first prefects, those in service between 1861 and 1871, have been analyzed by Ragionieri. He found that out of 59 prefects in 1861 31 came from the North, 11 from the Centre and 17 from the South of Italy. In 1871, after the annexation of Venice and Rome, 33 were born in the North, 15 in the Centre, and 19 in the South (2 unknown).[12] Regional origins have always drawn a lot of attention in the Italian historiography on public administration. To some extent, the somewhat negative idea of 'piedmontization' of the unitary state is largely due to the relatively large number of Piedmontese officials in the civil service, particularly in the higher ranks. Out of 65 higher officials (directors-general and division heads) working at the central offices of the Ministry of the Interior between 1870 and 1899 37 came from the North (26 from Piedmont), 13 from the Centre, and 15 from the South.[13] Out of the 69 prefects in function towards the end of the 1880s 38 originated from the North (17 from the former Kingdom of Sardinia), 9 from the Centre, and 22 from the *Mezzogiorno*.[14] The 46 prefects of this study show a slightly deviating picture: 17 from the North, 10 from the Centre, and 19 from the South (see Appendix). It is, however, far from self-evident, contrary to what is often implied, that the Northern majority did not sympathize with the more backward regions of the new state. First, many high

---

10 The regulations accompanying the new communal and provincial law of 1889 endorsed the various alterations to the original organization. The prefecture was divided into the cabinet, four divisions, the accountant's office, the office of the provincial director of studies (*provveditore agli studi*), and the office of public security.

11 'Regolamento interno della prefettura di Reggio Calabria', *Bollettino della prefettura di Reggio Calabria* (1868), 84.

12 Ragionieri, 136.

13 N. Randeraad, 'Gli alti funzionari del Ministero dell'interno durante il periodo 1870-1899', *RTDP*, 39 (1989), 210.

14 E. Gustapane, 'I prefetti dell'Unificazione amministrativa nelle biografie di Francesco Crispi', *RTDP*, 34 (1984), 1058.

officials were imbued with a true risorgimental spirit, dedicated to the goal of unity. Second, the careers of many civil servants, especially those of the Interior administration, led them through all parts of Italy. Prefects used to succeed one another rapidly. The province of Bologna had 20 prefects in 35 years. Hence, it could be argued that 'decentralized' career experiences were a more important factor than regional origins, when it came to knowledge of 'foreign' regions on the peninsula.[15]

The aristocracy was poorly represented in the Italian Interior administration. Historically, the presence of nobles was more restricted to the War Ministry and the Foreign Office. Before 1900 46.2% of the diplomats were of noble origins.[16] But in general the Italian public administration was much more a bourgeois stronghold than its French or German counterpart. At the end of the 1880s 11 prefects out of 69 were of noble birth.[17] Out of the 65 higher officials of the Ministry of the Interior in the last decades of the century only one belonged to the aristocracy.[18] 14 prefects out of the 46 listed in the Appendix of this study were nobles. This relatively high number can be explained by pointing to the importance of the prefectures of Venice and Bologna, which were required to be led by men who were accustomed to associate easily with the highest circles.

Although the powers conferred on the prefect seem limitless (the execution of almost every law involved his cooperation), acute observers noted that the provincial representation of the executive was soon broken up into various organs, notably the intendencies of finance established in 1869. The ministries preferred to rely on their own officials in the periphery rather than on an 'integrated' prefect.[19] Thereby the prefect gradually lost his unrivalled administrative authority. Nevertheless, throughout the liberal period the prefect remained a central figure in the administrative, social and cultural life of the province. A box of personal correspondence belonging to Giovanni Mussi, prefect of Bologna in the early 1880s, shows that he received countless letters, brochures and invitations of local associations and highplaced persons.[20] The prefects were required to present themselves in uniform at public ceremonies. The uniforms were meticulously prescribed by a royal decree of 1859: a

---

15 Randeraad, 235.

16 *La formazione della diplomazia italiana (1861-1915). Indagine statistica* (Rome, 1986), 63.

17 Gustapane, 1058.

18 Randeraad, 211.

19 See, on the 'unintegrated' characteristics of the job of the Italian prefect, in contrast with the French integrated system, Fried, 306-307 and S. Cassese, 'Il prefetto', 1453. The non-integration in the prefect's job had already been signalled by some nineteenth-century commentators, of whom the warnings of the ex-prefect Achille Serpieri are worth mentioning, A. Serpieri & D. Silvagni, *op. cit.*, 39-41 (as appears from the title page Serpieri annotated the first twelve articles of the law including those dealing with the powers of the prefect).

20 ASB, Pref., Gab., b. 351. In contrast with the French prefects, few Italian prefects have left memoirs. The only real autobiography, treating in particular Giolitti's period, is that of A. Nasalli Rocca, *Memorie di un prefetto*, edited by C. Trionfi (Rome, 1946). Consequently, there are few biographies, cf. V.G. Pacifici, *Angelo Annaratone (1844-1922). La condizione dei prefetti nell'Italia liberale* (Rome, 1990).

deep blue suit of military cut with gold-lace embroidery, a white waistcoat and tie, a sword with a golden hilt set off with mother-of-pearl, a black scabbard, and a hat *alla francese* trimmed with black feathers, with a golden buckle and national tassel (*nappa nazionale*).[21] Furthermore the prefects of the largest cities received large funds for official representation.[22] Most prefectures were housed in existing, distinguished and centrally situated palaces.[23]

At the beginning of this chapter several authors were cited, who poured scorn on the prefects. Although these were the opinions that were mostly picked up by later historians, some contemporary commentators close to the administrative reality highlighted the positive aspects in the prefect's job. Following De Sterlich Carlo Astengo, an experienced official in the Interior administration, gave a definition of the action of the state that went beyond the simple rule of law. He emphasized the 'potential initiative in all moral, economic and political novelties, whenever individualism is unable to bring them about and to regulate them'. A large part of the state's initiative fell within the tasks of the prefect: 'A very important part of his mission is that which the law does not mention, consisting of assiduous initiative aimed at germinating all living forces in the province, at promoting sociability, and at gathering and directing activity towards orderly moral, political and economic progress'.[24] The prefect's guiding role is also the leitmotiv running through the chapters that follow. Although the prefect, as representative of the state, directly or indirectly dealt with the entire administrative life in his province, only a few areas will be discussed here. One important omission needs some comment in advance. To the present day public opinion holds that the prefect is first and foremost a policeman. It is perhaps relevant to note that, notwithstanding the prefect's supreme command of the police forces, the office of head of police in the province was usually held by a *questore* (in provinces of lesser importance by an inspector). But apart from this reservation it is beyond doubt that law and order were principal themes throughout the nineteenth century and that the prefect was closely involved in the maintenance of public order – a job that calls for a similar analysis to that proposed here for civil administration. For basically the same problems connected with the relationship between state and society, between the enforcement of a specific perception of power and all kinds of obstacles, underlie the practices of symbolic and physical state violence.[25]

---

21   Royal Decree of 2 December 1859, see also ACS, Min. Int., Direzione Generale degli Affari Generali e del Personale, Atti Amministrativi, b. 15, f. 92.

22   E. Gustapane, 'I prefetti dell'Unificazione amministrativa nelle biografie di Francesco Crispi', *RTDP*, 34 (1984), 1051.

23   N. Randeraad, 'The State in the Provinces: the Prefecture as a Palace after Unification', in: *The Power of Imagery. Essays on Rome, Italy and Imagination*, edited by P. van Kessel (Rome, 1993), 98-108.

24   *Guida amministrativa ossia commento della legge comunale e provinciale (Testo unico 10 febbraio 1889)...*, edited by C. Astengo e.a. (Rome, 1889), 88.

25   See on this theme, J.A. Davis, *Conflict and Control. Law and Order in Nineteenth-century Italy* (London, 1988); R.B. Jensen, *Liberty and Order: the Theory and Practice of Italian Public Security, 1848 to the Turn of 1890* (Ann Arbor, Michigan University Microfilm International, 1987).

The actions of the prefects that will be taken into consideration are all concerned with the founding of a 'rudimentary modernity': representative bodies (the parliament and the provincial and communal councils), uniform and well-functioning local administration, and financial responsibility of local authorities. In the first decades after Unification public administration, despite the ambitions of the ruling class to encompass the whole of society, did not yet embrace the same wide array of services as in England or Germany in that period. Hence the largest part of this study deals with a phase in the development of administration that precedes the apex of the 'nineteenth-century revolution in government'.[26] One could perhaps argue that the objects of my research are a necessary condition for a successful and efficient further unfolding of the grip of administration on society. But it is not my purpose to go that far. My themes are divided up over the next five chapters, three of which deal with municipal government (mayors and local elections, the dissolution of communal councils, and municipal services), one with local finances and one with the conduct of parliamentary elections. In each of them the 'bipolar' function of the prefect will come out clearly.

As explained in the preface, many types of sources have been used. Two stand out in particular: the prefectural circulars gathered mostly in the *Bollettino della Prefettura*, and the regular reports on public affairs. The former is representative of a downward movement along the executive chain, the latter of an upward movement. In both cases the prefect and his staff had a filtering function: first, to spread instructions among the lower administrations; second, to relay information to the Ministry of the Interior. The *Bollettino della Prefettura*, compulsorily published by each prefecture from the communal and provincial law of 1865, was printed and distributed at the expense of the municipalities.[27] The information to be put in the bulletin included ministerial and prefectural circulars, laws and royal decrees (although it was stressed that these also had to be circulated separately), governmental regulations, and all other business that was relevant to the province. In a ministerial circular, signed by the secretary-general Giuseppe Alasia, the standards for the compilation and publication of the bulletins were laid down in some detail. A fair amount of liberty was allowed to the prefects: 'Their work experience and knowledge of places will guide the prefects in

---

26 Cf. the debate that followed O. MacDonagh, 'The Nineteenth-Century Revolution in Government: a Reappraisal', *The Historical Journal*, 1 (1958), 52-67. A recent assessment of the 'MacDonagh debate' can be found in R. MacLeod, 'Introduction', in: *Government and Expertise. Specialists, Administrators and Professionals, 1860-1919*, edited by R. MacLeod (Cambridge, 1988), 1-24.

27 In 1876 the *Bollettino della Prefettura* was replaced by the so-called *Foglio Periodico* (*Circolari del Ministero dell'Interno*, 5 and 15 September 1876, n. 31400) without any fundamental alterations. Only a supplement containing official legal and judicial announcements (*Foglio di annunzi*) was added, to be published at least twice a week. The new government of the *Sinistra* had decided to change the custom of entrusting official announcements to regular newspapers – a practice that had obliged these newspapers to favour governmental policy. After 1880 the expenses for the bulletin were no longer defrayed by the municipalities, but were put on the prefecture's budget, *Circolare del Ministero dell'Interno*, 20 July 1880. By R.D. 21 February 1897, n. 89, the bulletin was formally abolished.

chosing and treating subjects for the bulletin, and the Ministry relies for that on their careful judgement, adding only that one of the principal aims of the periodical in question is to succeed in uniting the administrative systems on the basis of general criteria issued by the central authorities'.[28] The prefectural bulletins were clear examples of bureaucratic decentralization. Some even went as far, much to the Ministry's annoyance, as to publish private advertisements, thus not only adapting national guidelines to local circumstances but also mingling the public and the private domain.[29] A glance at the *Bollettini* of Venice, Bologna and Reggio Calabria shows that there was indeed a wide divergence in their contents, due to different administrative needs, different traditions, and different degrees of diligence on the part of the prefects.[30]

The regular reports on public affairs (*relazioni sullo spirito pubblico*) were important sources of information for the central authorities. The *spirito pubblico* was held to reflect the will of the population to strive for happiness and progress; in other words, to share the intentions of the government. Article 1 of the regulations accompanying the communal and provincial law of 1865 prescribed that the prefects had to submit in November a yearly report on the general conditions of their provinces. Apart from this general report, which soon passed out of use, the prefects drew up periodical reports on public order and the political, administrative and economic conditions within their territory.[31] Initially the Ministry of the Interior kept a close watch on the drawing up of these reports: 'Because it is a principal task of civil governments to provide, with the most efficient means at their disposal, for the maintenance of public security, the protection of the life and property of citizens, and the immediate satisfaction of their legitimate interests, anyone can see that it is of great importance for this Ministry to be rapidly informed about public opinion and the moral, political, and economic conditions of the various provinces'.[32] In 1869, after a wave of social and political agitation in the North the Ministry called on the prefects to take their regular reporting very seriously: 'It is important for the government to know the real moral state of the people, and the real causes of discontent (where it exists), and to

---

28 *Circolare del Ministero dell'Interno*, 23 February 1866, n. 16067.

29 See *Circolari del Ministero dell'Interno*, 20 February 1870, n. 18100; 6 September 1870; 31 January 1874, 14 December 1879.

30 As for traditions, in the Kingdom of Naples a similar periodical was published, the *Giornale d'Intendenza*, A. Scirocco, 'Tra stampa amministrativa e stampa di regime: il Giornale d'Intendenza nel Regno di Napoli dell'Ottocento', *Rassegna Storica del Risorgimento*, 76 (1989), 476-490.

31 These reports were at first monthly (*Circolare del Ministero dell'Interno*, 31 October 1864, n. 15417), then quarterly (*Circolare*, 18 April 1865, n. 5499), again monthly from 1866 to 1870 (*Circolare*, 25 July, n. 9177), subsequently quarterly until 1874 (*Circolare*, 16 January 1870, n. 99). Then, in view of the growing political and administrative normality, the Ministry decided to make the reports semestral (*Circolare*, 16 March 1874, n. 1615). There are some striking similarities between the objectives of these reports and the Napoleonic practices, see S.J. Woolf, 'Les Bases sociales du Consolat. Un mémoire d'Adrien Duquesnoy', *Revue d'Histoire Moderne et Contemporaine*, 31 (1984), 597-618.

32 *Circolare del Ministero dell'Interno*, 25 July 1866, n. 9177 (confidential).

study its remedies, not in a vague manner, not by cherishing illusions, but practically and seriously. Of the moral diseases apathy is most detrimental in a country governed by public opinion; and it has to be cured in the interest of both order and liberty'.[33] The reports, required to go deep into the local conditions, thus acquired a central place among the prefectural routine. Every division drew up an account of its activities and the situation of the administrative field under its wing. The head of police also submitted a report to the prefect. Lazy prefects simply put these various pieces together and sent them off under their name. Immediately after their seizure of power in 1876 the government of the *Sinistra* made clear that it intended to use the regular reports as starting points for its electoral campaign. Through the prefectural reports it hoped to 'find out what judgement the country would give of the government's actions as well as of the reforms of public administration it intended to carry through'.[34]

The regular reports are an important source for the way the prefects saw the weal and woe of their provinces. In the absence of 'egodocuments' the reports are the most reliable source for a collective ideology of the prefectural corps. Yet the variations are great.[35] Some prefects evidently put much energy into their reports, trying to do justice to their role as advocate of local interests (by paying a lot of attention to the section 'needs of the province'); others wrote what they thought the Ministry wanted to read, which boiled down to the conclusion, justified or not, that things were going better than last year. Between the lines the writer's personal conviction often shines through, although it is sometimes hard to say whether the prefect himself is speaking or a member of his staff.

3 ADMINISTRATION IN THE FIELD

The variety of the prefect's actions is best illustrated by their day-to-day work in the provinces under their administration. The provinces of this study (Venice, Bologna and Reggio Calabria) have been selected not only for the archival reasons explained earlier, but also for their representativeness of markedly different regions in the Italian Kingdom. The three provinces obviously reflect the traditional division of Italy into North, Centre and South. But more than that, the three provinces typify different administrative, social and economic backgrounds, which had to be adapted to Piedmontese rule. As already discussed, all preunitary states had administrative systems that were characterized by a hierarchical centre-periphery relationship with prefect-like administrators as key-figures. In this sense, although many critics pointed

33 *Circolare del Ministero dell'Interno*, 28 June 1869, n. 119 (confidential).

34 *Circolare del Ministero dell'Interno*, 28 June 1876, n. 3556. A few months later the Ministry issued detailed instructions about the form of the semestral reports, *Circolare*, 4 December 1876, n. 6808.

35 P. Borzomati, 'Utilità e limiti delle relazioni dei prefetti', in: *Economia e società nella storia dell'Italia contemporanea. Fonti e metodi di ricerca*, edited by A. Lazzarini (Rome, 1983), 109-117.

to its excessive centralization, the Piedmontese model imposed on unified Italy was in keeping with existing forms of civil administration. It seems therefore not very rewarding to linger over centralization as such. Instead, one comes closer to the administrative reality by scrutinizing the effects of and reactions to centralism, especially when it was faced with a representative system and gradual enlargement of the electorate. Did centralism survive or was it even strengthened, as has been argued for the Second French Empire?[36] It is clearly unsatisfactory to study local administration in liberal Italy only from the top down; one should also try to assess the extent to which the periphery, or rather the peripheries, were able to respond to the challenges from above.

At this point the prefect's 'bipolarity' acquires its full meaning. The success of the exercise of his duties depended, first, on his ability to translate the national laws to the local situation; second, on his skill in forging consensus among the local elites. Through the combination of the limited franchise and the considerable power in the hands of municipal and provincial administrations, the local notables, mostly strongly attached to landed interests, preserved much of their traditional authority. But the question for the liberals in power was whether these notables were willing to put their authority to the service of the unitary state. One of the ways to serve the country and to keep an eye on local interests was to accept the office of mayor. Until the end of the century mayors were appointed by the government (except in larger cities, where mayors were elected already from 1889). We shall see that the nomination of mayors constituted a timeconsuming and difficult operation, for which the prefects were largely responsible.

The process of breaking down the old social hierarchy lasted through the entire nineteenth century, and strong remnants have nonetheless survived since. The evasive mentality or sometimes overt hostility towards the state was a corollary of the revolution in the centre-periphery relationship under Napoleonic rule.[37] The creation of new territorial units and the uniformization of the administrative organization marked a clean break with the Old Regime, and was a severe blow to the traditional elites. Their opposition rose, when the Restoration appeared to preserve many institutions of the Napoleonic state. This was particularly evident in the Kingdom of Naples. In 1820 many Neapolitan municipalities sent petitions to parliament, in which they voiced their grievances about a bill for a new communal law. One of the recurrent themes was the demand for the re-establishment of the old communal powers, from which the old elites had greatly benefited.[38] The autonomy

---

36 According to Zeldin Bonapartism was the means by which centralization solved the 'problem' of universal suffrage in France, T. Zeldin, *France 1848-1915*, vol. 1, *Ambition, Love and Politics* (Oxford, 1973), 522.

37 M. Broers, 'Italy and the Modern State: the Experience of Napoleonic Rule', in: *The French Revolution and the Creation of Modern Political Culture*, vol. 3, *The Transformation of Political Culture 1789-1848*, edited by F. Furet & M. Ozouf (Oxford, 1989), 489-503.

38 A. Spagnoletti, 'Centri e periferie nello Stato napoletano del primo Ottocento', in: *Il Mezzogiorno*

aspired to was that of the Old Regime, not in any way related to the interests of a unitary state. The resistance shown in the Napoleonic period and the Restoration should not necessarily be seen as having a direct, linear link with the opposition after Unification. Yet it remains true, particularly in the *Mezzogiorno*, that family rivalries stemming from changes of landownership in the early nineteenth century thwarted municipal government until well after 1860.

Preunitary practices and beliefs continued to interfere with the unfolding of 'good administration' in many ways. In the early 1860s the prefect of Palermo, Luigi Torelli, felt compelled to grant weekly 'hearings' to the public, as the viceroy had always done. In his memoirs Torelli recounts with annoyance how his Friday afternoons were invariably spoiled by lines of people begging for small favours or summary justice. He wanted to abolish the custom but 'all the locals told me that the result would be very bad, and that I should have patience and should persevere, because its sudden abolition would be dangerous'.[39] Many other forms of popular traditions hampering administrative modernization will be discussed.

Of the three provinces under consideration the prefects met, not surprisingly, with the greatest difficulties in the province of Reggio Calabria. The province of Reggio, covering an area of about 4,000 square kilometers, had been established in 1816 as Calabria Ulteriore Prima, a name it would carry for some time after Unification.[40] The transition from the old to the new regime was not accompanied by an insurrection. Garibaldi appointed Antonino Plutino, an anti-Bourbon exile, governor of the province. Plutino immediately issued a series of decrees, including one promulgating the Piedmontese constitution, which sealed the annexation to the Kingdom of Sardinia. The province was divided into three districts (Reggio, Palmi and Gerace), and comprised 106 (later 107) municipalities. In 1861 it had about 325,000 inhabitants, rising to 373,000 in 1881, and reaching 445,000 in 1901. Nature showed little mercy to them. The high inlands consisted of largely impenetrable mountains and forests. In the rainy season the swollen torrents flooded the few existing roads. Malaria was a dreaded disease in the lower marshes. The entire region lived under the threat of an earthquake that, like that of 1783, would devastate much of what men had built. Nature granted some potential sources of income too, but they were barely exploited or rapidly exhausted. Deforestation occurred on a large scale. The people only very slowly lost their age-old distrust of the sea. Most villages were high up in the mountains, where the earth was less fertile but the location was safer and the climate more salubrious. The harbour of Reggio was not geared to the requirements of modern shipping, and the city missed the opportunities offered by the opening of the Suez Canal. The specialized agriculture (mainly citrus fruits, olives and wine) was

---

preunitario. Economia, società e istituzioni, edited by A. Massafra (Bari, 1988), 383-384.

 39 Cited in A. Monti, *Il conte Luigi Torelli* (Milan, 1931), 177.

 40 In 1806 Calabria was divided into two provinces, Citeriore and Ulteriore. The latter had Monteleone as capital. Reggio was no more than a district. See U. Caldora, *Calabria napoleonica (1806-1815)* (Naples, 1960), 35-36.

not strong enough to pull the provincial economy through the long economic crisis that set in in the early 1880s.[41]

In the coastal area the land was divided up among smallholders, whereas large estates were predominant in the mountains. The division of the demesnes and lands of the Church – a project that was underway since the Napoleonic period – did not result in a more equal distribution. Many fertile areas remained uncultivated because of the unwillingness or, especially after the beginning of the agrarian crisis, the impossibility on the part of the landowners to invest. Economic stagnation perpetuated the existing social relations based on an authoritarion and clientelistic exercise of power. Under these social and economic circumstances the realization of the liberal project (good administration, primary education and road building) needed time and patience. The endurance of the state proved to be insufficient to overcome the counterforces at the local level. The failure of the state has always been stressed in the debates on the *questione meridionale*. Without wishing to prove this criticism false, I intend to pay particular attention to the mediation between state and society of the prefects, who were after all simultaneously representatives of that state and advocates of local interests.

Apparently, the prefect's job was easier in the province of Bologna. But, as we shall see, a different range of problems faced the implementation of 'good administration' in that region. The province of Bologna, extending over 3,600 square kilometers, had three districts: Bologna itself and surrounding communes, Imola and its plains, and the mountainous area of Vergato. The province had 58 municipalities (61 as from 1884), about 415,000 inhabitants in 1861, 461,000 in 1881 and 521,000 in 1901. The territorial and administrative organization had been reformed during the Napoleonic period, last in 1810.[42] During the Restoration, when the province was part of the Papal States, the system of control of local administration was maintained. Bologna became one of the 17 *delegazioni*, administered by a cardinal legate.[43] In 1859 the provinces of Emilia Romagna freed themselves from the papal regime, and a few months later joined the Piedmontese Kingdom.[44]

Bologna was a hub of economic, political and cultural life. Its university was the first and most prominent of Italy. Important exponents of the national political elite, like Minghetti, Pepoli and Codronchi, were from the area. It had a strategic location in the southeastern zone of the Po Valley; it commanded traffic routes from the North

---

41 L. Gambi, *Calabria* (Turin, 1978); G. Cingari, *Storia della Calabria dall'unità ad oggi* (Bari, 1982); Idem, *Reggio Calabria* (Bari, 1988); P. Bevilacqua, 'Uomini, terre, economie', in: *Storia d'Italia Einaudi. Le regioni dall'Unità a oggi. La Calabria*, edited by P. Bevilacqua & A. Placanica (Turin, 1985), 115-362.

42 A. Bellettini, *La popolazione del dipartimento del Reno* (Bologna, 1965), 34; M. Zani, 'Le circoscrizioni comunali in età napoleonica. Il riordino dei dipartimenti del Reno e del Panaro tra 1802 e 1814', *Storia Urbana* (1990), n. 51, 44-97.

43 E. Rotelli, 'Gli ordinamenti locali preunitari', in: Idem, *L'alternativa delle autonomie. Istituzioni locali e tendenze politiche dell'Italia moderna* (Milan, 1978), 96-117.

44 See on these events I. Zanni Rosiello, *L'unificazione politica e amministrativa nelle 'provincie dell'Emilia' (1859-60)* (Milan, 1965).

to Florence and the South, and from the Adriatic to the Tyrrhenian Sea. The main economic activity was agriculture. Bologna had long been the centre of hemp cultivation in Italy, but other crops were successfully grown as well. Small peasant property was predominant in the mountains, sharecroppers (*mezzadri*) were the largest peasant class in the foothills, and large and often prosperous estates, exploiting large numbers of day labourers (*braccianti*), were mostly found in the plains.[45]

The biggest challenge to administrative peace came, as the prefects often reported, from various 'subversive' movements. The anti-liberal clergy had a controlling influence on the scattered communes in the mountains of Vergato. The intransigent catholic opposition had its stronghold in the city of Bologna and long compromised the relations between Church and state. The authorities nourished a deep distrust of the various democratic organizations, which were supported by famous professors like Ceneri, Carducci and Filopanti. But the real danger, in the view of the ruling elites, came from the socialists, emerging in Imola and other towns in the countryside. The political actions of the prefects were more and more marked by direct and indirect surveillance of these groups. In addition to that, social and political protest regularly flared up among the rural proletariat, calling for incessant watchfulness.[46]

The province of Venice, stretching over a lagoon area of about 2,000 square kilometers, was characterized by the overwhelming prevalence of the city of Venice over the other municipalities. The province had about 338,000 inhabitants in 1871, of whom almost 40% lived in the city. In 1896 the population had risen to 386,000. The province had seven districts and 51 municipalities. As under Austrian rule, the districts, except Venice itself, were administered by *commissari distrettuali*, not by subprefects. In 1882 the commissioner's offices of Mestre, Mirano and Dolo were abolished, leaving only those of Chioggia, Portogruaro and San Donà intact.

Apart from the perennial problems posed by the regulation of the lagoon, the economic situation of Venice was somewhat alarming. Its harbour activities were declining, largely because the hinterland could not be opened up. The agricultural sector was backward and received few impulses. Many landowners lived in the city, and were unable to exploit their possessions efficiently. Much was expected from state subsidies to improve the infrastructure, but its interventions were scarce. The prefects, most of whom were fully aware of the special circumstances of the province, thus got into a difficult position: on the one hand, they were supposed to discharge their limited responsibilities as state officials; on the other hand, they frequently made a stand for the public works that the lagoon area so badly needed.

Just as in Bologna the state authorities considered the strong clerical presence a potential menace to the execution of the liberal programme. Moreover the prefects

45   A.L. Cardoza, *Agrarian Elites and Italian Fascism. The Province of Bologna, 1901-1926* (Princeton, 1982), particularly 13-67.
46   See the various contributions in: *Bologna*, edited by R. Zangheri (Bari, 1986).

often complained about the conservative mentality of the aristocracy, who, it was believed, tended towards short-term alliances with the Church.

For each province I have highlighted one municipality in particular: Melito Porto Salvo in Reggio, Medicina in Bologna, and Chioggia in Venice. These communes had nothing in common. Yet the law made them equal in their institutions. In each of them certain administrative deadlocks, often remnants of preunitary problems, hampered orderly communal government, and therefore put great strains on prefectural control. The procrastinated dissolution of the *partecipanza* (an ancient agrarian association) of Medicina, the old peasant rights in the district of Chioggia, and the question of the demesnes in Melito demonstrated each in their own way the limited effectiveness of the administrative instruments at the disposal of the prefects.

Chapter 3

Control of local government: 'childish tutelage' and emancipation

1 INTRODUCTION

Municipal government was a matter of continual worry to the Ministry of the Interior and to the prefects. Innumerable circulars on every conceivable aspect of communal administration were sent, from the Ministry to the prefects, and from the prefects to the mayors. But the mere repetition of information or incitement leads one to suspect that these verbal instruments were largely ineffective. In municipal government, more than in any other field, the tension between the expectations with regard to administrative life in the periphery on the one hand and its actual organization and development on the other, comes to light.

Administrative thinking in the first half of the nineteenth century was much concerned with the juridical position of the commune. The free and prosperous city-states of the Early Renaissance were still in the back of many minds, but it was generally accepted that the same independence could never be granted to the municipalities of the nineteenth century. The debate centred around the relationship between the state and the municipalities. On the one hand, until the end of the century many politicians and theorists, following Royer-Collard's famous words of the early Restoration, pointed to the 'pre-state' origins of the commune: 'the commune is like the family, prior to the state; the political law finds it and does not create it'. This maxim had lasting repercussions. It was, for example, very difficult to consolidate municipalities against their will (even though there were compelling financial motives to do so). On the other hand, whatever the degree of local autonomy, the science of administrative law and other administrative sciences developed the principle that the commune, 'first nucleus of the state', and the province, 'first image of the nation', were in the last resort subsidiary to the state.[1] If they failed to discharge their primary duties, the state was obliged to intervene. This idea had enormous practical implications after Unification. The formation of the national state was a necessary moment in the unfolding of the liberty of associations and individuals, but it burdened the municipalities and provinces with unprecedented responsibilities. All public administrations were being subordinated to the one goal of unity,

---

1 'Riforme dell'amministrazione comunale e provinciale e del contenzioso amministrativo', *RAR*, 2 (1851), 500.

and had to pay for that. The administrative doctrines of the Restoration proved very practical. Communes and provinces, an important commentator said shortly after Unification, were more than voluntary associations of private citizens; they derived their existence from the state, and were subject to its laws.[2] Hence, despite a certain liberalization the communal and provincial laws of 1848, 1859 and 1865, which were *grosso modo* identical, allowed for strict control from above. To what purpose this control was deployed and how it worked out in practice, are the underlying questions of the chapters that follow.

The degree of selfgovernment granted to the municipalities, irrespective of what critics of the centralized system had to say, was quite large by comparison with most preunitary states (Piedmont being the logical exception): though the franchise limited the number of voters considerably, each municipality elected its own representatives to the communal council. The will or 'capacity', however, of the municipalities to govern themselves in the way the founding fathers of Italy wished, was often insufficient. This gave the role of the prefects a particular cachet. They were not just the routine-ridden executors of state control, but, at least in the early years of the unitary state, they were supposed to guide the municipalities towards a more modern administration, based on representation and budgetary control.

This chapter is concerned with, first, the aims and the instruments at the disposal of the prefects, the representatives of the state, in exerting their control over municipal government; second, the obstacles that they had to overcome; and third, the highly ambivalent distinction between the 'educational' part of their job and unsolicited encroachments upon local interests. The popular characterization 'childish tutelage', coined by the jurist Giovanni de Gioannis Gianquinto to describe rigid surveillance from above, was perhaps exaggerated, but there were certainly great dangers in the prefectural discretionary powers.[3] Two features of local government will be discussed here: the appointment of mayors, and local (or administrative) elections. Another essential aspect, the dissolution of communal councils, will be the subject of a separate chapter. As at moments of crisis the margins of control are best visible, I have chosen to pick a number of examples of (in the eyes of the prefects) faulty communal government. They are perhaps not representative of everyday routine, but they show the fundamental ambivalence of the administrative system. Wherever possible the origins of the administrative deadlocks will be noted.

Despite the general euphoria it could not be expected that the transition towards administrative integration would be a smooth process. The first prefects, led away by

---

2 'Relazione (Bon Compagni) presentata l'8 marzo 1862 a nome della commissione della Camera dei deputati, sul progetto di legge presentato dal presidente del Consiglio il 22 dicembre 1861', published in: C. Pavone, *Amministrazione centrale e amministrazione periferica da Rattazzi a Ricasoli (1859-1866)* (Milan, 1964), 602.

3 Cited in G. Rebuffa, *La formazione del diritto amministrativo in Italia. Profili di amministrativisti preorlandiani* (Bologna, 1981), 82.

the enthusiasm of the early days of Unification, beat the drum for ambitious projects in their provinces. In September 1861 Raffaele Cassito, governor and later prefect of Reggio Calabria, exaltedly paid his respects to the newly installed provincial council. He praised its members for their courage in taking part in the making of Italy. He stressed that they were required not to follow an established system, but to re-create public administration on new foundations. He listed the aims of the new institutions: setting up public education, beginning public works, providing economic assistance, and so on.[4] A year later the atmosphere had completely changed. The high hopes had been replaced by grim pragmatism. The then prefect Giuseppe Cornero opened his speech announcing 'few and harsh words, because the grave conditions and worries of his days did not consent him to say more'. Cornero, knowing the province from an earlier mission at the beginning of 1861, considered most municipalities unprepared for the new liberties: 'the communes, especially the smallest and most mountainous, were caught by surprise, and, since almost all confused liberty with licence, they were unfit to sustain the new institutions'.[5]

Massimo Cordero di Montezemolo, prefect of Bologna from 1862 to 1865, describing in December 1862 the situation of the province, attributed shortcomings in communal government to low morale: the absentee large landlords took little interest in the administration of the municipalities where they had their possessions; the smaller landowners, omnipresent in the communal councils, had no 'moral authority' over the rural population.[6] Before the unifying administrative laws of 1865 were promulgated, the prefecture and the local administrations had to find their way through what was left of old legislation that dealt with areas not yet covered by the new legislation. In the spring of 1863 Cordero reported that 'one treats administrative matters rather with the arbitrariness of common sense and with rules that are gradually asserted without unity and without conceptual continuity, so that it gets very difficult to point out the

---

4 'Discorso del governatore', in: *Atti del consiglio provinciale di Calabria Ulteriore Prima per l'anno 1861* (Reggio Calabria, 1862), 14-25. In many provinces the prefects gave an annual account of administrative life to the provincial council. In the Kingdom of Naples (but not only there) this had been a regular custom. The importance of such a report, which was to facilitate the work of the council, had already been stressed by P. Liberatore, *Institutzioni della legislazione amministrativa vigente nel Regno delle Due Sicilie dettate nel suo privato studio di diritto* (Naples, 1836-38), I, 52. In 1858, for the Kingdom of Sardinia, Cavour had laid down precise instructions for the structure of the annual report to the provincial council, *Circolare del Ministero dell'Interno*, 1 September 1858, published in: *RAR*, 9 (1858) 611-615. After Unification, however, the prefects were less and less eager to bear this responsibility. After Crispi's new communal and provincial law of 1889, which abolished the prefect's presidency over the provincial deputation, the annual reports to the council got into disuse.

5 'Relazione del prefetto funzionante da commissario del Re', in: *Atti del Consiglio Provinciale de Calabria Ulteriore Prima nell'anno 1862* (Reggio Calabria, 1863), 9-10. On the earlier mission of Cornero, see D. De Giorgio, 'La provincia di Reggio dopo la liberazione del 1860. La missione Cornero', *Historica*, 11 (1958), 163-169.

6 ASB, Intendenza Generale, Archivio riservato (1862), b. 13, letter of the prefect to the Ministry of the Interior, 21 December 1862.

47

defects in the procedure, which cannot be said to have been definitively established'.[7]
The royal commissioner and first prefect of Venice, Giuseppe Pasolini, energetically
began his term of office by requesting the district commissioners to draw up a
detailed report about the administrative services under their control. He simultaneously stressed the importance of 'the control and the educational action which the
governmental officials had to exert under certain circumstances'.[8] Until then the
district commissioners (who had held their office after the annexation) had acted as
secretaries for the smaller municipalities, assisting them in their day-to-day administration and during the sessions of the communal council. It took the municipalities
some time to adjust their administrations to the fresh, more autonomous situation.
The prefecture tried to help by sending regular circulars about the implementation of
the new legislation. The first aim was to instruct the district commissioners and to
urge them to study the new laws: they could no longer act as municipal secretaries,
but were tolerated as 'judges of regularity' at the meetings of the councils.[9]
Subsequently, the mayors were approached; a prefectural circular, issued by Luigi
Torelli at the end of 1867, encouraged the mayors of the province to pursue their
'mission', since communal administration had still made little progress.[10]
Whereas, understandably, in all three provinces discussed here the Piedmontese
administrative system met with problems of adaptation, the extent to which it
succeeded over the years in penetrating the radius of local government varied from
province to province. In the mid 1860s, especially after the promulgation of the
communal and provincial law, the revolutionary spirit seemed to have calmed down,
and the 'era of administration' commenced. In 1865 the prefect of Naples Vigliani
almost solemnly contended, in the same way as some of his Napoleonic predecessors
had done, that: 'In the first period of the revolution, the political element usually
absorbs the administration because of the supreme necessity to bring about in people
and things the transformation that corresponds with the form and spirit of the new
government. This could be said to have come to an end, and therefore should be
followed by the administrative period, in which the care of administration is not
disturbed by the agitation of politics'.[11]
In Reggio Calabria the breaking down of the old order was a painstaking process,
and one wonders whether the state has ever effectively made its presence felt at the
local level. The local communities lived according to their own rules, which were
inviolable for outsiders. On the one hand the large landowners who dominated the
existing power relations feared to lose the privileges enjoyed under the Bourbon
regime. Without getting actively involved in local government, they looked down on

---

  7   ASB, Pref., Gab. (1863), b. 69, answer of the prefect (20 April 1863) to the ministerial circular of 18
March 1863, n. 8812-789.
  8   *Circolare della prefettura di Venezia*, 24 October 1866, n. 33.
  9   *Circolare della prefettura di Venezia (riservato e urgente)*, 20 January 1867, n. 565.
  10   *Circolare della prefettura di Venezia*, 2 November 1867, n. 2322.
  11   Cited in the *RAR*, 16 (1865), 726.

those who did. Achille Serpieri, prefect of Reggio from 1868 to 1871, bitterly recorded that the richest men were the first to oppose roads and schools. 'A real general civil renewal of this province was far away with such coefficients', the prefect pessimistically noted.[12] On the other hand the new local administrators – from the mayors down to the municipal secretaries – lacked the know-how or the willingness to come up to the liberal expectations. Serpieri lamented the absence of 'all local life, since all administrative acts were reduced to a burden and to simple matters of form'. The prefecture had to interfere in every minute act of the municipalities; consequently, there was no time to make initiatives to bring about more general improvements. He set himself the task to *'prepare with expedient regulations local life itself in order to enable it to absorb the administration'* (my italics).[13] Although ten years had passed since Unification, it would be foolish, according to Serpieri, to entrust the municipal government fully to the local population (by which he obviously intended only the notables). The administrative project to be carried out in Reggio Calabria (and in the South in general) consisted not only in executing laws and regulations, but came near to proposing a massive societal reform. With a handful of state officials in each province and many bridges to cross it could not be expected that this formidable task would be accomplished within a few years. One cannot be surprised to find that until the last decade of the century the prefects continued to report the unwillingness or indifference of the local elites in administering their municipalities.

Economic backwardness, poor communications and uncooperative local elites were one set of obstacles; political interests were another. Technically, the municipalities of the provinces of Bologna and Venice found less difficulty in making their administrations work, although, as will be shown, numerous exceptions proved the rule. But, especially in Bologna, the prefects had their hands full with the 'politicization' of many communal councils, by which they meant interference by supralocal interests. It is true that from the 1870s onwards clericals, radicals and internationalists turned communal politics into their battlefield. The aim of the state representatives was usually to try to calm the emotions roused by the presence of these so-called subversive elements in the councils. In this connection one could add the fast growth of associations in Emilia-Romagna, which put great strains on the prefect's task of keeping all tendencies towards subversive action under surveillance. In Venice the threats to the unfolding of the liberal administrative system came from clerical and conservative parts. Particularly in the city of Venice, which administratively dominated the rest of the province, strong elite groups represented a forceful opposition to the striving for pacification pursued by the prefects.

---

12 ASRC, Pref., Gab., b. 62, f. 981, report of the prefect to the Ministry of the Interior, 5 July 1870.
13 *Ibidem*, report of the prefect to the Ministry of the Interior, 10 October 1871.

2 THE APPOINTMENT OF MAYORS

The legislation concerning the appointment of mayors (*sindaci*) remained unchanged between the Piedmontese edict of 1847 on local administration, which laid the foundations for the reforms of 1848, and Crispi's communal and provincial law of 1889: they were nominated by the King from within the communal council for a period of three years. Since 1889 the councils of cities with more than 10.000 inhabitants were free to appoint their mayor. Eventually, in 1896, all councils acquired this right.

Appointment from above was not a rare procedure in nineteenth-century Europe. The Piedmontese legislation derived, not only on this point, from the Belgian communal law of 1836. The Kingdom of the Netherlands had a similar system (introduced in 1851), leaving the choice fully to the King. Likewise, the French municipal act of 1831 laid down that the mayors had to be nominated from within the municipal council. Under the Second Empire the clock was turned back, but after 1871 the relevant laws gradually reintroduced election from within the council. The only real exception was, of course, Great Britain, where no comparable function (i.e. a mayor responding to a higher state authority) existed.[14]

In Italy the appointment of mayors fully complied with liberal administrative thought, as it developed before and after Unification. The mayor – the communal and provincial law of 1865 recapitulated – is at once the head of the municipal administration and a governmental official. This duality, according to the doctrines, was logical and necessary to ensure that the mayor kept a watchful eye on both local and general interests. The authoritative *Rivista Amministrativa del Regno*, from its first years onwards, regularly paid attention to the mayor's duties. In 1854 the review stressed the importance of a lasting agreement between the state and the municipalities, and between the municipalities and their residents: 'The commune is, so to say, a minor whose tutelage is entrusted to the mayor (...). The mayor has to put together the different and sometimes repugnant interests of the persons making up the commune, and he has to make sure that the administration of property fulfils, as far as possible, everybody's need'.[15] A ministerial circular of 17 November 1868 still echoed the early liberal ideology: 'The mayors are called upon to show the living and true idea of liberty that goes together with authority; of local interests that intermingle and form a whole with general interests; of good administration that constitutes and expresses good politics, under the protection of the institutions and the laws'. To some extent, the mayor was closer to the grass roots of administration than the prefect. 'Wherever the law', a publicist wrote, 'seeks and affects people and goods individually, it makes use of the mayors' arm. The prefects transmit the action,

---

14 A. Malgarini, 'Del modo di nominare il capo del comune secondo la legislazione comparata', *Archivio Giuridico*, 30 (1883), 347-412; L. Frezzini, entry 'Sindaco', *Digesto Italiano*, XXI, parte 3ª, sezione 1ª (Turin, 1895-1902), 459-460. See also, J. George, *Histoire des maires, 1789-1939* (Paris, 1989).

15 *RAR*, 5 (1854), 6.

watch, direct, and control; the mayors execute'.[16] They combined in themselves virtually all the administrative powers of the state. These powers, Frezzini acutely noted in his entry in the *Digesto Italiano*, augmented in inverse relation to the size of the municipality governed by the mayor, 'because it is exactly in minor communes that the number of offices and governmental officials is less, as a result of which one can say that in small communes the government manifests and fulfils itself in the mayor'.[17] The most important tasks of the mayors in their quality as government officials were the publication of laws and regulations, the keeping of the registry office, and maintaining public order.[18]

The system of appointing the mayor from above seemed, to its supporters, in perfect accordance with the double role of government official and head of the municipal administration. Luigi Tegas, prefect and deputy, wholeheartedly justified it: 'Herein lies the real point of contact between the state and the communes. From this double nature it follows that local as well as central authorities have to take part in his nomination. If election, either by the council or by the inhabitants, is involved in the nomination, the mayor ceases *ipso jure et facto* to represent the state: in the same way as he would cease to represent the commune, if the government could chose him from outside the council. In the current manner of appointment both powers are really present, all the more so because the government is required to make a choice from the majority among the councillors, whose support is essential to the mayor'.[19] Tegas spoke for most of his colleagues. A ministerial investigation carried out in 1869 brought to light that a majority of the prefects preferred to leave the appointment of the mayors in the hands of the executive.[20]

It is, on the other hand, quite clear that the dual nature of the mayor's job, in practice, could give rise to profound clashes of interests. Acting on behalf of his municipality, the mayor might infringe upon the state's pursuit of uniformity; following blindly the government's wishes, he could well remain isolated in the communal council. Both rendered efficient administration very difficult. Some publicists, taking their cue from decentralization theories, questioned the appropriateness of the appointment from above. In V. Conti's view state officials were not very well informed about local circumstances; hence, they tended to nominate persons

---

16 Malgarini, 351.

17 Frezzini, 477.

18 A general, elaborate work on the mayor's functions was written by the municipal secretary of Naples, A. Romano, *Il sindaco del comune italiano. Guida teorico-prattica preceduta da nozioni generali di pubblica amministrazione* (Naples, 1884).

19 L. Tegas, *Interesse generale e interessi locali. Studi* (Brescia, 1871), 67-68.

20 The aggregate results of the investigation were published in AP, CD, legisl. XIII, sess. 1876-77, Documenti, no. 33A, report of the commission (spokesman A. Marazio) on the bill of Nicotera for a reform of the communal and provincial law (*all.* H). Some reports written in reply to the ministerial circular were published in the *Rivista Amministrativa* of 1869. The inquiry has been discussed exhaustively by R. Romanelli, 'Tra autonomia e ingerenza: un'indagine del 1869', in: Id., *Il comando impossibile. Stato e società nell'Italia liberale* (Bologna, 1988), 77-150 (particularly 115-129 on the mayor).

whose only virtue was their loyalty to the government of the day.[21] In the following we shall examine, first, to what extent the two sides of the mayor's job were compatible in the changing political and administrative climate; second, what influence the prefects were able to exert in the mayor's appointment and in the exercise of his duties.

The first mayors after Unification were appointed under the various transitory regimes (e.g. in the province of Reggio Calabria by decree of the *luogotenenza generale* of Naples, and in Bologna by decree of Farini). The attitude towards the revolution was the prime criterion, although not infrequently incumbent mayors kept their office. Thus the first round of 'normal' appointments took place in 1863. Unfortunately, there is little material left in the prefectural archives of Reggio Calabria and Bologna to shed light on the nominations in the early years. Nevertheless, some salient aspects of the procedure show through.

It is evident that the proposals made by the prefects to the Ministry of the Interior were of overriding importance. But it is also clear that they had to rely on information from third parties: because of their continual replacements the prefects were mostly unfamiliar with grass roots local government. It was therefore quite normal that in October 1863 the prefect of Reggio Calabria, by confidential dispatches, asked the local judges, the commanders of the *carabinieri* stations, and the provincial councillors to give their opinion on the sitting mayors and on new candidates.[22]

Requesting information from state officials stationed in the municipalities became a regular practice. Every three years a time-consuming procedure was begun in order to appoint some 8000 mayors throughout the Kingdom. Shortly after the yearly partial elections for the communal council the Ministry used to press the prefects to submit their proposals. A first indication for the prefects was the election of the *giunta* (the body of aldermen assiting the mayor in the day-to-day administration), which told him which councillor was most accepted in the council. Making this man mayor would at least prevent conflicts between the mayor and the council. In general, finding and nominating the right candidate required considerable conciliatory skills. It was always a relief for the prefects when a well-to-do, influential, liberal citizen with some administrative experience accepted the job. But it regularly happened that after the first scrutiny the most preferred candidate refused. The richest and most powerful men often chose not to get involved in the intricacies of local government. Then, if the first candidate continued to resist the powers of persuasion, the search for the right man, including another round of inquiries, started all over again.

In the smaller municipalities the 'supply' of suitable candidates was heavily limited. The subprefect of Palmi (Reggio Calabria) bitterly observed: 'in these provinces,

21 V. Conti, *Il sindaco nel diritto amministrativo italiano. Studi di legislazione e di giurisprudenza* (Naples, 1875), 151-152.
22 ASRC, Pref., Gab., b. 1, f. 1, letters of the prefect, 21 October 1863.

where unfortunately education is so sparsely diffused, especially in the small centres, I was seriously embarrassed in making a convenient choice; and often, for want of personnel, I had to be satisfied with mediocrity, and sometimes, for fear of the worst, I had to ask for the reconfirmation of mayors who were hardly active and not at all worthy of the trust of the government'.[23] Particularly in the *Mezzogiorno*, because of the persistent personalistic, sometimes feudal power relationships, the choice of a particular candidate was often a hazardous one. To appoint an exponent of one of the usual two factions was to add fuel to the flames, or, at best, created a 'new feudalism', in which the group in power held dominion over the municipality.[24]

Mayors could lose their office in the unlikely event that they were not reelected as member of the municipal council in the partial elections. Moreover, much to the prefect's regret mayors frequently handed in their resignation before their term of office had expired. This happened in San Donà (Venice) in 1867. Only two months after his official appointment – in April 1867 – G. Bartolotto announced his intention to resign because he had miscalculated the work load. The prefect Luigi Torelli first tried to persuade him change his mind by writing him a friendly letter. After this attempt had failed, he summoned Bartolotto to Venice. Although there is no written evidence to sustain this, the prefect probably managed to put off the resignation until after the summer elections. He had, however, another letter of resignation on his desk in October. Subsequently, Torelli urged the district commissioner of San Donà, the chief of police in Venice, and the commander of the *carabinieri* to designate a successor. They all found it extremely difficult to find a man suited for the job. The district commissioner declared that 'for the time being at least, that is until the periodical renewals bring new elements into the council, it is not easy to chose as mayor someone who finds favour with public opinion and does not saddle himself with other troubles'. He enclosed a list of communal councillors, giving for each one an account of his scarse suitability for the job: two held the office of mayor elsewhere, some had no administrative experience, others would create too much tension in the council. In the meantime Bartolotto continued to perform his duty, which was taken as a tacit agreement to stay on. Nevertheless, in February 1868 Bartolotto again handed in his resignation; this time – but not before June – it was accepted. A substitute, F. Ferraresco, was appointed, who, as ill luck would have it, was among the councillors that were to be reelected in the partial elections of that summer. Fortunately, he returned with a majority of votes in the council, and the district commissionar did not hesitate to push him forward as a serious candidate. His qualities were evident: he was one of the most wealthy landowners in town; his family was widely respected; he had a distinguished lifestyle; and, last but not least, he held moderate principles. Alas, he already held the office of mayor in a nearby municipality. Ferraresco preferred to stay on as mayor there, but accepted governing

---

23 ASRC, Pref., Gab., b. 1, f. 3, letter of the subprefect to the prefect, 16 October 1869.
24 Romanelli, 129.

San Donà as senior alderman (*assessore anziano*) in April 1869. Hence, the prefecture had no choice but to await the end of the three year period, and to hope that Ferraresco could be persuaded to switch.[25]

Similar ordeals in the appointment of mayors were of the order of the day. Contrary to the government's wishes and the requirements of good administration the prefects often left the municipalities without an official mayor.[26] The subprefect of Palmi overtly reported in 1888 that the absence of a regular mayor in the preceding three years had worked out well for Molochio: public opinion had had a chance to reorientate itself, and a major shift had occurred after the last elections for the council. A new man, in the meantime appointed as mayor, had emerged, who otherwise would not have been spotted by the higher authorities. The subprefect even went as far as to state that, in general, leaving a municipality without a regular mayor and entrusting the senior alderman with the attendant duties was less risky than giving the office to someone who could seriously embarrass the government's trust.[27] Indeed, many mayors were found to betray the confidence put in them by the higher authorities. An appendix to Nicotera's draft for a new communal and provincial law (1877) contained alarming evidence. It showed that from 1 January 1873 to 23 November 1875 penal proceedings were started against 221 mayors for criminal offences, and another 601 incurred a fine.[28]

An important condition for becoming mayor was the fixed residence in the municipality in question. Nevertheless, many smaller municipalities were ruled by absentee mayors, because the wealthiest and most authoritative men used to prefer the luxury of the city to the hardship of country life. Their absence tended to accumulate power in the hands of the communal secretaries, which could be detrimental to the municipal administration. Particularly in the South, the secretaries usually did not have the license required by the regulations that followed the communal and provincial law of 1865.[29] Accordingly, their suitability for the job left much to be desired. Furthermore, it was not easy for the mostly low-paid communal secretaries to maintain an independent position between rivalling factions. On the other hand, there is also

---

25 ASV, Pref., Gab. (1866-71), f. 5, 4/1, various letters.

26 The ministerial circular of 30 September 1868, n. 8984, said that the law provided for the replacement of the regular mayor by an alderman, but this situation was to be avoided in order to safeguard good administration. Another ministerial circular, 3 January 1873, n. 16300, inquired into the state of the mayoralty in the municipalities. It appeared that in 1872 in the province of Venice four municipalities had been without a mayor because of resignations or refusals, ASV, Pref., Gab. (1877-81), rubr. 5, 4/1, letter of the prefect to the Ministry, 15 January 1873. Shortly before the triennial renewal for the period 1875-1877 12 municipalities in the province of Bologna did not have a regular mayor, ASB, Pref., Gab., b. 240.

27 ASRC, Pref., Gab., b. 3, f. 24, letter of the subprefect of Palmi Beniamino Battistoni, who held the office since 1882, to the prefect, 5 May 1888.

28 Report of Marazio on Nicotera's bill of a new communal and provincial law (1877), *op. cit.*, all. F.

29 On the municipal secretaries between Unification and World War I see R. Romanelli, *Sulle carte interminate. Un ceto di impiegati tra privato e pubblico: i segretari comunali in Italia, 1860-1915* (Bologna, 1989).

much evidence that they used their function and experience to tyrannize over a municipality. We encounter such a situation in Casal Fiumanese, a small town of ca. 3500 inhabitants in the subprefecture of Imola, in the mid 1870s. For many years Antonio Barbieri held the office of mayor, despite the doubts expressed by the subprefect shortly before the triennial renewal for 1875-77. Barbieri lived in Imola and totally relied upon his secretary for the day-to-day administration. It had come to the prefect's attention that this secretary did not always exert his function for the benefit of the municipality, and, what was worse in his eyes, the man used his influence to favour the clerical party.[30] The subprefect of Imola, asked to investigate the matter, could not but endorse these allegations. The *giunta* rarely met and the meetings of the communal council were usually postponed until the last moment to give the mayor time to settle his personal affairs. Barbieri, though weak, was known as a gentleman and respectful of the law. He was, according to the subprefect, supported by the majority, because he uncomplainingly did what others wanted. Sant'Andrea, the municipal secretary, was the man behind the show: 'Hence, unfortunately, I cannot but believe that whatever mayor is appointed among the citizens of Casal Fiumanese, he would be forced to suffer the influence of Sant'Andrea, and at the same time I am convinced that the municipal affairs would gain a lot by changing secretary, since experience has shown that these old municipal employees are good for nothing but preserving a bad status quo, which enables them to live prosperously without minding that the communal administration remains sterile, idle and on the verge of breakdown'.[31]

The appointment of mayors in the larger cities, before the new communal and provincial law of 1889 made the office of mayor eligible, posed particular problems. On the one hand, the prefects did not want to antagonize the local power elites. Hence, they tended to follow the preferences of the communal council by nominating the alderman with the highest votes. Or they appointed a leading local administrator who was also active on the national political level. Gaetano Tacconi, mayor of Bologna for many years in the 1870s and 1880s, was a distinguished member of Parliament. On the other hand, the rapidly shifting alliances in urban politics rendered a stable appointment almost impossible. The political controversies in the communal council of Venice, which were particularly vehement in the late 1860s and 1870s, gave the prefects little to go on; accordingly, several mayors succeeded each other within a relatively short time.

---

30 ASB, Pref., Gab., b. 256, letter of the prefect to the subprefect of Imola, 16 September 1875.
31 *Ibidem*, reply of the subprefect, 29 September 1875.

3 POLITICAL INTERFERENCE IN THE NOMINATION OF MAYORS

The definition of 'government official' given to the mayor and his appointment from above rendered guidance along ministerial lines always an easy option. It would be interesting to see if this happened in 1876, the year of the the parliamentary swing from the *Destra* to the *Sinistra*, which is always said to have had such a corrupting influence on the political and administrative culture. The actual 'revolution' had taken place in March 1876, and had come too late to affect the triennial renewal for the period 1876-1878. There is, however, some evidence that the vacancies still to be filled fell victim to political interference. In Spinea, a village of 2,000 inhabitants near Venice, the membership of the communal council of the incumbent mayor expired in the summer of 1876. In spite of his reelection the new prefect Sormani Moretti had his eye on another candidate, who 'showed himself convinced of the goodness of the programme that the current cabinet intends to impose on public administration, and is prepared to accept public office in order to cooperate in that sense'.[32] Shortly after the appointment of the prefect's man all hell broke loose; the old mayor managed to persuade his supporters (who held a majority in the council) to resign. This convinced the new mayor that it was no use staying on; he resigned together with his aldermen. The general elections that followed after the dissolution of the council restored the old mayor's majority, and from that circle a new mayor was eventually appointed. Thus the municipalities had an effective weapon – deliberate obstruction – to protect themselves against unwanted encroachments upon their interests, even if these concerned the appointment of the mayor.

On the other hand, not only the municipalities, but the prefects too were subject to control from above. During the scrutiny of candidates the Ministry of the Interior often came up with names that circulated in the central offices. The prefects were professionally required to check these proposals, but they were not too pleased with this way of going about things. In 1878 the Ministry continued to throw up names for the office of mayor in Crevalcore, a town of 10,000 inhabitants in the district of Bologna. The prefect Nicola Petra, duke of Vastogirardi, stuck to the incumbent mayor, because, as he stated with some irritation, 'unpleasant disagreement in that municipal representation would be avoided, as well as further recommendations to the superior Ministry, which have no other significance than being inconsistent with each other and revealing ever more the difficulties which the proposal of mayors puts to those who want to have nothing to do with the parties nor, to put it better, with the various political cleavages dividing the villages'.[33]

Not only had the prefects to respond to the proposals that more or less officially arrived from the Ministry of the Interior, but they also had to deal with the parlia-

---

32 ASV, Pref., Gab. (1877-81), rubr. 5, 4/1, confidential letter of the prefect to the Ministry of the Interior, 24 September 1876.
33 ASB, Pref., Gab., b. 378, letter of the prefect to the Ministry of the Interior, 27 May 1878.

mentary deputies and senators of their province. Here the line between neutral information and personal interests was naturally very thin.

This can be further illustrated by the procedure for the appointment of mayors in the period 1878-80, which went through many channels. The prefect appoached the usual state officials (commanders of *carabinieri* stations, the subprefects, the prefecture's head councillor, etc.); but he also asked some deputies and senators for advice: Gustavo Vicini and Cesare Lugli (local members of parliament), Gaetano Tacconi (mayor of Bologna and member of parliament), and Francesco Magni (senator). It seems that the prefect took all opinions into account, and finally presented a well-considered list to the Ministry. As political conflicts grew more heated (nationally and locally), the appointment of mayors got more difficult. In 1886-87 the prefect of Bologna and the Ministry could not agree upon the mayor of San Lazzaro di Savena. There were two candidates, who were both 'good and honest citizens'. It appeared that the controversy could be reduced to two deputies having opposite ideas. The matter was further complicated by allegations of clericalism about one of the candidates. A Solomonic judgement eventually came from Giacinto Scelsi, a highly respected prefect from Crispi's circle, who carefully assessed the information available in his archive. He chose the man that, according to the local justice of peace (*pretore*), enjoyed the confidence of the majority of the council, and was able to settle some long-standing administrative problems.[34]

The influence of parliamentary deputies remains a fairly shadowy affair. The local press, inextricably tied to specific lobbies, liked to proclaim conspiracies of mayors, deputies and prefects from the rooftops. A parliamentary commission studying the desirability of the election of the mayor wrote: 'The mayor is inclined to offer his support to the deputy, on condition that he is supported by the government; the deputy is inclined to oppose the nomination of a mayor who was not his partisan at the elections; the government is inclined to avail itself of the mayors to obtain a favourable electoral result for its candidates '.[35] But it is difficult to find hard evidence to sustain these allegations. It seems that from the middle of the 1880s deputies tended to occupy themselves more actively with the nomination of mayors. In 1885 Pasquale Cordopatri, deputy for Catanzaro II, wrote from Rome to the prefect of Reggio Calabria to propose his brother as mayor of Rizziconi, because, he alleged, the subprefect would, for personal reasons, certainly not put him forward.[36] On the other hand, the deputy was not necessarily the prefect's patron. After the administrative elections of 1889 Rocco De Zerbi, deputy in the province of Reggio, let the prefect know that 'the victors and the defeated in Polistena assailed me with recommendations for the nomination of the mayor. I do not want to find myself in conflict

34 ASB, Pref., Gab. (1887), cat. IV, letter of the prefect to the Ministry, 15 August 1887.
35 AP, CD, Leg. XVIII, 1ª sess. 1892-93, Documenti, no. 88 e 89A, report of the commission Tittoni (spokesman) concerning modifications to art. 123 of the communal and provincial law (election of the mayor).
36 ASRC, Pref., Gab., b. 3, letter of P. Cordopatri to the prefect, 3 February 1885.

with you, nor do I have a preference for one or the other. What would you like me to do? (...) You are on the spot and you have a high and fair perception, so you can judge better than me'.[37] In December 1891 and January 1892, perhaps under the influence of the Calabrese Nicotera, at that time minister of the Interior, all deputies of the province of Reggio occupied themselves busily with the renewal. After the first prefectural proposals had reached the Roman corridors, Vincenzo De Blasio hastened to push forward his candidates for his district. He claimed to have only the public good in mind, since 'modesty apart, (...) my electoral power is not the mayors, but to have succeeded in convincing the voters that it is up to them to beg me to stand for parliament, not up to me to beg them to vote for me'.[38] One wonders why he insisted so much on this point. Taking their cue from the prevailing feeling at the Ministry, the deputies eventually went along with the prefect's proposals, Francesco Tripepi (another member of parliament) reported to the prefect.[39] Finally, Saverio Vollaro, an ardent supporter of the *Sinistra*, complained about the long *Via Crucis* of the appointments, but did not feel the need to push any further.[40] All in all, from the end of the 1880s onwards the local deputies of Reggio Calabria were quite entangled in the nomination of mayors. Their influence, however, is difficult to measure. It seems that they usually endorsed the opinion of the prefects.

In a letter to his subprefects, dated 10 October 1887, the prefect of Reggio Calabria pointed to the special conditions of the province, which imposed some constraints on the persons qualified for the office of mayor. First, good candidates ought to be able to deal personally with the communal administration; in other words, those who lived during the greatest part of the year outside the municipality, were not suitable for the job. Second, the mayors-to-be ought to guarantee that they would use their authority for the public benefit. Thus, those who were involved in other public or private affairs, those who were in debt to the municipality, and those who 'for their social position, their weakness of character, or lack of education' were susceptible to influences from outside, were excluded from the office of mayor.[41] The contents of this letter followed to some extent the confidential ministerial circular of 2 July 1887. It is, however, telling that some requirements defined by the Ministry were apparently superfluous for the Southern province. The circular was very clear in highlighting the political colour of the future mayors, i.e. liberal-monarchical. These prerequisites were repeated in another confidential circular of 3 December 1887, which also laid down that mayors should not belong to illegal political parties. The political requirements were obviously a minor problem in Reggio, compared to the tremendous difficulties in finding capable and decent administrators.

37 *Ibidem*, b. 4, f. 26, letter from De Zerbi to the prefect, 17 November 1889.
38 *Ibidem*, b. 4, f. 30, letter of De Blasio to the prefect, 9 January 1892.
39 *Ibidem*, b. 4, f. 30, letter of Tripepi to the prefect, 21 January 1892.
40 *Ibidem*, b. 4, f. 30, letter of Vollaro to the prefect, 5 February 1892.
41 ASRC, Pref., Gab., b. 4, f. 24.

The general administration elections following the promulgation of the new communal and provincial law (1889) showed that national politics still played a secundary role. The choice of the mayors was predominantly a matter of weighing up local interests (even though these could be entangled with the interests of deputies from the area). The subprefect of Palmi, for example, making his proposals for the nomination of mayors after the general elections of 1889, gave a short biography of each alderman. He tried to manoeuvre between the factions dominating the municipalities, and invariably gave preference to those candidates who had some experience in administration and were expected to be able to handle the constant conflicts. There were no hints at political affiliations.[42]

By that time, a number of communal councils in the provinces of Venice and Bologna had become the scene of fierce battles between parties with strong political ties transcending local rivalry. The function of mayor, there, had ceased to be a matter of mere local interest. Perhaps the clearest example is the appointment of the mayor of Imola, a town of more than 10,000 inhabitants (hence its mayor was to be elected by the communal council). Early in 1889, in a report on the public services in his district, the subprefect of Imola, reiterating the liberal belief in a clearcut distinction between politics and administration, wrote that 'in a district where politics were such a large part of the life of the citizens it was a natural, albeit regrettable fact that politics, invading the orbit of the communal administrations, caused substantial damage to the public services'.[43] The general administrative elections of 1889, the first after the widening of the local franchise, resulted in a radical majority, the first in Italy. The question of the mayoralty thus became a very arduous one, which attracted the personal attention of Crispi, minister of the Interior and premier. The subprefect closely followed the election of the mayor, and kept the prefect continually informed. The first to acquire the confidence of the Imolese council was Luigi Sassi. He thanked his audience in rather audacious words, declaring that he accepted no other authority than popular sovereignty. Crispi, after being briefed about the event, immediately reacted by telegram: 'If the words of Luigi Sassi are true, it is not necessary to ask him for explanations but to sack him. Furthermore, since his words constitute an offence according to article 471, he ought to be served with a writ of libel'.[44] The prefect, Giacinto Scelsi, preferred a more cautious approach. He pointed out that Sassi was not officially in function, and that he would certainly refuse to take the mayor's oath. The council then would have to withdraw its nomination, which it would probably not do. At that point there would be a legitimate motive for the dissolution of the council. A clever commissioner would be able to steer the subsequent general elections to a more convenient end. All this would circumvent the fuss

---

42 ASRC, Pref., Gab., b. 4, f. 26.
43 ASB, Pref., Gab. (1890), cat. 9/1, report of the subprefect of Imola, Vincenzo Lugaresi, to the prefect, 3 January 1889.
44 ASB, Pref., Gab. (1889), cat. 4/1, telegram of Crispi to the prefect, 11 November 1889.

to be expected from a lawsuit against Sassi.[45] Thus the prefect more or less let the municipal representation disunite itself. The councillors of the liberal minority soon resigned en bloc. The majority, made up of socialists, republicans and radicals, became divided, and one municipal executive succeeded the other. Finally, in May 1893 the government found a reason for the dissolution of the council in the municipality's overt support for the May Day celebrations. The elections that followed were full of venom: on the one hand, the commissioner and the subprefect tried to purge the electoral rolls in order to reduce support for the socialists; on the other, the latter actively and sometimes unlawfully fought the electoral contest.[46] What interests us here, is that the socialists managed to win and that they successfully defended their hard-won position against the 'legal' ways the state authorities tried to obstruct them. Not before February 1894, however, could the council appoint a mayor who was to retain his office for more than a year.

4 LOCAL ELECTIONS

Administrative thinking in the Kingdom of Sardinia, leaning heavily on French Restoration doctrines, tended to be in two minds about the place of the municipalities in the polity: on the one hand, the municipalities, as long as they stayed within the orbit of local interests, were accorded an advanced form of selfgovernment unknown under the Absolutist regime; on the other, they were placed at the lower end of the administrative hierarchy. These two lines of thought were perfectly reconcilable through the distinction between general and local interests, or, in other terms, between politics and administration. In 1848 Cavour himself contended: 'It is an undisputed truth in more liberal countries that the communal councils should not constitute independent political bodies; that is why it is necessary to distinguish carefully between the rights of the municipalities, which are administrative rights, and political rights. This is (...) an essential condition of a wise constitutional system, which should aim at reconciling the liberty of the people with a strong and united central power'.[47]

The communal and provincial law of 7 October 1848 set up representative bodies at the local level; the municipalities became *enti morali e giuridici sui generis*. Concurrently, the law provided the intendants (the precursors of the prefects) with considerable executive power. The municipalities were not considered voluntary associations, but were subject to requirements imposed by the state. In this way the initiative to install forms of local autonomy was immediately counterbalanced by a stronger presence of the state. This mixture of liberal and preconstitutional elements

45 *Ibidem*, telegram of the prefect to the minister of the Interior, 12 November 1889.
46 *Ibidem* (1894), cat. 4/1.
47 C. Cavour, 'Legge elettorale. 1. Diritto politico e diritto amministrativo' [1848], in: *Tutti gli scritti di Camillo Cavour*, edited by P. Pischedda e G. Talamo, 4 vols (Turin, 1976-78), III (1976), 1091.

made itself felt well into the unitary state, and became more problematical as the representative system unfolded itself.

The first and foremost prerequisite of public administration in the periphery were properly conducted local elections. Each summer a fifth of the communal council had to be renewed (the size of the communal councils depended on the number of inhabitants). In keeping with the administrative thinking just noted the municipalities were responsible for the organization of the elections. They were to draw up the electoral rolls annually, to establish (if necessary) the electoral subdistricts, and to fill the seats of the provisional electoral committees.[48] Officially, the prefects only had a controlling function: they were required to oversee the correct execution of the relevant laws and regulations. The trickiest part of the elections, however, the control of the electoral rolls, was entrusted to the provincial deputation. Nevertheless, as the municipalities were not too keen on carrying out the legal prescripts, the prefects were prominently present in the electoral process. Furthermore, the separation of local and national interests, so much striven for, gradually became harder to sustain. Already in 1867, and again in 1869 and 1872, the Ministry of the Interior warned the communal and provincial councils not to make political statements; the prefects were told to annul immediately deliberations to that effect.[49] In the years that followed socialists and catholics tried to 'invade', as staunch moderates used to say, the local representative bodies, and to use them as a springboard to broader action. More and more, the prefects were asked to protect the sphere of national interest, checking on the deliberations of the communal councils but also preventively interfering in local elections.

As to the technical aspects of prefectural control, the problems arising from the annual revision of the electoral rolls demonstrate the poor responsiveness from below. Although the provincial deputation presided over by the prefect was responsible for the final approval of the electoral rolls for local elections, the prefecture kept a watchful eye on the drawing up of them. First of all, year after year the mayors were exhorted to revise the rolls, and to put the item subsequently on the agenda of the spring session of the communal council. A ministerial circular, issued in 1863 by the then general secretary Silvio Spaventa, called on the *giunte* to carry out this task seriously, 'because sometimes the communal councils, driven by the necessity to deliberate many other matters of local interest, in the short period allowed for their session, do not minutely examine the rolls, but refer to the work of the *giunta*; and the governmental authorities and provincial deputations, which are not on the spot, do not always have sufficient factual knowledge and elements on which to base their judgement to discover omissions and to correct unlawful registrations made by the

---

48 A precise account of the different stages of the electoral process has been given by A. Signorelli, 'Partecipazione politica, diritto al voto, affluenza alle urne: contribuenti ed elettori a Catania negli anni Settanta dell'800', *Quaderni Storici* 23 (1988), 873-902.

49 *Circolari del Ministero dell'Interno*, 8 November 1867, 28 June 1869, n. 880, and 28 May 1872, n. 15673-14.

local administrations'.[50] The *Rivista Amministrativa del Regno* contributed to the education of the municipalities by inventing a communal council discussing the revision of the electoral rolls. The discussion, treating appeals against the provisional rolls, included references to the most recent jurisprudence on the subject. The fictitious councillors dealt with the registration or otherwise of a non-naturalized foreigner, a blind man, a son of the village pharmacist, a non-resident with propery in the commune, etc. Thus many questions about the qualifications necessary for voting, such as wealth, 'capacity', education and literacy, were systematically passed in review.[51]

The organization of the voting itself required stringent measures. Numerous circulars pointed to the importance of regular elections, and several manuals explained the rights and duties of the voters.[52] Again the *Rivista Amministrativa* offered assistance: it published a role play, which accurately illustrated the proceedings (and many possible attendant problems) on polling day.[53] The function of the prefect was apparently subsidiary: after the elections he received the results and had to check the reports of the electoral committees. Since the communal and provincial law of 1889, magistrates had to fill the seats of the electoral committee, and the prefect, in agreement with the president of the *Corte d'Appello*, determined the date of the polling day.[54]

Not only were the municipalities reluctant to organize the local elections in accordance with the legal procedure, but an additional problem was that a large part of the electorate stayed at home. The administrative suffrage, based on wealth and 'capacity' (measured by education, profession, etc.), limited the percentage of registered voters to 3.9% of the total population in 1865 (still about twice as much as the percentage of political voters); the percentage slowly rose to 5.8% in 1878, to 6.3% in 1883, to 11.2% in 1889 (after the widening of the administrative electorate); it sank, however, to 8.9% in 1895 (general elections). The actual number of voters, expressed

50   *Circolare del Ministero dell'Interno*, 7 March 1863.

51   'Un consiglio comunale in azione. Seduta per la revisione della lista elettorale amministrativa', *RAR*, 20 (1869), 89-108.

52   F. Rosati, *Manuale sull'elettorato amministrativo* (Ancona, 1873); A. Baschirotto, *Vademecum per l'elettore amministrativo* (Padua, 1875); G. Pintor-Mameli, *Giurisprudenza sulle elezioni amministrative* (Rome, 1875); A. Civardi, *Manuale dell'elettore amministrativo* (Chiavari, 1883); G. Caramelli, *Elettorato ed eleggibilità amministrativa e governo locale: osservazioni pratiche* (Bologna, 1887); S. Acossato, *Manuale dell'elettore amministrativo* (Turin, 1889); R. Drago, *Manuale dell'elettore amministrativo* (Genoa, 1889); F.P. Tuccio, *Guida per l'elettore amministrativo* (Palermo, 1889); E. Magni, *Gli uffici elettorali amministrativi: guida teorico-pratica* (Venice, 1891); C. Testera, *Elettorato amministrativo e liste ed elezioni comunali e provinciali* (Turin, 1894).

53   'Assemblea degli elettori comunali', *RAR*, 13 (1862), 321-376; also published in *Guida amministrativa ossia commentario della legge comunale e provinciale del 20 marzo 1865...*, edited by C. Astengo e.a., 3rd ed. (Milan, 1865), 107-132.

54   In the parliamentary discussions on the new law this provision of the law was critized because it was said to increase the interference of the executive in the elections. Others defended the new rule, noting that now the choice of the polling day was less prone to partisanship, cf. the comment to art. 64 in A. Santini, *Codice dei comuni e dell provincie ossia manuale dei sindaci e dei consiglieri...* (Rome, 1889), 218-219.

in relation to the number of registered voters, was surprisingly low: 37.8% in 1865, 43.8% in 1878, 59.9% in 1889 (general elections), 63.5% in 1895.[55] In our core provinces the proportion of actual to registered voters was below the national average in Venice and Bologna and above the average in Reggio Calabria (which fits in with the general divergence between the North and the South).[56] The Ministry of the Interior on several occasions expressed its worry about this absenteeism, which, according to a circular, 'damaged the good course of administration and the prestige of liberal institutions'.[57] The prefects were urged to make the mayors mobilize potential voters. We shall examine whether it is possible to ascribe the prefects' incitements to revise the electoral rolls to a particular motivation: was it a genuine quest for participation, or a guided mobilization?[58]

Initially, the low turn-outs were attributed to lack of knowledge and unwillingness on the part of the population. The municipal elections held in the summer of 1866 raised little interest in the district of Imola: just 340 voters were counted (out of 1819 men registered, 2.9% of the population). The subprefect Polidori said he did not believe the easy explanation that this poor turn-out was due to the past war; he rather held the view that lower motives lay at the root of the problem: 'Unfortunately a large part of the electorate is still cursed with blatant ignorance of everything that concerns civil rights and attendant duties; another part, sulky because of envious vexation, abstains from participation in operations from which it expects a result which does not meet its own desires; and a final part (that of systematic opposition) does not show up, thinking that this would prejudice the right it arrogates to itself to rail against the acts of people, and the elections in which it would have participated in some way'.[59]

Although, as we have seen, the statistics were slightly more encouraging in Reggio Calabria than in Venice and Bologna, the participation in the elections of Reggio left

55 R. Romanelli, L'Italia liberale (1861-1900) (Bologna, 1979), 446-47. His figures are from Istat e Ministero per la Costituente, Compendio delle statistiche elettorali italiane dal 1848 al 1934, 2 vols (Rome, 1946-47).

56 We have provincial figures only for the years 1866, 1870-78, and 1887: the proportions for Venice were in 1866 37.7%, in 1870 25.4%, in 1878 40.4%, and in 1887 35%; for Bologna respectively 29.1%, 21.3%, 37.7%, and 32%; for Reggio Calabria respectively 43.3%, 46.8%, 53.9%, and 51.8%. Sources: Statistica del Regno d'Italia. Elezioni politiche e amministrative. Anni 1865-66 (Florence, 1867); MAIC, Direzione Generale della Statistica, Statistica elettorale amministrativa. Composizione del corpo elettorale amministrativo secondo le liste definitivamente approvate per l'anno 1887 e numero dei votanti nelle elezioni comunali avvenute nello stesso anno (Rome, 1888). The aggregate figures given in these statistics differ slightly from those given by Romanelli, which are based on a more recent source.

57 Circolare del Ministero dell'Interno, 8 July 1872.

58 A. Signorelli (op. cit.) has found for the case of Catania not only a low turn-out, but also a suprising divergence between the number of registered voters and that of persons who on the basis of their wealth were entitled to figure on the electoral rolls. He concludes that the formation of the electoral rolls should be further investigated, and that, because it is difficult to define those who were entitled to vote, there were large margins in the extension of the electorate: participation and mobilization were in his view closely connected.

59 ASB, Pref., Gab., b. 177, report of the subprefect of Imola to the prefect, 3 September 1866.

much to be desired. In August 1869, basing himself on partial results, the prefect Achille Serpieri noted the 'usual sluggishness of the voters'. He negated any political motivation behind the absenteeism of the electorate: 'to look for political motives to explain the origins of the local inertia where it concerns the public cause, is an easy way to cover the real causes'. He rather attributed it to 'a very imperfect consciousness of the value of the right to vote'. Even if the need to change the composition of the local representative bodies was felt, there were no suitable men to assume the responsibility. Not only was administrative capacity lacking, but also willingness to get involved in public affairs. At best, public office was accepted in the hope of personal profit. Serpieri, not satisfied with the adverse mentality, tried to win over 'honest men' by starting to improve the state of communal services, hence his project to approve the overdue final statements and check the electoral rolls. He admitted, however, that in the two years of his prefecture, despite massive involvement, little was achieved, and that the work had to be continued with full commitment: 'only good administrative conditions can render the country calm and confident, and with the practical sense of the Italians wholly bring back political questions to their real proportions'. In the same report he went on to describe the municipal elections in Reggio itself. Throughout the first decades of Unity the communal council of the provincial capital was divided into moderate liberals, clericals, and progressive liberals of various opinions. The coalitions between them, however, were variable, based on personal preferences and short-lived alliances.[60] In the year 1869 the progressive opposition managed to win all open seats. Serpieri suspected that gerrymandering had contributed to its victory (the number of ballot-cards did not correspond with the number of voters), but none of the parties entered a protest, which, according to the prefect, was 'the clearest example of how muddled the ideas were, and how artificial the agreements; and it is impossible to see in these elections a true expression of public opinion, as unfortunately is almost always the case'.[61] In another report Serpieri, looking back on the administrative elections of that year, recorded that the number of voters had somewhat increased, but that it fell short of 'the progressive rise that the development of liberal institutions should have produced'. The electorate was usually larger in the smaller municipalities: the required level of wealth was lower, and the division of the demesnes had produced many smaller landowners. In the more important towns, however, the prefect noted a widespread lack of interest among the taxpayers.[62]

While in these early years the officials in the periphery expressed their concern for the prevailing unfamiliarity with the representative system, the temptation of the government to interfere was, also from the beginning, irresistible. This interference manifested itself more clearly as openly anti-liberal movements got involved in the

---

60 G. Cingari, *Reggio Calabria* (Bari, 1988), 68-71.
61 ASRC, Pref., Gab., b. 1, f. 9, report of the prefect to the Ministry of the Interior on the administrative elections, 2 August 1869.
62 ASRC, Pref., Arch. Gen., inv. 14, f. 73, s.f. 10, undated report of the prefect.

local administrations. Initially, the liberal ruling class seemed to believe sincerely that the majority of the population (that is, the majority of those entitled to vote) was liberal and in favour of the unitary state. Hence the calls for registration in the electoral rolls. The premier and minister of the Interior Giovanni Lanza, during whose term of office Rome had been taken, acknowledged in 1872 (see n. 57) that the clericals participated in the administrative elections only 'in order to contribute to the ruin of liberal institutions and the state'. Therefore, he regarded voting as a sacred duty of the true liberal, 'not so much to deny the enemies of unity and liberty a victory, which they will never gain, but to show to civilized Europe that opposed to them is the great majority of Italians, prepared for every sacrifice in order to defend the rights of the nation, and to frustrate the attempts of a party, which under the pretext of upholding religion, wants to reconquer temporal power, irretrievably lost for the benefit of Italy, civilization and religion itself'.

The implications of these guidelines were evident in the province of Venice, in the early 1870s administered by Carlo Mayr. He had held high office in the provisional government of Emilia-Romagna after the fall of the papal regime (1859-60). Perhaps this experience in the ex-papal territories had fed his anti-clericalism. At any rate, in his four years of office (1872-76) he displayed great zeal in combatting the catholics who in his view aspired after political power. In March 1873 Mayr reported to the Ministry of the Interior that the clericals had already started their electoral campaign by exhorting their supporters to register themselves as voters. Shortly after this had become known to him, he issued a circular to urge the municipal *giunte* to be as thorough as possible in the yearly revision of the rolls.[63] Simultaneously, he tried to convince the liberals to take action, calling on their newspapers to raise the alarm. He promised the minister 'to intervene with the proper discretion and to use my guidance, so that from the elections only councillors come forward who are truly devoted to the government and to liberty'.[64] Lanza immediately replied, urging the prefect to 'to promote, with all lawful means, the registration of the citizens omitted on the electoral rolls, and the enlightenment of public opinion; and to lend, in one word, vigorous support to liberal elements'.[65] The results of the elections in the city of Venice, however, demonstrated that the activities of Mayr were not too successful. Shortly before polling day a third party, consisting of the aristocratic opposition to the then ruling majority, involved itself in the campaign, and allied itself with the clericals. This coalition managed to win half of the votes, although it was later said that the clericals had abstained.[66] The turn-out in the entire province was exceptionally low, about 20%: 'The disproportion between the registered voters and those who presented themselves at the polls, has to be ascribed, in general, to the deplor-

63   *Circolare della prefettura di Venezia*, 7 March 1873, n. 4029.
64   ASV, Pref., Gab. (1872-76), cat. 5, 3/1, confidential letter of the prefect to the Ministry of the Interior, 13 March 1873.
65   *Ibidem*, confidential and personal letter of Lanza to the prefect, 15 March 1875.
66   *Ibidem*, confidential report of the prefect to the Ministry, 31 July 1873.

able apathy towards administrative life, which paralyzes the eminently liberal aim intended by the law; in particular, to the simultaneity in four communes (...) of the elections on one day, and in two (...) on the same day as the elections in Venice, where many of the same landowners are electors'.[67] In general, absenteeism among the landowners was high, since many of them were in the countryside in the hot summer months.

The next year, Mayr again tried to find support against the rise of the clericals. He called on the district commissioners and other administrative heads to be alert and to urge their subordinates to vote liberal: 'It is by now time to recognize that it is wrong to think that the local elections do not have a political character; they acquire it from the moment that a party opposed to the government and hostile towards our national institutions hints that it avails itself of the elections to fight the government, and to undermine the institutions'.[68] The extreme vehemence of the prefect's appeal was prompted by the programme of the first catholic congress held in Venice. On this occasion, the liberals woke up to the threat in time. The turn-out for the municipal elections of Venice was higher than usual, 2036 voters out of 5281 registered, but still discouraging. The entire list of liberal candidates was elected; unfortunately, since the last two were not registered (a singular sign of carelessness), their places were taken by clericals. In his report to the Ministry the prefect defended himself against the allegations, made by the conservative press, of interference in the elections. He stated that he had only recommended the union of the various liberal factions, and had called for a high turnout: 'That was my duty, and I have scrupulously fulfilled it, respectful of the freedom of action of the other party'.[69] Along these lines, in June 1875 Mayr issued another confidential circular to the heads of the administrative services in his province to persuade their subordinate civil servants to show up at the polling stations. To his regret, this circular was intercepted and published in a Milanese newspaper. The clerical opposition adroitly made use of the event, and 11 of its candidates (for 15 available posts) were elected. Mayr, however, found himself to have a clear conscience, because, as he wrote to the Ministry, he had warned the liberals in time.[70] The conservative victory threatened to effect the resignation of the incumbent *giunta*. The Ministry did not like the idea and rapidly informed the prefect that he had to do his best to prevent a crisis. The prefect managed to put enough pressure on the mayor and the aldermen to stay on until the autumn session. But by then their resignation was unavoidable. It was not only the fear of total victory for the catholics in the event of new general elections, but also the striving for peace in the council which guided the prefect in his attempts to hold the councillors at bay. First, he closely followed the official and informal meetings of

---

67 *Ibidem* (1877-81), rubr. 5, 3/1, report of 15 September 1873.
68 *Ibidem* (1872-76), cat. 5, 3/1, confidential circular to the heads of various administrative services, 2 July 1874.
69 *Ibidem*, report of the prefect to the Ministry, 31 July 1874.
70 *Ibidem*, confidential report of the prefect to the Ministry, 13 July 1875.

the various factions in the council, but in the end, when he saw that no agreement could be reached, he personally persuaded the then eligible aldermen to take over the job. He thought it better not to try to appoint a regular mayor, but to leave the office in the hands of the senior alderman – a not unusual procedure, as we have seen, to wait to see which way the wind would blow.[71]

From 1874 onwards the Ministry of the Interior kept official records of the tendencies that manifested themselves in local elections.[72] Political interference, however, was still of secundary importance in the province of Reggio Calabria. The report of the prefect Francesco De Feo confirmed the discouraging descriptions given by Serpieri. The checking of the electoral rolls took a long time, and the municipalities were lax in forwarding the announcements of the polling day to the prefecture. Hence, the provincial deputation had no choice but to fix the date on 31 July, the last day allowed by law. For some municipalities, as they could not be reached in time by telegram or courier, the date was even postponed until August. De Feo characterized the electoral struggle by pointing to the absence of any political interest, but instead personal antagonism and petty ambitions.[73] In the following years the tone of the prefectural reports did not change much. In 1877 the elections of some municipalities were held on the basis of the rolls of the previous year, because the communal councils had been too negligent in the spring sessions. Again, the prefect attributed the 'apathy' to the 'little faith the voters put in our institutions, or their ignorance as to what importance one was supposed to give to them.[74] In 1878, under Filippo Lamponi, the prefecture mounted a full-scale operation in order to approve and revise the electoral rolls in time. It took the initiative to examine the lists and presented them fully revised to the provincial deputation officially charged with this task. Only the lists of two municipalities (Cosoleto and Polisteno) were lacking, for reasons of irreparable negligence. The prefecture thoroughly studied the requirements to be registered, and even consulted the tax registers. In this way it was not necessary, unlike earlier years, to make special inquiries or to send commissioners – methods that had been widely used before without success. The results of the operation, however, show that the councils had far greater margins than the state authorities in revising the rolls (see table 1).

Yet the share of the electorate relative to the total population in these elections was considered rather low (about 4%). It was expected to stay that way, although the number of taxpayers increased and many municipalities had less than 2000 inhabit-

---

71 *Ibidem*, confidential report of the prefect to the Minstry, 15 September 1875.

72 *Circolare del Ministero dell'Interno*, 29 July 1874, n. 15600-19, calling, among other things, for a 'qualification' of the electoral struggles in the main towns.

73 ASRC, Pref., Gab., b. 2, f. 17, report of the prefect to the Ministry, 8 September 1874,

74 *Ibidem*, b. 62, f. 987, report on the communal administration, prepared by the secretary Pietro Ferri, January 1878.

Table 1 Revision of the electoral rolls in the province of Reggio Calabria (1878)

Added to by the councils (without Cosoleto and Polisteno)	Reggio	725
	Palmi	350
	Gerace	285
	Total	1360
Cancelled by the councils (without the same)	Reggio	441
	Palmi	414
	Gerace	232
	Total	1087
Added to by the Deputation	Reggio	65
	Palmi	40
	Gerace	76
	Total	181
Cancelled by the Deputation	Reggio	37
	Palmi	18
	Gerace	88
	Total	143
All voters (without Cosoleto and Polisteno)	Reggio	5850
	Palmi	4726
	Gerace	4175
	Total	14751

ants (which rendered a small income sufficient to be entitled to vote). According to a prefectural official, the reason for this lay in the poor spread of public education; consequently, the number of voters would increase very slowly.[75] The prefecture continued to examine the electoral rolls before submitting them to the provincial deputation. It asked for missing documents, investigated the appeals, and tried to apply the criteria of literacy, wealth, and capacity according to the spirit of the law.[76]

The administrative elections in the province of Reggio remained the scene of battle of local conflicts. This could have different consequences for the surveillance to be exerted by the prefecture. Local factions tried to fill the electoral rolls with their

75 *Ibidem*, b. 62, f. 988, report written by the prefectural secretary Ferri on the communal administration, 29 July 1878.
76 *Ibidem*, b. 62, f. 989, report of Ferri, July 1879. From a later prefectural report it emerges that in 1885 the prefecture still provided the provincial deputation with the material required for final approval, cf. P. Borzomati, *La Calabria dal 1882 al 1892 nei rapporti dei prefetti* (Reggio Calabria, 1974), 138.

supporters, and simultaneously appealed to the higher authorities to cleanse the rolls of their opponents. Control had to be intensified, and the high rate of appeals, once welcomed as a sign of growing participation, became a thorn in the flesh of the prefects. Furthermore, the checking of the rolls was spoiled by voters crossed off from the lists presenting themselves at the polling stations after having submitted their appeals to the judicial authorities. They were usually allowed to vote, without the lawsuit ever taking place.[77]

The political colour of the councillors and candidates, of no real relevance in Reggio Calabria until the beginning of the 1890s, became a matter of growing interest for the government in Venice, because of the strong clerical opposition, and in Bologna. Unfortunately, the prefectural archives of Reggio and Venice shed hardly any light on the role of the prefects in the local elections of the 1880s and early 1890s.[78] The municipality of Bologna remained firmly in the hands of the moderates, even during the rule of the *Sinistra*. Carlo Faraldo, prefect in the years 1878-80, reported to the Ministry that the municipal administration had always kept its distance from political influence, a praiseworthy attitude in the prefect's view. In 1879 moderates and progressives agreed upon a common list of candidates; the prefect was asked to communicate the proposals made by the progressives to the moderate leaders who were members of the provincial deputation. Faraldo, not unsympathetic towards the progressives, wholeheartedly accepted this role as mediator, but did not refrain from notifying them that the presence of an uncomprimising radical in their ranks rendered his support quite difficult: 'I am in favour of a high degree of liberty and tolerance, but I think a prefect, without betraying his duty, cannot support (...) someone who seizes every occasion to behave as an enemy of the *Sinistra* and of the current cabinet'.[79]

The real test case for prefectural interference in local elections came with the widening of the suffrage for local elections in 1889. The greatest innovation was the weight given to wealth over census for being registered as voter (the ratio had been 9 to 1 in 1887, and became 5 to 5 in 1889). The relative number of voters rose from 6.7% in 1887 to 11.2% in 1889, but declined to 8.9% in 1895 after the general revision of the electoral rolls ordered by the law of 11 June 1894, n. 286.[80] Already before the promulgation of the new law Crispi, still just minister of the Interior, had issued a confidential circular calling for precise reports about the outcome of the elections. The circular not only asked for statistical data about the number of voters, but also

---

77 ACS, Min. Int., Gab., Rapporti dei prefetti, b. 18, f. 53, s.f. 5, report of the prefect on public opinion in the first half of 1888, 5 October 1888.

78 The role of the prefects in the dissolution of communal councils, for which there is evidence, will be discussed in the next chapter.

79 ASB, Pref., Gab., b. 333, confidential report of the prefect to the Ministry of the Interior, 16 June 1879.

80 G. Schepis, 'Le elezioni comunali e provinciali', *Amministrazione civile*, 5 (1961), n. 47-51, 283-85. For a profound statistical study on the consequences of the new franchise, see L. Leoni, 'Il personale elettivo', in: *Le riforme crispine*, III, *Amministrazione locale* (ISAP Archivio, n.s. 6, Milan, 1990), 789-857.

requested information about the political colour of the voters and the elected (whether they were monarchical constitutionalists, clericals or reactionaries, radicals, or inspired by 'administrative' criteria), about the reception of the outcome by the public, and about possible corruption.[81] By then, the political importance of local elections was fully accepted, and feared.

Again, as in the section on the mayors, the case of Imola (and of other municipalities in the district) is emblematic. With the new suffrage Costa and his followers saw their chance to put the socialist programme of 'taking possession of the communes' in practice.[82] In several municipalities where socialist tendencies gained ground, the dissolution of the councils was a matter of waiting for or creating the right occasion. The rise of the socialists made possible by the extension of the franchise had cut across the existing balance of power, and was most unwelcome to the old liberal elite. The opportunity of dissolution was often seized to revise the electoral rolls to the detriment of the progressive opposition. The prefects, though not personally involved, used to acquiesce in these operations; for example, as in the case of Molinella by postponing the general elections a few days, which necessitated the drawing up of new lists.[83]

The general revision of the electoral rolls in 1894-95 carried out by a special provincial commission led to a substantial decline in the electorate. The parliament had called for this revision, because it believed that in many municipalities the rolls, through illegal registrations, had become an instrument of local politics. Once this defect was removed, the electorate would be brought back to real proportions and more closely reflect public opinion. The prefects, who were not themselves members of the commissions, were requested to determine 'at a single and comprehensive glance' the dates of the polling day, in order to feather the nests of the liberals.[84] All in all, 8,948 men were crossed off the lists of 1894 (consisting of 60,025 registered voters), and 1,617 were added. The most salient changes, however, did not occur in Imola (246 cancelled and 188 added out of a total of 3,747), but in the district of Vergato (in Camugnano 454 out of 720 were cancelled!).[85] It is unlikely that the electoral rolls were purged for political reasons only. One would have expected greater changes in the district of Imola (and it is unclear whether the cleaning up in Vergato affected the traditionally strong clerical party in particular). Nevertheless, the advantages for the liberal parties were evident. The well-considered choice of the polling days in the various districts may have contributed to the over-all victory of

---

81 *Circolare del Ministero dell'Interno*, 3 July 1887, n. 15600-7. After the general elections Crispi, now also premier, called for similar politically orientated information about the elected councillors, see *Circolare del Ministero dell'Interno*, 25 October 1889, n. 6686.

82 E. Ragionieri, 'La formazione del programma amministrativo socialista in Italia', now in: Idem, *Politica e amministrazione nella storia dell'Italia unita* (Rome, 1979), in particular 202-249.

83 ASB, Pref., Gab. (1894), cat. 4, letter of the prefect to the Ministry, 8 May 1893.

84 *Circolare del Ministero dell'Interno*, 15 February 1895, n. 15600-3.4.

85 ASB, Pref., Gab. (1895), cat. 4, statistical report of the prefect to the Ministry, 28 February 1895.

the liberals (except in Imola, Medicina, and some minor municipalities). The prefect had notified the Ministry months before the elections were due that in Imola they had to be held before the political elections in order to prevent splits in the liberal party; that in Vergato they should not be held before the month of July because most registered voters were working in other parts of Italy until then; and that in Bologna the date depended on the alliances of and within the liberal factions.[86]

5 CONCLUSION

The establishment of the liberal system of local government was a painful and lengthy process, which did not naturally ensue from the political revolution of Unification. The centralized hierarchy in which the municipality played a subordinate role was taken over from the Restoration, but most parts of united Italy were unaccustomed to representative bodies and free elections. The prefects were the obvious persons to set up these administrative novelties. Yet the administrative revolution could only become a success if it was accompanied by a social revolution. Even though it would be exaggerated to say that the *risorgimento* was totally foreign to the greater part of society, the traditional elites were reluctant to abdicate their position and the *homines novi* fell back on local paternalistic relations rather than put their faith in the national state. Therefore, at least as important as the 'technical' aspects were the social aspects of the prefects' job. In order to make local administration work, they needed the support of the notables. To sustain this 'dialogue' was an important prerequisite of success for an official in the field. Any serious disturbance of the relations between the prefect (and other members of his staff for that matter) and local authorities sufficed to bring about the transfer of the former.

The most efficient instrument in the hands of the prefect seemed the appointment of the mayors, which was largely his responsibility. In a certain sense the mayors, according to the law both heads of the municipal administration and officials of the government, were the real administrative link between state and society. They were supposed to keep local interests from interfering with general interests, and simultaneously to guarantee the implementation of national and uniform administrative rules. Whereas in theory these two sides of the mayor's office were perhaps compatible, in practice they were certainly not. On the one hand, mayors of small villages often represented the interests of one family and its clientele instead of the interests of the entire municipality. Personal gain often got the upper hand over administrative responsibility. On the other hand, political or other supralocal interests easily got entangled with the mayor's duties in larger towns. In both cases the prefect had to keep the mayors on the right track.

---

86 *Ibidem*, cat. 5, letter of the prefect to the Ministry, 4 March 1895.

Selection for the office of mayor proved to be a highly delicate operation, confronting the prefecture every three years (and often in between) with serious difficulties. The customary procedure passed through many channels, from local state officials to parliamentary representatives. Frequently, the Ministry of the Interior also put its oar in. Whereas the sometimes unscrupulous consultations involved in finding 'the right man' (rich, liberal, with administrative skills) underline the discretionary powers of the higher authorities, obstacles at the local level show that centralism had its limits. Particularly in the *Mezzogiorno* it could happen easily that there was no one who matched the profile and could be accepted as the 'government's official'. It was even more difficult to find somebody who stood above the local factions. Those who did, were reluctant to stick their neck out. Absenteeism and abuse of power further eroded the office of mayor. Almost invariably the prefects proposed the alderman who had received most votes, so that at least conflicts between the council and the mayor were avoided. With the politicization of local government, especially in Venice and Bologna, the function of mayor became the object of political control. Nevertheless, the prefects were often more interested in keeping administrative peace than in triggering political conflicts; this often led them to accept the municipalities being ruled by the senior alderman.

The striving for pacification constituted the most preferred strategy in dealing with local representative bodies. In the early period of the unitary state (and particularly in the South) this entailed frequent interventions to conciliate rivalling families or factions. In later years the prefect's role extended to that of political mediator. The direct duties of the prefect concerned the organization of the elections. This was no minor task, since many municipalities showed a great lack of interest in the matter. What emerged in particular, were the attempts to raise the turnouts (which remained low, at a level of about 40%). Gradually the prefects got more involved in the control of elections themselves and their outcome. It has been shown that in Bologna after 1889 the revision of the electoral rolls was used to 'adjust' the composition of the electorate. In other words, the quest for new voters gave way to the exclusion of unwanted voters.The annual revision of the electoral rolls, carried out by the municipalities themselves, had to be supervised with meticulous care (even though the final approval was up to the provincial deputation). Many communes tended to neglect their responsibility. Some local authorities tried to utilize the revision to favour their supporters. Such falsifications became a plague after the widening of the suffrage for local elections in 1889. The control of the revision of the rolls will be further discussed in the chapter on parliamentary elections. The seemingly most efficient measure to bring badly functioning municipal administrations to heel was the dissolution of the council. That is the subject of the chapter that follows.

Chapter 4

The dissolution of municipal councils: administration and politics

1 INTRODUCTION

At the turn of the century Gaspare Finali, in a speech to the Senate, sounded a note of warning: 'The dissolution of a communal or provincial council is not an ordinary act of administration; it is an extraordinary instrument of government, it is dictatorship applied in the realm of local administration'.[1] By then, the annual number of dissolutions had reached the levels of the early years of Unification, and had become a much debated issue inside and outside the parliamentary Chambers. Finali's statement was not exaggerated. Indeed, one of the most grave interferences of central government in municipal government was the power embodied in the former, in the event of serious violation of public order or for reasons of bad administration, to dissolve the communal council and appoint a special agent. The agent took over the local administration until new elections had been held.[2] The power to suppress the legitimate representation of a municipality, laid down in all communal and provincial laws from 1848 onwards without fundamental alterations, leads us right to the heart of the ambivalence inherent in the liberal administrative system: the dichotomy between authority and liberty. To recapitulate, on the one hand, the municipality had a certain degree of autonomy through an elected organ, the communal council; on the other, the state maintained wide powers of supervision over the activities of the municipality. In liberal thought the potentially divergent powers were reconcilable through the distinction between local interests and national interests. The two spheres of interest determined the range of action of local and national administration. Although the municipalities could freely attend to their local interests, it was generally accepted, even among the supporters of decentralization, that the state ought to have the power to intervene in local affairs, if they obstructed national interests.

The dissolution of municipal councils fitted in perfectly with this doctrine; it was argued that this act of *summa potestas* was only a temporary infringement upon communal autonomy and that, eventually, the initiative was returned to the voters,

---

1 AP, Sen., legisl. XX, sess. 1898-99, Discussioni, 5 June 1899.
2 The communal and provincial law also allowed for the dissolution of the provincial council. In practice, however, this rarely happened. Therefore, I only deal with the dissolution of municipal councils.

since they were enabled to re-elect their representatives. Arabia and Adorni, officials of the Ministry of the Interior, said in their comment on the communal and provincial law of 1865: 'Some people find that the government's power to dissolve elected bodies is illiberal; they are wrong. What does the executive do when it orders a dissolution? It appeals to the commune, represented or rather assembled in the electorate; it calls on the commune to judge the controversy that underlay the dissolution. The commune decides in favour of the government, if it gives its votes to new persons; against the government, if it reelects the outgoing councillors. Furthermore, under the moderate monarchy the sovereign, through his ministers, is the regulator of administration; and whomsoever, body or official, takes part in it, is subordinate to the sovereign. If in an elected body a conflict arises, what other remedy is there but a dissolution and appeal to the commune?'.[3]

That the power to dissolve was not a dead letter, is proved by the much-discussed dissolutions of the municipal councils of Florence in 1874 and of Naples in 1876; the council of Genoa, for example, was dissolved six times between 1857 and 1882![4] It is, however, not easy to compound the scattered evidence into a comprehensive time series: until 1889 there were no periodical statistics. The annual number of dissolutions (which, out of a total of approximately 8000 municipalities, never reached extraordinary high figures) was only occasionally published in the yearly reports on the administrative services (see table 2).[5]

Francesco Tommasini made an elaborate statistical analysis of the dissolutions between 1890 and 1893. He paid particular attention to the regional differences and found that the number of dissolutions in the South, especially in Sicily and Campania, was much higher than elsewhere. He attributed this difference, first, to the lack of experience in selfgovernment in the South; second, to the bad economic conditions, which frustrated the regular conduct of public administration; third, to the reign of personal clienteles and political corruption. He pointed in particular to the break with administrative tradition in the *Mezzogiorno*, where the suffrage suddenly confronted the old ruling elites with emerging social groups.[6] It is not my intention, mainly because the evidence is so scattered, to analyze the quantitative trend in dissolutions. I shall try, on the other hand, to assess the place of dissolutions in the relationship between state and municipalities.

---

3   T. Arabia & M. Adorni, *La legge comunale e provinciale del Regno d'Italia commentata* (Florence, 1865), 246. Their line of thought was followed by many authoritative commentators, see G. Capitani, entry 'Scioglimento del consiglio comunale e del consiglio provinciale', in: *Digesto Italiano*, XXI, parte 1ª (Turin, 1891), 805: 'A consequence of our constitutional system is precisely the King's power to take measures, whenever a blow is dealt to general interests, by submitting the representatives of local interests to the judgement of the voters, who should elect, without bias, better representatives'.

4   R. Drago, *Lo scioglimento dei consigli comunali e i delegati straordinari* (Genoa, 1886), 106.

5   Some of these reports, starting to appear in the 1870s as a sequel to the first statistics after the law of 1865 on the administrative services, were published in the *Gazzetta Ufficiale*. They were addressed to the King. Only Nicotera, minister of the Interior in 1876-77 and 1891-92, submitted his reports to Parliament.

6   Tommasini, 252-54.

Table 2 Annual number of dissolutions (1869-1902)

1869	121	1890	80
1870	176	1891	96
1871	?	1892	113
1872	148	1893	136
1873	110	1894	83
1874	90	1895	83
1875	69	1896	120
1876	89	1897	152
		1898	145
		1899	154
1887	87	1900	139
1888	84	1901	186
1889	66	1902	205

Sources: *Circolari del Ministero dell'Interno*, 28 September 1870, n. 18801 and 16 May 1871, n. 18400; *Gazzetta Ufficiale*, 19 August 1875; AP, CD, legisl. XIII, sess. 1876-77, Documenti, no. 33A, report of the commission (spokesman A. Marazio) on the bill of Nicotera for a reform of the communal and provincial law; 'Relazione sull'andamento dei servizi dipendenti dal Ministero dell'Interno dal 9 febbraio al 30 settembre 1891, presentata dal ministro dell'Interno (Nicotera) nella tornata 25 november 1891', in: AP, CD, legisl. XVII, 1ª sess. 1890-91, Documenti, no. 26; F. Tommasini, 'Osservazioni sull'istituto dello scioglimento dei consigli comunali e provinciali', *Archivio di diritto pubblico*, 5 (1895), 241-320; G. D'Ambrosio, 'Lo scioglimento dei consigli comunali e provinciali', *Il Filangieri*, 28 (1903), 566-597.[7]

In nineteenth-century public opinion it was commonly held that the dissolution of a municipal council represented an authoritarian interference in local affairs. Indeed, the various communal and provincial laws left much room for arbitrary interpreta-

7 For the period 1876-86 there are no figures available. In the 19 months between 1 April 1876 and 31 October 1877 180 councils were dissolved, AP, CD, legisl. XIII, sess. 1876-77, Documenti, no. 23, 'Relazione sull'andamento dei servizi dipendenti dal ministero dell'interno dal 1º aprile al 31 ottobre 1877, presentata dal ministro dell'interno (Nicotera) nella tornata del 22 novembre 1877'. After 1902 the upward trend continued, cf. S. Serra, *Le amministrazioni straordinarie dei comuni ed i poteri dei rr. commissarî* (Catania, 1906), who claimed that over the preceding five years 940 councils had been dissolved. D'Ambrosio gathered his figures for the period after 1889 mainly from the *Gazzetta Ufficiale*, claiming that the *Direzione Generale di Statistica* as well as the Ministry of the Interior, in reply to his enquiry, had contended that no official statistics on dissolutions existed (p.576). A note in the archives of the Ministry of the Interior confirms this, ACS, Min. Int., Direzione Generale dell'Amministrazione Civile, Comuni, b. 366, letter of the Ministry to D'Ambrosio, 18 April 1900 (I have found, *ibidem*, a list, made up by the Ministry, of dissolutions between 1889 and 1898, which slightly differs from the one given by D'Ambrosio. The memory of the Ministry, in its answer to D'Ambrosio, was (perhaps deliberately) short. A note of 7 July 1895 proves that at that time statistics did exist: 'Apart from rare exceptions this grave measure always hits the same communes with an interval of two or three years, *and the statistics on the last two decades proves this*' [my italics], ACS, Carte Francesco Crispi, Roma, sc. 28, f. 616. Unfortunately, these statistics have not been preserved.

tions.[8] This was acknowledged by most commentators, for examply by the influential Carlo Astengo: 'Former communal laws, including that of 20 March 1865, lacked regulations for this grave and delicate subject, in which the government's power was absolute; this could easily (and unfortunately there are many examples) lead to arbitrary acts'. It is not very difficult to find practical examples of the discretionary powers involved in dissolving a council. The prefect of Bari, Biagio Miraglia, proudly wrote to the Ministry in his report on the administrative services and the public spirit of the second semester of 1882 that, in view of the national elections, he had dissolved various important councils: 'In the last political elections a complete victory has been gained. This was due, on the one hand, to the liberal spirit of the intellectual classes and the benevolence of the voters; on the other hand, as far as it was up to me, I have tried to achieve this success by dissolving important municipalities, notably Bari, Andria and Noce'.[9] The observations of the prefect Amadeo Nasalli Rocca were, in their succinctness, even harsher; without waisting more words on the matter, he claimed that during his tenure of office in Campobasso (November 1900 – January 1903) he had dissolved some 20 councils for reasons of bad administration.[10]

Although the prefect had no legally defined function during the dissolution of a municipal council (in the rare event of the dissolution of a provincial council the prefect assumed the administrative powers belonging to the provincial deputation, see art. 201 of the 1865 law), he usually was the key figure in the entire process: he proposed the dissolution to the Ministry of the Interior, he suggested a special agent, he kept in touch with the course of the municipal administration under the extraordinary regency and he informed the Ministry about the most important developments.[11]

In contrast to most nineteenth-century commentators, I believe that the dissolutions represented not just an act of negative restriction but also, particularly in the first decades of Unification, the opportunity to make positive provisions for communal services (and, in a wider sense, for the modernization of the municipal infrastructure). It cannot be denied, however, that there was a certain shift in the motivation for the dissolutions, that is, from the striving for administrative appeasement (and hence the emphasis on 'real' adminstration) towards a more overtly political manipulation of local representatives.

---

8 *Guida amministrativa ossia commento della legge comunale e provinciale (Testo unico 10 febbraio 1889, n. 5921)...*, edited by C. Astengo et al. (Rome, 1889), 1624-25. Likewise, Grizzuti, though in general not against dissolutions, criticized the vague formulation of the law, C. Grizzuti, *Dello scioglimento dei consigli secondo la nuova legge comunale e provinciale* (Portici, 1890).

9 ACS, Min. Int., Gab., Rapporti dei prefetti, b.3, f.7.

10 A. Nasalli Rocca, *Memorie di un prefetto*, edited by C. Trionfi (Rome, 1946), 157.

11 M. Sterio, *Dello scioglimento dei consigli comunali e della amministrazione dei regi commissari* (Messina, 1904), 42.

2 THE LEGAL BACKGROUND

The prerogative of dissolving a communal council, as a corollary to the introduction of local elections, appeared for the first time in the Piedmontese *Regio Editto* of 1847. This edict was a product of the final phase of the Restoration in the Kingdom of Sardinia and functioned as a *trait d'union* with the communal and provincial law of 1848, which in its turn laid the foundation for the post-unitary administrative laws. Despite the definitive establishment of the representative system, the law of 1848 showed, not only in the articles dealing with the dissolution of representative councils, the legislator's firm intention to keep a close watch on the local ruling classes. Interestingly enough, as far as the dissolution of municipal councils is concerned, the Piedmontese law of 1848 deviated from its Belgian model of 30 March 1836, in which this kind of infringement was impossible. Moreover, in most European countries the power to dissolve representative bodies did not exist.[12] In fact, only French legislation (from the municipal law of 1831 to that of 1884), which seems to have greatly influenced the Piedmontese and Italian communal law on this point, maintained the possibility of dissolving communal councils.[13]

The dissolution of municipal councils was treated at some length in an editorial of the *Rivista Amministrativa del Regno* in 1854. First of all, the 'absolute silence of the law' was mentioned; but it was accepted that 'domestic discord', 'systematic opposition in the execution of governmental decrees' and 'illegal demands that aim to offend the independence of government' were legitimate grounds for dissolution. Furthermore, the expediency of the measure was regretfully recognized: 'These generically described grounds are not simply hypothetical; they are reality, undeniable though sad, for those who carefully examine the state of many communal administrations and of the affairs dependent on the communal affairs of small villages, in which the influence of the educated citizen pales into insignificance compared to the majority, whose learning and qualities are only weighed against wealth'.[14]

In the decades that followed, the subject more or less disappeared from the public stage. A parliamentary debate between Baldacchini and Peruzzi in 1863 (when grave perturbations of public order were still scourging the South) underlined the great delicacy of dissolving communal councils. Baldacchini had his doubts about the advantages of the measure. Especially in smaller communes, he argued, where families rather than political parties reigned, the intervention of government only conferred the victory upon one of the factions. Hence, 'only the discontent of some people is dispelled, but things continue more or less in the same way'. Peruzzi, minister of the Interior, recognizing some of Baldacchini's complaints, pointed to the

---

12   D'Ambrosio, 568; Tommasini, 244.
13   M. Block, *Dictionnaire de l'administration française*, 3rd edition (Paris, 1862), 1202; G. Sautel, *Histoire des institutions publiques depuis la Révolution française. Administration – justice – finances* (Paris, 1978), 517.
14   *RAR*, 5 (1854), 12.

extraordinary circumstances under which the Southern provinces lived, and therefore considered dissolution 'one of the most necessary though temporary measures to accustom the population to the exercise of rights sanctioned by the liberal laws that govern us'.[15]

In the early 1880s Minghetti and Turiello, leading spokesmen of the Destra, touched upon the matter in their writings, and set the tone for the long-lived critical opinion. Minghetti wrote: 'The dissolution of a provincial or communal council is a very grave event. The law provides for it, but it states as a condition serious motives of public order (art. 235). What guarantee is there that the minister has such motives and is not driven by party interests? None whatsoever. Here one does not even consult the Council of State, nor is a report justifying those grave motives published in the *Gazzetta Ufficiale*; what is more, it has become customary not to publish a decree of dissolution at all. This very important act in local life remains virtually an internal affair. And even if now and then, when large cities are concerned, someone endeavours to raise a question in parliament, the dissolution of small communes passes by without others knowing of it, particularly when it is done in agreement with the local deputy, or in order to serve his wishes'[16] Following this line of reasoning, at the beginning of the new century, Guglielmo D'Ambrosio argued that the dissolution of a communal council represented a powerful weapon in the hands of the government in order to curtail those councils that opposed pro-government deputies.[17]

The silence of the law, lamented by the *Rivista Amministrativa* in 1854, persisted until the reforms of Crispi. The communal and provincial law of 1865 was in full accord with its 1859 precursor. The two articles concerning the dissolution of municipal councils (they were rather incoherently inserted in the law as article 151 and 235, which reflected their misplacement in the previous laws) prescribed that the King, in the event of grave disturbance of public order, could dissolve a municipal council and entrust the administration of the municipality to a special delegate, who had to organize new elections within three months. The definition 'grave motives of public order' was rather vague and left room for arbitrary decisions of the controlling authorities. One of the leading commentators of the communal and provincial law, Carlo Astengo, anticipating the law of 1889, wrote in the third edition (1865) of his manual: 'The dissolution of the communal council can be rightfully declared when it is upset by internal discord or when it pursues systematic opposition in the execution of governmental decrees, or continues to make illegal requests, which offend the goverment's liberty to amend those regulations which are considered useless'.[18]

---

15 AP, CD, legisl. VIII, 2ª sess. 1863-64, Discussioni, 3 June 1863.

16 M. Minghetti, *I partiti politici e l'ingerenza loro nella giustizia e nell'amministrazione* (1881), now in: Idem, *Scritti politici*, edited by R. Gherardi (Rome, 1986), 674. See also, for a comparable view, P. Turiello, *Governo e governati in Italia* (Bologna, 1882), 253; and N. Colajanni, *Le istituzioni municipali. Cenni ed osservazioni* (Piazza Armerina, 1883), 119-120.

17 D'Ambrosio, 570.

18 *Guida amministrativa ossia commentario della legge comunale e provinciale del 20 marzo 1865 e del relativo*

Nicotera's report of 1877 on the administrative services of the preceding year mentioned bad administration, quarrels within the council, resignation of councillors and non-compliance with the law as causes of dissolution.[19] It should be noted that the yearly renewal of a fifth of the councillors often represented a destabilizing factor in the balance of power within the municipal council, and thus could bring a dissolution nearer (although sometimes the annual reelection came just in time to restore the peace).

In the decades after 1865 various reforms of the communal and provincial law were proposed, which included changes of the dissolution policy. They centred on the need for a more precise definition of the circumstances that could give rise to a dissolution, and for greater guarantees to the municipalities, for example a prior consultation of the Council of State, a detailed report before dissolution and a specification of the special agent's powers.[20] None of these proposals, however, were voted through. Finally, Crispi's law of 1888, included in the new *testo unico* of 1889, adopted some of his predecessors' proposals: not only disturbance of public order but also persistent violations of obligations prescribed by law on the part of the communal council were now explicitly mentioned as grounds for dissolution. In practice, as we have seen, these and other transgressions had already been accepted as sufficient grounds. The *Manuale Astengo* wrote in 1893 that the dissolution of a council often had its origin in the delicate financial conditions of the municipality: 'The most common cause for the measure lies in the financial situation of the commune, which the administrators do not wish or intend to repair. For popularity's sake or for other reasons the citizens hesitate to take the matter energetically in hand; hence the work is entrusted to royal commissioners. Practice has shown that that is the only way to repair the deficit of the budgets'.[21] Furthermore, it was laid down in the communal and provincial law of 1889 that the term of new elections could be prolonged to six months, that every dissolution had to be preceeded by a report listing the reasons for the act, that the royal decrees of the dissolution had to be published in the *Gazzetta Ufficiale*, and that every three months a list of these decrees had to be passed on the Senate and Chamber of Deputies.

During the parliamentary debates on the reforms the deputies Paternostro and Ercole proposed further guarantees for the municipalities (a 'deliberative vote' of the Council of state), but they collided with Crispi's determination. For he resolutely dismissed the expediency of an intervention of the Council of state and he claimed for the public administration its own sphere of influence, replying that the dissolution 'is an act of authority which can be examined and judged by parliament alone'.[22]

---

regolamento..., edited by C. Astengo et al. (Milan, 1865), 1225.

19 'Relazione sull'andamento dei servizi dipendenti dal ministero dell'interno dal 1° aprile al 31 ottobre 1877..', *cit.* See also Capitani, 805, for the causes of dissolution occurring in practice.

20 Notably the bills of Nicotera (1876) and Depretis (1882). See also on this subject, Drago, 8.

21 *Manuale degli amministratori comunali e provinciali*, 32 (1893), 329.

22 AP, CD, legisl. XVI, sess. 2ª, Discussioni, 18 July 1888.

In his thorough study of the dissolutions Melchiore Sterio, municipal secretary of Messina, dwelt on the duties of the *regio commissario delegato*, which he considered from a moral and a juridical point of view. As far as ethics were concerned, the special agent should acknowledge the exceptional character of his mission, 'as a pathological moment in the administrative life of the commune'. Therefore he should comply with local experiences (if they had proved useful) and bear in mind that, for example, municipalities in mountainous areas required a markedly different approach from those in the plains: 'It is necessary to have an exact knowledge of the precedents, the needs, the habits, as well the local prejudices'. A first impression of the administrative situation could be obtained from the municipal budget, 'which in the simplicity of the figures speaks louder and clearer than whatever report that preceeds the decree of dissolution'.[23]

The powers of the special agent slowly expanded: they had not been defined in the first communal and provincial law of 1848. In the laws of 1859 and 1865 they were limited to those of the *giunta*. In the jurisprudence it was gradually accepted that the special agent, in case of emergency, could assume the powers of the council as well.[24] His decisions, however, always needed ratification, once a new council was installed. With the law of 1889 the powers were officially extended to those accorded to the mayor and *giunta*.

Until 1902, when a permanent commission for the purpose was set up, the appointment of a special agent was poorly regulated.[25] Usually, the prefect proposed an agent to the Ministry, often an official from within his administration. With the ministerial circular of 23 October 1872, n. 16200 the prefect was asked to look for a special agent outside active service (because of the shortage of manpower in the organs of state administration), e.g. a capable municipal secretary or a provincial councillor. According to Quarta-Guidotti, these instructions had little effect: it often happened that the prefect only learned of the name of the special agent in the *Gazzetta Ufficiale*, in the decree of dissolution. Furthermore, the author maintained that frequently private citizens were nominated.[26]

The *regio delegato straordinario* received an indemnity at the expense of the municipal treasury. In order to avoid burdening the municipalities excessively, the Ministry established, in the circular mentioned above, that the special agent refrain from publishing his final report (except for larger cities).

At first sight the powers of the special agent were limitless. He could virtually engage in all administrative areas: the dismissal of municipal servants, the reorgani-

23 Sterio, 269-271. A list of qualities expected to be possessed by the special agent had also been drawn up by S. Severino, *Del regio commissario straordinario* (Siracuse, 1894).

24 'Parere del Consiglio di Stato', 6 September 1871, n. 3195-1806, see *RAR*, 24 (1873), 395-396.

25 *Decreto del Ministero dell'Interno*, 25 July 1902, 'Sulla scelta dei RR. commissari per i comuni e le opere pie'.

26 L. Quarta-Guidotti, *Lo scioglimento dei consigli comunali e le attribuzioni del r. commissario straordinario...* (Lecce, 1890), 16-17.

zation of the offices, the execution of taxes imposed by the council, the drawing up and execution of the budget, etc. There were, however, several checks and balances to his powers; some were imposed by law, others by the nature of his job. First, as was reiterated by most commentators, the term of three months (six after 1888) was often insufficient for carrying out all the necessary measures that were meant to put the municipal administration back on the 'right track'. Second, the special agent had no legal power to prevent trouble-making councillors from being re-elected in the new elections. Hence, the dissolution of a communal council could be entirely fruitless, if the voters and the elected persisted in their will to obstruct the demands of the higher authorities. For example, the prefect of Agrigento, Enrico Falconcini, lamented in 1863 an agent's impossibility to revise the electoral rolls (which, by changing the number of voters, could influence the outcome of the elections): the dissolution of Racalmuto had little effect, because the same members of two rival families were returned to the council.[27] Later, it became possible for the special agent, acting in place of the *giunta*, to revise the electoral rolls. Finally, as we shall see, the primary aim of the special agent was the pacification of conflicts within the municipality, which in one form or another were always at the root of the trouble. Therefore, he had to prepare his strategy carefully and could not ostentatiously support a particular cause in municipal disputes.

3 THE DISSOLUTION IN PRACTICE

The dissolution of large municipalities had to be a carefully planned operation. The voting behaviour of the urban electorate was not entirely predictable, and could very well turn against the government's preference. Hence, only in the last resort did the prefects and the Minister of the Interior, who was usually personally informed about an impending crisis in big cities, ask the King to sign the royal decree of dissolution. The annexation of the Veneto to the Italian state in 1866 was barely two years old when the municipal council of Venice itself was dissolved. The dissolution took place in a period of profound crisis in the city. The economy was touching its nadir, hordes of unemployed were threatening public order and the 'risorgimental' government of count Giustinian, which had been installed under the regency of Pasolini (the royal commissioner and first prefect of Venice), did not succeed in finding sufficient support among the different factions in the council.[28] In this context it was perhaps not surprising that the massive resignation of councillors after the yearly elections in the summer of 1868 led to an impasse in municipal government. For some time, the prefect of the period, Luigi Torelli, tried to dissuade the Ministry from dissolving the council, proposing supplementary elections as a solution to complete the council:

---

27 E. Falconcini, *Cinque mesi di prefettura in Sicilia* (Florence, 1863), 56-57 and 86 of the appendix.
28 E. Franzina, *Venezia* (Bari, 1986), 49.

'The royal commissioner, without grave motives, is a measure to be avoided for the moment, and since all the operations for the supplementary elections are in progress, it would not be opportune now without discrediting the authorities and displeasing all those who have taken the rights of the voters most seriously'.[29] But the minister of the Interior, Carlo Cadorna, insisted on the dissolution: 'Not to order it would mean that the government takes sides, and would turn it into a political question; if the government lost in partial elections, it would be a political checkmate, and seriously harm authority. Some of the few remaining councillors have asked for a dissolution, which is also a more regular, liberal measure, about which nobody can complain'.[30] But as Torelli had foreseen, the act caused a considerable fuss among the members of the departing council. Councillor Manetti deplored that, under the new national government, this extreme measure had to be taken, whereas nothing to that effect had ever happened under the Austrian regime.[31]

The *regio delegato straordinario* was Ferdinando Laurin, a high prefectural official and ex-right hand of Pasolini. From his report, rather hastily published in 1868 (his term of office lasted from 18 August to 10 December), it clearly appears how far-reaching the powers of the special agent were. To a certain extent, this is only natural, since he had to guarantee the continuation of the municipal administration (which for a large city like Venice was no small enterprise). The most salient interference of Laurin related to the municipal administrative organization. He mentioned two main defects: first, the lack of a 'unity of direction' in the handling of administrative affairs by the various sections and, second, the incomplete documentation of almost all acts due to the obsolete filing system. Laurin's objective was clear: the increase of efficiency in order to integrate the preunitary administrative order into the new one. He directly addressed himself to the councillors: 'If I mention some irregularities, which are imputable rather than to people to the novelty of the laws, or perhaps also to a lack of skill in handling public affairs, and to the special circumstances of a time in which reforms and innovations were hastily pushed through, I do so because I think it is my duty to point to reforms which I had to carry through or, because I did not have the time, which I find appropriate for you to carry through'.[32] Following this cue, he reorganized the division of labour between the different offices, putting into practice regulations that had already been approved by the council; he put a secretary general in command of all sections in order to supervise and to study the necessary improvements; and he followed the model of the prefectural archives to rearrange the municipal filing system.[33] Furthermore he checked the existing regulations for all

   29 ASV, Pref. Gab. (1866-71), cat. 5 3/1, letter of the prefect to the Ministry of the Interior, 10 August 1868.

   30 *Ibidem*, telegram of the minister of the Interior to the prefect, 12 August 1868.

   31 *Atti del consiglio comunale di Venezia*, 25 August 1868, 67.

   32 F. Laurin, *Relazione fatta al consiglio comunale di Venezia dal regio delegato straordinario nella seduta 10 dicembre 1868* (Venice, 1868), 9.

   33 *Ibidem*, 10.

administrative branches and proposed adaptations to the unitary laws (many municipal regulations went back to the preunitary period). Finally, he arranged a loan of 200,000 lire in order to meet the most pressing expenses.

There are some striking similarities with the dissolution of the municipal council of Bologna, which occurred in the same period. Gaspare Bolla, a high official of the prefecture of Bologna who had been appointed special agent, meticulously highlighted in his final report the bottlenecks in the municipal bureaucracy and proposed a series of reforms. In this connection, most fields pertaining to the communal administration were passed in review. Bolla laid his finger on many 'technical' problems and suggested the revision of the regulations involved. He concluded his report by pointing to the urgency of a new loan, for which he had already made the first provisions.[34]

The municipality of Venice was dissolved a second time towards the end of 1882. In the partial elections of 1881 and 1882 the clerical party had augmented its number of councillors to 27 (out of a total of 60), and was therefore capable of exerting considerable influence on the composition of the *giunta* and on the municipal administration in general. The progressive liberals, hardly represented, repeatedly called for the dissolution of the council. The prefect Giovanni Mussi (an ex-deputy of the *Sinistra*), though deploring the small number of progressives, did not simply endorse their opinion. He recognized that it was difficult but necessary to achieve an alliance between moderates and progressives to counterbalance the clericals.[35] Nevertheless, the resignation of the *giunta* as many as three times ultimately led him to propose its dissolution to the Ministry with conviction.[36] He only asked to postpone the official announcement of the dissolution until after the council had approved the budget for 1883, so as not to overload the future special agent with work (he managed to persuade the *giunta* to stay on in order to have the budget legitimately approved). The special agent appointed was the seasoned Carlo Astengo, then inspector of the Ministry of the Interior and, formerly, *regio delegato straordinario* in Bari and Genoa.[37] The progressive and moderate liberals were brought to agree upon a common list of candidates. The prefect was proud to say that he had given his full support to this coalition (from which a conservative minority dissented), and that the progressives

---

34   G. Bolla, *Relazione letta dal cav. avv. G.B. R. Delegato straordinario per il Municipio di Bologna nell'atto che il giorno 7 novembre 1868 insediava il nuovo consiglio comunale*, Bologna, n.d. The report has been discussed by A. Alaimo, *L'organizzazione della città. Amministrazione e politica urbana a Bologna dopo l'unità (1859-1889)* (Bologna, 1990), who points to the 'succinct and technical style which was unusual in the town's documents of those years' (p. 142).

35   ASV, Pref., Gab. (1882-87), serie 2, cat. 1, f. 4, letter of the prefect to the Ministry, 16 September 1882.

36   *Ibidem*, letter of the prefect to the Ministry, 4 November 1882.

37   It is interesting to see that the Ministry first proposed the experienced prefect Giacinto Scelsi (at the time not in active service) as special agent. Mussi, however, thought it unwise to appoint an official higher in rank than himself, which would create an atmosphere of distrust towards the prefecture, *Ibidem*, letter to the Ministry, 8 November 1882.

were expected to enter the council.[38] As was hoped for, the coalition gained electoral victory: 'The purpose for which the elections were proclaimed has been attained, that is, all the clerical leaders were excluded, which reduced that party to a small minority in the council'.[39] Astengo's final report, leaving the political situation totally out of the picture, underlined the importance of an all-embracing view of the communal administration. Generally, he was quite satisfied with the state of the municipal services in Venice, calling nevertheless for strict observance of the regulations. Discussing briefly all administrative areas, he proposed to modify the existing regulations here and there, such as for the porters and loaders, in order to discipline this highly important service (for Venice at least) after many years of neglect. He also succeeded in bringing the addition of Malamocco to the municipality of Venice to a successful end.[40]

The emphasis on improvements in administrative organization is particularly evident in some dissolutions in the Bolognese countryside during the 1860s. The municipality of Savigno, south-west of Bologna in the lower hills, had been dissolved in 1864 but this had not produced any long-standing effects. In 1866 the prefect Giuseppe Cornero informed the Ministry that administratively Savigno still had countless shortcomings; the council was indifferent to the development of education and the building of roads, and for the fulfilment of any urgent operation a prefectural commissioner had to be sent. Allegedly, this 'very depressing administrative situation' corresponded to the clerical tendency of municipal politics. Altogether the prefect held the time ripe for another dissolution.[41] The Ministry agreed, appointing the prefectural secretary Antonio Ragusa as *regio delegato straordinario*. After one month in office Ragusa wrote to the prefect that his mission was proving anything but simple. The root of the problem lay in the geographically unfavourable location of Savigno and in its long-drawn-out shape.[42] Between the two far ends, badly interconnected, prevailed significantly divergent interests. Out of a total of 5000 inhabitants there were only 130 voters, from whom no initiative was to be expected: they were, in Ragusa's words, imbued with an 'obstinate venality' and a 'sickening stinginess'. In fact, the only effective but hardly feasible solution would be the subdivision of the various parishes among other municipalities.[43] As the authorities

38 *Ibidem*, confidential letter of the prefect to the Ministry, 4 February, 1883.

39 *Ibidem*, letter of the prefect to the Ministry, 16 February 1883.

40 C. Astengo, *Relazione del regio delegato straordinario al consiglio comunale di Venezia, letta nella seduta d'insediamento del 21 febbraio 1883* (Venice, 1883), 34.

41 ASB, Pref. Gab., b. 126, letter of the prefect to the Ministry of the Interior, 29 May 1866.

42 On the Napoleonic remaking of the municipal boundaries in Bologna, which to a great extent persisted throughout the Restoration, see M. Zani, 'Le circoscrizioni comunali in età napoleonica. Il riordino dei dipartimenti del Reno e del Panaro tra 1802 e 1814', *Storia Urbana* (1990), no. 51, 44-97.

43 ASB, Pref., Gab., b.177, letter of the *regio delegato straordinario* to the prefect, 25 September 1866. The changing of communal boundaries, particularly through the consolidation of several municipalities into a new one, encountered strong resistance among the 'localist' elites, nor was it in accordance with the widely

feared, the communal elections did not change the face of the council. What was worse, the conflict between the centre of Savigno and the countryside only intensified.[44] Nevertheless, in his final report to the communal council Ragusa made a strong plea to act to the benefit of the municipality. He frequently resorted to remarks about the formidable task of the unitary state, but also listed many administrative activities in arrears, which varied from rather insignificant paperwork to laxness in planning roads. Opposition to the development of communications and education were depicted particularly as a slap in the face of true progress. Ragusa introduced many improvements in the municipal archives ('the archive is the compass of administration', he didactically wrote), he fulfilled the periodical requirements of the municipality towards the prefecture, he drew up new municipal police regulations. But most importantly, he prepared the budget for 1867, including a considerable loan for starting up the road building.[45] The budget, however, needed the approval of the new council – a stumbling block for many reforms proposed by the special commissioners.

In 1869 a number of municipalities was dissolved as a result of the *macinato* riots (following the introduction of a tax on the grinding of cereals). During this grave social conflict popular fury was frequently directed against the municipal authorities and sometimes ended in the ransacking of the town hall. In other words, these were classic cases of severe violation of public order and, hence, dissolution was a legitimate measure. For example, in the first days of 1869 (when the taxation officially took effect) some 3000 men armed with sticks descended upon the village of Pianoro and tried to enter the town hall. The local *carabinieri* could barely prevent further escalation. Nevertheless, the mayor and his municipal servants were too frightened to stay in their posts. Therefore, at the beginning of February the prefect proposed to the Ministry to dissolve the council and to appoint Francesco Sugana, secretary of the prefecture, as special agent. In the tense atmosphere of those days – the army had been sent to prevent another wave of violence –, the Ministry agreed to the proposal. Sugana proceeded very cautiously by convoking the members of the outgoing council and some of the most influential heads of families. He mentioned in his first note to the prefect that the dissolution had been a justified measure for other reasons as well, because he had discovered many serious arrears of administrative affairs.[46] Continuing his consultation of his superiors at the prefecture, Sugana paid some visits to the mill-owners (obliged but unwilling to collect the new tax, they played an essential role in the conflict). Simultaneously, he occupied himself with the drawing up of the communal final statements of the preceding years and with other administrative

accepted liberal idea of the pre-state origin of the commune. The government's attempts to unite municipalities, therefore, were largely abortive.

44   *Ibidem*, b.127, letter of the *regio delegato straordinario* to the prefect, 3 December 1866.

45   ASB, Pref., Arch. Gen. (1866), tit. 15, rubr. 4, report of the *regio delegato straordinario* to the communal council of Savigno, s.d.

46   ASB, Pref. Gab., b. 164, f. 2, letter of the *regio delegato straordinario* to the prefect, 5 March 1869.

check-ups.[47] The final report of the prefect to the Ministry about the dissolution was fairly positive: 'A large part of the old council has returned in the new council, but I must make it clear that in a small rural village it is not realistic to imagine that the largest and wealthiest landowners, who through their agents and tenants have great influence, can remain excluded from the council'.[48] Nevertheless, the six new members of the council signified an 'important and radical improvement', because they were known to be devoted to the government.

Illustrative of what was in the long run the limited power of the state *vis-à-vis* the municipalities is the case of the communal administration of Melito Porto Salvo, a small town of 3,000 to 4,000 inhabitants in the province of Reggio Calabria. Melito acquired some fame from the landing of Garibaldi in 1860, the first step to the liberation of the southern mainland, but this moment of glory rapidly vanished from public memory. Internal conflicts split the communal council, and rendered the office of mayor precarious. In 1873 the councillor Domenico Alati, not very much trusted by the then prefect, put a 'black paper' to press, in which he accused the municipal government of gross malversation. Yet the prefect De Feo postponed any interference until April 1875. He justified his late reaction by pointing out that a dissolution and the attendant general elections would probably bring no new men into the council. Since the large landowners of the municipality lived far away, the council was composed of small landowners, constantly divided by infighting. But finally an example had to be set.[49] The *regio delegato straordinario* Temistocle Tannarelli, secretary at the subprefecture of Taranto, started out at the root of the administrative problem, the question of the demesnes (see also chapter 6 for a more elaborate analysis of this problem). He put the agent charged with the division operations to work, reorganized the municipal finances, drew up police regulations, made provisions for road building and schools, and reordered the municipal archive (there was not even a collection of laws, nor any administrative manual). The electoral campaign was heated; 121 men (out of 155 registered voters) went to the polls! The elections even had to be postponed to allow the *Corte d'Appello* to give a verdict on a number of appeals made against the cancelling of voters from the rolls (the inclusion of these voters was held to work against the special delegate). The local archpriest, supporter of the dissolved majority, made an unsuccesful attempt to prevent the elections being held in the communal church. But despite these parentheses the results of the election were quite satisfactory according to Tannarelli's standards: 16 of the 20 councillors belonged to the 'honest party'.[50] The prefect was equally content with Tannarelli's work: 'It was not only a matter of reorganizing the commune's disordered administration materially, but also of putting into effect a new legal and moral mentality and

47 ASB, Pref., Arch. Gen. (1869), serie 2ª, Pianoro.
48 ASB, Pref., Gab., b. 164, f. 2, letter of the prefect to the Ministry of the Interior, 17 June 1869.
49 ASRC, Pref., Gab., b. 20, f. 86, letter of the prefect to the Ministry, 6 April 1875.
50 *Ibidem*, report of the *regio delegato straordinario* to the prefect, 29 September 1875.

making its advantages felt'.[51] This made it all the more painful for the prefecture to find three years later that the communal administration had again ended up in an abyss. The communal archive was still neglected, and the financial situation was utterly deplorable; but since all local administrators were to some extent involved in the misconduct, there was little hope of immediate repair.[52] In December 1879 another inspection into Melito's administration was held. The outcome was invariably the same: enormous financial and administrative problems, but no solution at hand.[53] In the end, the prefect proposed the dissolution of the communal council to the Ministry, justifying the measure by pointing to the danger of an uprising of the poor, 'because these poor citizens, put under severe strain to pay levies and taxes, see the fruits of their efforts and sweat dissipate in favour of the vampires who, not satisfied with having enriched themselves by usurping the property of the proletariat, revel in seeing the population suffer'.[54] The Ministry agreed and appointed the prefectural councillor Aristide Bossi special agent. After the dissolution Domenico Alati became mayor. He had shown, according to Bossi, a certain degree of independence and sense of justice in trying to claim the demesnes for the residents of the village.[55] This appointment, as could be expected in the social setting of Melito, gave rise to many charges against him in the years that followed. The prefect, however, continued to support him until the end of 1884. Subsequently, the internal conflicts were kept at bay until the early 1890s. But towards the end of 1890 Melito's justice of the peace notified the prefect that the management of the municipal finances had deteriorated to such an extent that a special commissioner would need at least a year to repair the situation.[56] In 1891 citizens of Melito twice lodged a complaint against the municipal government. The prefect came to the conclusion that, although family relations would continue to hamper the orderly course of the municipal administration, it was time for another dissolution. The question of the demesnes was still pending, and the checking of the last final statement had brought to light many irregularities. On his advice, by a decree of 31 December 1891 the council was dissolved for the third time. The continuing story of administrative malpractice and dissolutions shows the structural dilemma of the prefect. On the one hand, when things got out of hand, he could always resort to the dissolution of the council; on the other, since there were no new persons to be elected in the council, the measure was bound to lose its potential advantages as soon as the new council was installed.

In contrast with the prevalence of administrative and public security motives, the dissolutions of Noale, Cavarzere and Chioggia (province of Venice), in the first half

---

51 *Ibidem*, letter of the prefect to the Ministry, 8 October 1875.
52 *Ibidem*, report of the inspection held by the prefectural councillor Giacomo Maglieri, 3 April 1878.
53 *Ibidem*, report of Maglieri to the prefect, 31 December 1879.
54 *Ibidem*, letter of the prefect to the Ministry, 10 April 1880.
55 *Ibidem*, letter to the prefect, 27 November 1880.
56 *Ibidem*, letter of the justice of the peace to the prefect, 11 November 1990.

of the 1870s, show a greater political involvement of the higher authorities. The council of Noale, a village of just over 4000 inhabitants in the district of Mirano and with approximately 200 registered voters, was deeply divided over the appointment of a teacher at the local elementary school. The strong clerical faction boycotted a liberal candidate, which in October 1874, shortly before the parliamentary elections, caused the resignation of 11 of the 20 councillors. The prefect of Venice, Carlo Mayr, communicated to the Ministry that, since the number of councillors was reduced to less than half, there was no choice but to dissolve the council and to prepare new elections. He proposed Luigi Benozzi, an influential member of the municipal council of Noale itself, as *regio delegato straordinario*. This choice had been suggested by the ex-deputy and now candidate of the electoral district to which Noale belonged.[57] The political interest for Noale's liberal party as well as for the local candidate to Parliament is more than evident. It was no surprise that the anti-clerical block turned out to be the winner of the elections. Afterwards, Benozzi suggested that the mayor who had resigned to provoke the dissolution and had now been re-elected ought to be appointed to his former office: 'The entire educated, sensible, honest and liberal class has no doubts that he will be confirmed in the office of mayor, which he has held honourably until now and had to lay aside in order to paralyze the influence of the parish priest in administrative affairs'.[58]

The dissolution in 1873 of Chioggia, after Venice the most important town of the province, had its origin in the lingering social, economic and political crisis of the city. For years peasants' riots had swept the countryside of the district, of which Chioggia (ca. 28,000 inhabitants in 1871) was the capital, in defence of the *vagantivo* (an old grazing and fishing right of the peasants and fishermen).[59] The city itself, in the middle of the lagoon and connected to the mainland by one bridge, was going through a period of painstaking economic reconstruction. It was, as the district commissioner in the early 1870s Domenico Monterumici put it, balancing on the edge between progress and decadence.[60] The main economic activity of the local population – fishing – was threatened by the outflow of the Brenta into the southern part of the lagoon. In 1881 the Italian parliament passed a law to change the river's direction, but the works continued until 1896. The road conditions of the district were poor, and the city badly needed a railway connection with the hinterland. The railway, however, was not finished until 1887, without an essential last section connecting the centre with the

---

57   ASV, Pref. Gab. (1872-76), cat. 5, 4/1, letter of the prefect to the Ministry of the Interior, 28 October 1874.

58   *Ibidem*, letter of the *regio delegato straordinario* to the district commissioner, 9 December 1874.

59   M. Berengo, *L'agricoltura veneta dalla caduta della Repubblica all'Unità* (Milan, 1963), 124.

60   Monterumici wrote two profound statistical monographs on Chioggia: *Raccolta di alcune notizie statistiche sul cholera nella provincia di Venezia e nel distretto di Chioggia (invasioni 1855, 1867, 1873)* (Treviso, 1874); *Il distretto di Chioggia. Illustrazioni statistiche amministrative* (Treviso, 1874).

harbour. Chioggia's economic isolation, therefore, was bound to linger on.[61]
The death in 1869 of Antonio Naccari, mayor of Chioggia between 1841 and 1851, and from 1859 onwards, marked the beginning of a prolonged period of administrative imbroglios. Already in November 1869 the prefect Torelli predicted the dissolution of the council, if no suitable and strong mayor could be appointed.[62] In the years that followed it became clear that his premonition would come true. The district commissioner informed the prefect in November 1871 that the new mayor was often away, even in the months that the autumn session of the communal council was to be held.[63] The financial situation of the commune clearly suffered from the lack of unity in the local administration. For several years the local administrators did not take heed of the budgets in their expenditure. With the passage of time it became more and more difficult to find the resources to meet the ordinary expenditure for salaries, schools, roads, etc.[64] Initially, the prefect Mayr and the district commissioner Palomba hesitated about proposing the dissolution. They agreed to wait for the yearly elections (to replace one fifth of the council), hoping that new persons would be elected. In the new council, on the contrary, a clerical majority was chosen, which immediately decided to reopen a recently closed seminary. This led, in turn, to a series of resignations which, added to the deficitary municipal economy, rendered the dissolution unavoidable. The personal antagonism was aggravated by the by now desperate financial situation. The prefecture had returned the budget of 1873 (already long overdue), because it was full of mistakes and contained a series of fictitious receipts.[65]
The dissolution that followed, however, did not have durable effects. In September 1874, after new partial elections, the district commissioner noticed that the old problems cropped up again: it appeared impossible to elect a *giunta* that would satisfy the rival parties in the council. Again this led to many resignations, which rendered the municipality even more ungovernable. The district commissioner saw all his attempts at reconciliation fail and informed the prefect: 'The government and its officials employed every possible means to lead the difficulties that thwarted the communal administration of Chioggia in another direction, but their efforts did not suffice, because it was impossible to say whether it was more difficult to overcome the obstacle constituted by the catastrophic financial situation, or to fight the pertinacity of its councillors who excluded everything that did not correspond to their principles or convictions. I beg you to forgive me if I express myself so vivaciously, but being on the spot and in close contact with these people, among whom I do not

61 A.M. Scarpa, 'La situazione economica di Chioggia nel periodo 1859-1873', *Ateneo Veneto*, 7 (1969), 21-38; U. Marcato, *Storia di Chioggia. I fatti e i monumenti più caratteristici. Le prospettive di sviluppo* (Chioggia, 1976).
62 ASV, Pref., Gab. (1866-71), confidential letter of the prefect to the Ministry, 17 November 1869.
63 *Ibidem*, letter of the district commissioner to the prefect, 22 November 1871.
64 ASV, Pref., Gab. (1872-76), cat. 5, 4/1, report of the district commissioner to the prefect, 16 May 1873.
65 *Ibidem*, letter of the prefect to the Ministry, 6 August 1873.

detect any noteworthy virtue, I very much feel the effects of this wearisome situation'.[66]

Since the higher authorities were not capable of repairing the two main evils (the bad financial situation and the obstinacy of the local administrators), the council of Chioggia was dissolved again in October 1874. The Ministry recommended the appointment of an impartial *regio delegato straordinario* from the neighbourhood, since the organization of the new elections was primarily a matter of managing the local rivalries. At the suggestion of the district commissioner the provincial councillor Agostino Zennaro was appointed. A week after his appointment, however, a disturbing message from the Ministry arrived at the prefecture (the second ballot of the parliamentary elections had just been held), warning the prefect that Zennaro was an ardent supporter of the opposition's deputy Alvisi. The prefect responded comfortingly but promised to keep an eye on the situation.

After the inauguration of the new council peace returned for a while, but a new impasse threatened to present itself at the end of 1875, when a new mayor had to be nominated. The district commissioner prudently informed himself about possible candidates. Finally, he came up with the name of Filippo Baffo, an enterprising young man without a full education but, what was more important, not involved in the local strife: 'I think it opportune to try to leave aside the men of letters, the nobility, the rich, and to put someone in command of Chioggia (a town devoted to sea trade, fishing and shipbuilding), who is skilled and comes from the commercial class, and is therefore more capable of discerning the needs and of exercising influence on the majority of the population'.[67] The only disadvantage of Baffo was his support of Alvisi's party but this problem seemed to have been overcome by the time the *Sinistra* had taken power. Baffo, however, was forced to resign in 1877 due to serious dissension about the route of a railway connecting Chioggia to the mainland – another problem that divided the local administration. Hence, with increasing irritations, the factions continued to live in discord. Their struggle affected the entire population: 77% of the voters (an unusually high turn-out) showed up at the administrative elections of 1877. In 1879 the lower classes of Chioggia broke out in revolt because of the heavy tax burden and the deteriorating fishing grounds (which was attributed to reluctance of the state to intervene). The municipal government was unable to control the riots. The prefect ordered a detachment of troops to the city, and proclaimed the dissolution of the council (23 May 1879). At the end of his stay the special agent, Pietro Pavan (communal secretary of the city of Venice), emphasized the abominable state of the communal finances (see chapter 6). His guidelines for recovery, however, explained in his final report to the new council, were not followed up.

---

66   *Ibidem*, letter of the district commissioner to the prefect, 23 September 1874. See also the letter of 27 July 1874 about the partial elections.
67   *Ibidem*, letter of the district commissioner to the prefect, 20 February 1876.

In October 1881 the district commissioner notified the prefect that it was again difficult to form a *giunta*. He put forward as a reason the lack of willingness to tackle the financial crisis. Rumour had it, he went on, that among the local elite another dissolution was expected, but 'this would certainly be an illusory solution, since experience shows that in Chioggia new elections have never changed the communal council'.[68] Nevertheless, as the economic crisis deepened and the councillors seemed more impotent than ever to conquer it, the Ministry of the Interior and the prefect agreed on the dissolution (22 December 1881). Once more the measure had little success. The financial plans drawn up by the special agent Matteo Maggetti (alderman of the city of Ravenna) went too far in the view of the Ministry; and, what was worse, the electoral victory went to the clericals, because the liberals begged off. Never before had so few voters shown up, and nobody recalled since 1848 any priests being elected to the council.[69] The acting prefect, Vincenzo Colmayer, was not at all pleased with this result and, thus, with Maggetti. He had, according to Colmayer, taken up an isolated position, thwarting rather than promoting the unity between moderate and progressive liberals. For example, at the feast for the birthday of the King Maggetti turned down the invitation to be present at the *Te Deum*, and had left the city. All municipal servants, consequently, were absent from the cathedral. This left behind a bad impression with the population, and it was even whispered that he was anti-monarchical (which was nevertheless contradicted by the prefect).[70] Maggetti had ignored the basic rule for the attitude of a *regio delegato straordinario*, namely to conform himself as much as possible to the local milieu.

The result was that the position of Chioggia's municipal administration was more vulnerable than ever. The new council remained fundamentally divided over the solution to its financial problems. Many councillors resigned. Attempts at reconciliation by the district commissioner were fruitless. A fifth dissolution announced itself: 'One cannot but conclude that since the most vital interests of the town as far as the present and future are concerned, and personal conflicts have flared up after the last heated discussions, there is no other way to solve the crisis but by letting the voters declare themselves in favour of one or the other programme'.[71] At first, the Ministry was totally opposed to another dissolution, but when it was told that it became necessary to send a prefectural commissioner for every administrative action, the Ministry gave up its resistance. For the second time Pavan was appointed *regio delegato straordinario* (25 August 1882). The general elections resulted in a resounding victory of the progressive liberals.[72]

---

68 ASV, Pref., Gab. (1882-1887), serie 2, cat. 1, f. 4 (A-Z), letter of the district commissioner to the prefect, 8 October 1881.

69 *Ibidem*, confidential letter of the district commissioner to the prefect, 3 April 1882.

70 *Ibidem*, letter of the prefect to the Ministry, 20 April 1882.

71 *Ibidem*, letter of the prefect to the Ministry, 1 August 1882.

72 There is no archival material preserved on the period between the dissolution of 1882 and the end of 1884 but a short report of the prefect to the Ministry, 1 December 1882, ASV, Pref., Gab. (1882-87), serie 2, cat. 1, f. 4.

In January 1885 the faction struggle came to a new peak. The solution to the question of the local finances offered by Pavan in 1882 had never been put into practice.[73] The prefect invited the leaders of the factions to his office in order to establish a temporary pact. He thought he had created an atmosphere of consent, but the following council meeting again ended up in chaos. Hence, the prefect informed the Ministry that another dissolution seemed desirable.[74] History repeated itself. Neither of the parties succeeded in attaining a clear majority, and the future looked dreary. The district commissioner noted that after the elections the newly installed communal council listened to Pavan's report with an unconcealed lack of interest. Since no councillor was found capable of managing the communal affairs, the council was destined to fall victim to another crisis.[75] In sum, the structural economic depression, from which the city could impossibly escape without massive state support, and the weak and divided local elite, which because of the limited franchise continued in power, led Chioggia from one dissolution into another.

The crisis of the district of Chioggia was also highly felt in Cavarzere, a rural municipality of 15,000 inhabitants. For years, the countryside around the town had been the scene of popular protest. In 1872 the municipal council had already been dissolved but in the summer of 1874, after the partial elections in which the clerical party succeeded, the prefect advised the Ministry to consider another dissolution. However, the Minister, through secretary general Gerra (an ex-prefect), did not immediately agree. He reminded the prefect that the number of councillors in office still had not fallen below the legal minimum and that there was hope that the outgoing councillors could be persuaded to take their seats again 'by making them understand that the electoral struggle, even on the local level, was a condition of countries that were liberally governed, and that lack of confidence and negligence infused audacity into the opposing party'. His subsequent reasoning took an extremely interesting turn: 'It is good to remove once and for all the suspicion that in the present circumstances the government wants to utilize the dissolution of municipal administrations as an electoral weapon. Nevertheless, either because of the refusal of the resigning councillors to take up their office again; or because of the resignation of others; or if for other reasons it is impossible to modify the current majority and if this majority really pursues a course which is incompatible with the commune's interest or with public order (in which case art. 235 of the communal and provincial law can be applied according to the spirit of the letter), I shall not hesitate, if necessary, to take the extreme measure of dissolving the administration'.[76]

These considerations demonstrate that the Ministry did not cynically seize every opportunity to dissolve a municipal council for political purposes. But despite the

---

73 *Ibidem*, report of the district commissioner to the prefect, 31 January 1885.
74 *Ibidem*, letter of the prefect to the Ministry, 7 February 1885.
75 *Ibidem*, letter of the district commissioner to the prefect, 8 May 1885.
76 ASV, Pref., Gab. (1872-76), cat. 5, 4/1, letter of the Ministry of the Interior to the prefect, 18 August 1874.

Ministry's hesitation, the dissolution of Cavarzere proved inevitable. The provincial councillor Giacomo Fiori was appointed special agent. He succeeded in restoring peace in the village, so that in February 1876, after the nomination of a new mayor, the district commissioner could rightly say that the municipal crisis was over.[77]
The evidence from the province of Venice shows that the involvement of the higher authorities in municipal government cannot be reduced to a single purpose. It is true, on the one hand, that the prefect – and indirectly the Ministry – did not hesitate to instrumentalize the dissolutions for their own political purposes. On the other hand, the administrative problems of the dissolved municipalities were real. Large parts of the Veneto went through a period of profound economic crisis that inevitably affected the municipal administrations. Furthermore, in the anticlerical climate of the early 1870s, it was highly improbable that the government would be resigned to the rise of the clerical party in local administrations.
The combination of a structural economic crisis (like the lingering question of the demesnes in Melito Porto Salvo and the isolation of Chioggia) and a strong diversity of opinions (often reinforced by the economic difficulties) in the communal council was a breeding ground par excellence for regular dissolutions. Likewise, the question of the *partecipanza* constituted a permanent stumbling block to the municipal adminis-tration of Medicina (district of Imola, Bologna). The *partecipanza* of Medicina, like a few others in Emilia, was an ancient private institution, administering its large estates without any state interference. Its history, inextricably bound up the commune, went back to the Middle Ages; but only with the Restoration of 1814 (after the French regime had allotted its property to the 'new' municipality) had it become an autono-mous body independent of the municipality. Every five years the older families of Medicina – the *partecipanti* – received their share of the proceeds. By an old decree the *partecipanza* was bound to pay a considerable sum to the municipality for education and public health. In 1859 it was established that the administrative council of the *partecipanza* be elected by universal suffrage. That this organization would be a serious impediment to both the municipal administration and the prefect, was already noted by Cordero di Montezemolo in 1862: 'These *partecipanze* indeed show perpetual substitution in the transference of property, whereas present-day legislation tends to abolish such bonds'.[78] First, conflicts were likely to arise between the *partecipanti* and the excluded families; second, the sum to be transferred to the municipality was bound to cause disagreement; and third, it was unclear whether the prefecture was authorized to intervene in the quarrels. Oreste Regnoli, who was called on to give his opinion, reasoned that the prefectural authorities were qualified to deal with possible conflicts, and that eventually the municipality was empowered

---

77 *Ibidem*, letter of the district commissioner to the prefect, 4 February 1876.
78 ASB, Intendenza Gen., Arch. Riservato, b. 13, report of the prefect to the Ministry of the Interior, 21 December 1862.

to divide the premiums among the 'shareholders'.[79] But the *partecipanza* remained a juridical and practical stumbling block.

The triple problem culminated in a first dissolution of the council on 31 December 1864. At stake was the presence of *partecipanti* in the communal council. Since they were involved in a lawsuit against the municipality, they could be legally excluded from the communal council. It was, however, evident to the prefect that in the long run the exclusion of half of the potential electorate was absurd. It took until 1873 (including another dissolution of the municipal council of Medicina) before the dispute was settled. As a consequence the prefect Capitelli decreed on 18 September 1874 that from then on the *partecipanza* would be free of state interference (it must be remembered that the communal and provincial law of 1865 had already abolished administrative justice by the prefectural councils). Even though at the time this measure was hailed as the herald of liberty, the decay of the corporate body itself and the inadequacy of internal control created administrative chaos. The special judicial administrator appointed by the Court of Bologna, Augusto Bordoni, concluded in 1881 that the heart of the problem was the premium paid out to the *partecipanti*, which was too high for the body's means to bear. The redistribution of the debts and the replacement of the head of the day-to-day administration were part of the verdict reached by Bordoni.[80] But the immediate result was that the old head started a smear campaign against the new one. More and more voices were heard to abolish the *partecipanza* as an anachronistic remnant of feudalism.[81] The internal conflicts, sometimes leading to riots, inevitably affected the communal administration. The communal council fell prey to the same differences of opinion as were prevalent within the *partecipanza*. Furthermore, the 'spectre of socialism' that was about in many parts of the district of Imola also afflicted Medicina. Particularly after the defeat of the socialists and the republicans in the political elections held in the spring of 1886 they were, as the prefect put it, nourishing social unrest among the population. For these reasons the municipal government of Medicina, without a regular mayor since 1883, was in no position to continue in office.[82] The dissolution of the council seemed in order.

The general elections following the dissolution brought, to the relief of the authorities, 'good elements' to power. The *regio delegato straordinario* Aldo Goretti, secretary of the Ministry of the Interior, investigating the entire municipal administration,

---

79 O. Regnoli, *Dei diritti del comune di Medicina* (Genoa, 1862).

80 ASB, Pref., Gab. (1884), cat. 12, confidential memoir of A. Bordoni to the prefect, 1 October 1881.

81 See for example, *Sullo scioglimento delle partecipanze. Memoria del municipio di Medicina ai ministri di Grazia e Giustizia e dell'Interno* (Bologna, 1882). Also, *All'illustrissimo Tribunale Civile di Bologna. Dei diritti del comune di Medicina sul patrimonio medicinese. Esposizione di fatto e di ragione pel comune nella causa contro la partecipanza* (signed, among others, by P.S. Mancini and O. Regnoli) (Bologna, 1872).

82 *Ibidem* (1888), cat. 4, letter of the prefect to the Ministry, 17 June 1886.

indicated the *partecipanza* as the great obstacle to the recovery of Medicina.[83] Its dissolution was not long in coming. But whereas the *partecipanza* lost its influence after its possessions were dispersed, the rivalling factions continued to thwart the administration of Medicina.[84] The general elections of 1889, after the widening of the suffrage, produced a radical turn in the communal council. The liberal mayor, appointed by the council in 1889, resigned in October 1890 together with his aldermen. A socialist *giunta* took over their place. The liberal councillors chose to keep their options open by letting things run their course: 'This fact evidently demonstrates that if the communal council of Medicina consists of a majority of people devoted to order (as it actually does), it nevertheless nourishes the idea, like other municipalities in the province, that the communal administration should be left to turbulent elements, so that the masses may rapidly see that they are bound to give a bad proof of their capacity to administer public office. It is my conviction that such elements can hardly stay long in charge of the administration of Medicina, and doubling my strict control over the interests of that administration I shall propose the necessary measures to you as soon as I discover signs of bad administration and overt violation of the laws'.[85]

The strategy seems to be same as in the case of Imola discussed in the previous chapter. The opportunity for the dissolution of the council came rapidly. The new *giunta* of Medicina made such an enterprising start that many councillors of the liberal opposition resigned. The number of councillors thus ended up below the number legally required to make valid deliberations. The *regio commissario straordinario* (the title was slightly changed by the communal and provincial law of 1889) Giustiniano Bonfigliolo ably organized the general elections. He managed to placate the working classes by initiating 'soup kitchens'. The elections were a resounding victory for the liberals.[86] This success, however, was short-lived. The general elections of 1895 and the following partial elections of 1896 brought again a large number of socialists into the council. The rest of the story takes us beyond our period (other dissolutions took place in 1898, 1899, and 1905!); but it is abundantly clear that the government's policy was directed towards frustrating socialist municipal government, and vice versa. The prefect, hence, often got caught between two fires, between the striving for administrative peace and continuation on the one hand, and the presence of 'subversive' elements in the municipal government on the other.

---

83 *Relazione letta al consiglio comunale di Medicina dal Regio Delegato Straordinario Avv. Aldo Goretti* (Medicina, 1886).

84 Cf. the remarks of the subprefect in January 1889, before the general elections later that year: 'By now the "partecipanza", which was meant to support many families of day labourers, is hardly worth its name. Apart from seriously harming the working classes, the dissolution of the extensive property contributed to aggravate the hatred', ASB, Pref., Gab. (1890), cat. 9/1, report of the subprefect to the prefect, 3 January 1889.

85 ACS, Min. Int., Direzione Gen. dell'Amministrazione Civile, Comuni, b. 122, f. 15811.12, letter of the prefect (Scelsi) to the Ministry, 11 November 1890.

86 *Ibidem*, letter of the prefect to the Ministry, 19 March 1891.

4 CONCLUSION

In the period between 1860 and 1889, even if the immediate cause of the dissolutions was political (dissension within the communal council) or if it was a matter of violation of public order, a strong element of administrative mobilization was involved. The activities of the *regio delegato straordinario* were not limited to the organization of the elections but extended over all services pertaining to the municipal administration. Frequently, the special agent took advantage of the dissolution to 'update' affairs that were in arrears, such as final statements, municipal regulations and personnel policy. In this way, passing over the usual procrastination by local employees, the state was able to impose uniform rules for communal administration. Although the prefect did not have a legally prescribed task before or during a dissolution, he was the fulcrum of the entire process, from the first messages to the Ministry about impending municipal crises to the final report on the work of the special agent and the outcome of the general elections. The prefect was the most obvious contact outside the commune for the special agent. As the special agents were not always experienced officials, assistance from the prefectural staff could be quite substantial. Occasionally the prefect could ask for the replacement of the agent. In many cases the prefects tried to prevent dissolution, in particular when past experience made it likely that the measure would not lead to lasting administrative quiescence. On the other hand, repeated dissolutions were often unavoidable. Municipalities in which financial chaos went hand in hand with personal antagonism within the ruling elite were prone to interventions from above. Every province used to have a few of such municipalities (those of Chioggia in Venice, Medicina in Bologna and Melito Porto Salvo in Reggio Calabria have been discussed); but most dissolutions occurred in the *Mezzogiorno*.

The dissolution of a communal council was a risk. The primary aim – the reconstitution of the entire body – could easily be missed by the return of the outgoing councillors; it could even turn into a major disaster, if so-called subversive parties gained victory. The return of old councillors was almost certain in small communes, where the right to vote and eligibility were reserved to a few dozen men. Other obstacles also foiled the success of dissolution. First, many special agents and prefects lamented its relatively short duration. Within three or at most six months it was impossible to cut the many Gordian knots that the dissolved municipalities presented. Second, the powers of the special agent were limited to those of the *giunta* (although in an emergency he could take on the powers of the council too). He could, therefore, only issue executive orders; more structural interventions, such as the drawing up of the budget and the allocation of large investments, needed ratification by the newly elected council. The municipality, therefore, always had a weapon to undo the agent's work. The revision of the electoral rolls, which could considerably influence the outcome of the elections, was for long excluded from the powers of the special agent. On the one hand, this rendered it difficult for him to change a communal council; on the other, it precluded the possibility of seizing dissolution to manipulate the local representative bodies.

Improvements of the administrative organization were also part and parcel of the work of special agents when they were called in to administer large cities. It has been shown that the dissolutions of Bologna in 1868 and of Venice in 1868 and 1882 were used to make provision for specific services. The main motive for dissolution, however, was political, even though the reports drawn up at the end of the temporary government never touched upon this aspect. The confidential correspondence between the prefect and the Ministry shows that the dissolution of the council of an important city was a carefully planned operation in which even the interests of central government were at stake.

The rise of the catholics, and later of the socialists, made dissolution a tempting measure to alter rapidly the composition of the communal council. There is evidence that at the beginning of the 1890s some prefects pressed the Ministry to issue decrees of dissolution in order to thwart the socialist rise in the communal councils (by then the special agent had the power to modify the electoral rolls). It seems that the increase in dissolutions in the 1890s was partly due to the more complicated political situation. They became the straws which the authorities tried to grasp in order to maintain the liberal order. Conversely, the increase also points to a stronger self-confidence of emerging social and political groups at the municipal level.

Chapter 5

Control of municipal services:
uniformity and tradition

1 INTRODUCTION

The pursuit of stable local administration was accompanied, or rather preceded, by attempts to organize the municipal services on uniform and rational standards. In continuation of the tradition of the Restoration, 'good administration' was, after public order, the basis of the proper functioning of local government, not the other way round. Good administration meant taking care of municipal properties, the urban and rural police, road building and maintenance, local public services, education, poor relief, etc. As the ups and downs of the municipalities were inextricably bound up with the prosperity of the state, so – as the theory would have it – the execution by local authorities of national rules in the field of administration was of paramount importance to the central government. Hence, the legislator had given the prefects, who represented the executive power in the province, far-reaching tasks in the field of the control of municipal administration. In the opening years of the unitary state the administrative project prepared by Cavour and Rattazzi was zealously executed. Central and peripheral administrators shared a 'liberal-authoritarian' view of the development of municipal administration: on the one hand, the 'free' elections were hailed as the breakthrough of liberalism (the extent of their freedom has been amply discussed in the previous chapter); on the other, the municipal governments chosen in these elections were required to adopt a certain number of uniform rules for their administration. When the first national statistics on the administrative services appeared, it became clear that the high aims of the 'men that built Italy' could not be attained in the short term. But whereas many prefects remained loyal to their administrative mission for some time, the political centre soon lost its openness towards the general problems of civil society, substituting it with a system of favours in exchange for electoral support. It is the purpose of this chapter to assess this development, in particular from the vantagepoint of the prefects.

For many parts of the peninsula, Unification entailed stricter regulation of the services rendered by local authorities. The communal and provincial law of 1865 and, in particular, its attendant regulations laid down a number of rules for the examinations and duties of communal secretaries; for filing methods to be applied in the communal archives; for inventories of communal properties, communal debts, and communal roads; for municipal police, health, and building regulations; and for beginning a collection of official documents (such as the acts of the communal council and the *giunta*, electoral rolls, laws and decrees of the Kingdom, budgets and final statements (*conti consuntivi*), census and land registers, conscription records, etc.). The *conditio sine qua non* of the execution of these rules was the presence of capable communal secretaries. Complaints about their capacities, however, were legion. Until well into the 1880s the prefects, especially those stationed in the *Mezzogiorno*, frequently lamented the inefficiency of the municipal employees. But as long as the law was not broken, there was little they could do about it. Whereas it was not too difficult to get rid of poorly functioning mayors, the prefects had to put up with unlicenced secretaries and the attendant delays. Moreover, the municipalities were free to appoint who they wanted (and pay them an extremely low salary), provided that the candidates had passed a relatively easy exam organized each year by the prefecture (the questions, however, were drawn up by the Ministry of the Interior).[1] The unreliability of the municipal secretaries was particularly high in the South. Before 1865 no official diploma was demanded from the aspirants to a municipal office, and many kept their job afterwards. Achille Serpieri, prefect of Reggio Calabria, described the secretaries of his province as one of the greatest obstacles to good administration. In 1871 98 out of 107 municipal secretaries did not have the license prescribed by the law of 1865. In Serpieri's experience they were incapable of exercising their office to any acceptable degree. On the other hand, he acknowledged that the exceptionally low salaries could hardly be an incentive to do a good job. While twenty municipalities paid their secretaries a mere 500 lire, only two went beyond 1000 lire (the lowest-paid prefectural official earned 1500 lire in 1871).[2]

Elementary legal and administrative education, therefore, was absolutely essential, both for prospective secretaries and for secretaries in office. A flood of small administrative periodicals, manuals, and monographs, often written by civil servants but privately published, spread over the country. Some of them literally dictated what was expected from the municipal secretaries. In his guide for municipal offices Carlo Beltrami listed, month per month, the duties to be performed by the secretaries. Order and neatness were the first requirements for running the municipal offices efficiently. The secretaries should have a conviently arranged agenda for affairs to be completed. The draft acts had to be divided according to the authority involved (council, *giunta*, or other administrative body), and kept in boxes with the names of these authorities on them.[3] The communal secretaries were further required to keep a register for all outgoing papers, so that at the end of June they could easily draw up the 'summary of regular duties' to be forwarded to the prefecture. In this way the prefect could check the workings of the communal offices at one glance. Taking the secretaries by the hand like this, the higher authorities of the Interior administration

---

1 See on these issues R. Romanelli, *Sulle carte interminate. Un ceto di impiegati tra privato e pubblico: i segretari comunali in Italia, 1860-1915* (Bologna, 1989), 67-118.

2 ASRC, Pref., Gab., b. 62, f. 982, report of the prefect to the Ministry of the Interior on 1870 and the first trimester of 1871, 15 April 1871.

3 C. Beltrami, *La nuova guida per gli uffizi comunali*, 2 vols (Turin, 1871-73), I, 19.

hoped to bring some order into the municipal administration. But clearly the fate of municipal administration did not rest solely on the shoulders of the secretaries. The real initiatives, insofar as they were needed, came through the prefectural channels.

2 MEETINGS OF THE COMMUNAL COUNCIL

The most recurrent incentive coming from the prefecture concerned the sessions of the communal councils, the most obvious manifestations of well-functioning local self-government. Apart from extraordinary sessions (which had to authorized by the prefect until the communal law of 1889 changed this check on municipal discretion), the councils met twice each year, in spring and in autumn. The law imposed that in these sessions the most essential matters of municipal administration were to be discussed: in spring the electoral rolls and the final statement of the previous year, in autumn the election of the *giunta*, the budget for the coming year, and the appointment of the auditors for the final statement. These obligatory sessions were considered the pivot of local administration; without strict observance of the guidelines laid down in the law and in the ministerial and prefectural circulars, the Ministry of the Interior firmly stated in 1869, further liberalization of local administration was impossible.[4] Taking this cue, almost every year (until well into the 1880s!) the prefects of Venice, Bologna and Reggio Calabria issued circulars calling for a regular ordering of the sessions. Sometimes they simply brought up subject matters previously neglected by the municipalities; at other times they went as far as to induce the councils to accept certain expenditures considered vital for further economic development. In September 1872, for example, the prefect of Venice drew the attention of the local administrators to the usual trinity of liberal aims: education, public health, and road building. In his words: 'The communal councils have to take public education, hygiene and road building very much to heart; and though it is their duty to be frugal with other expenditure, they have to be free with these things, insofar as is allowed by their means, because on them depend public health and the material and moral prosperity of the commune'.[5] Similar arguments, linking up seemingly routine council deliberations with the highest aims of liberal policy, can be found in many prefectural circulars of the 1870s. Later these ideologizing guidelines disappeared and gave way to purely technical explanations.

From 1870 the Ministry wished to receive a separate annual report on the deliberations of the communal councils during the spring session.[6] It had become clear that

---

4 *Circolare del Ministero dell'Interno*, 30 August 1869, n. 5261.

5 *Circolare della prefettura di Venezia*, 20 September 1872, n. 15919.

6 *Circolare del Ministero dell'Interno*, 5 April 1870, n. 15100. In 1878 the Ministry allowed the prefect of Venice to stop drawing up this report and to integrate it in his half-yearly report on public affairs and the administrative services, cf. a letter of the Minstry of the Interior, 19 July 1878 (in response to a request made by the prefect of Venice 15 June 1878), ASV, Pref., Arch. Gen. (1877-81), f. 1, 54/3. Since no reports

many municipalities systematically failed to discuss the required matters. The reports of the prefects of Venice, drafted by one of the councillors (Alessandro Bonafini), were always quite extensive.[7] They were not limited to a dry account of the number of municipalities that had not submitted their final statements, or had not approved the electoral rolls, but also treated the most important single deliberations. Thus the Ministry was informed about special investments in public works, changes in municipal police regulations, the establishment of schools, and other minor affairs.[8] The aim of the prefecture was of course to direct the flow of subsidies for public works or to influence possible reforms considered by the Ministry. But it is questionable whether Palazzo Braschi used this detailed information in any other way than for bureaucratic reasons, particularly since the Ministry soon made clear its readiness to suspend these reports.

The instructions given by the prefect of Reggio for the ordinary sessions were usually precise, virtually offering a blueprint of the meeting itself. Shortly before the arrival of the new prefect (Achille Serpieri) the chief councillor Vitelli, foreshadowing the zeal of his superior, issued an exhaustive list of subjects of discussion. He assembled all relevant articles of the communal and provincial law and of other legal texts in a very succinct circular. He concluded with a general plea for good and honest administration: 'The communal administrators ought to keep in mind that in the ordinary spring session they have a most serious duty with respect to the population, namely that of drawing up the accounts, and that of taking care of electoral rights; both are the pivot of a good and honest administration'.[9]

In the years that followed Serpieri stuck to this line, expressing legal regulations in high-flown terms. The passive sabotage perpetrated by the municipalities, however, was not easily defeated. In 1870 he noted: 'But since many municipalities have shown in the past year that they have not paid attention to the rules as they should have, or that they have not sufficiently understood them, I put them again in front of the municipalities with some further warnings and clarifications'.[10] And unremittingly he reiterated the formal rules for the sessions of the communal councils. Under Filippo Lamponi, prefect from 1877 to 1881, another large-scale attempt was made to

drawn up later than 1877 have been found elsewhere, it seems reasonable to assume that the permission to stop was given to other prefects as well.

7 Alessandro Bonafini (born 1820) was one of the pillars of the prefectural offices of Venice; he served until 1884 in Palazzo Corner, most of the time as councillor charged with communal and provincial administration. The reports on municipal services, the sessions of the communal councils, the financial management of the municipalities, etc. were invariably in his hand. He perused the administrative manuals, particularly the one edited by Carlo Astengo, as is shown by his personal collection of circulars and countless marginal notes on administrative issues, later deposited in the state archives of Venice, cf. ASV, *Dono Bonafini*.

8 See for example the annual report on the deliberations of the municipalities during the ordinary session of the councils in the spring of 1877, ASV, Pref., Arch. Gen. (1877-81), f. 1, 54/3.

9 *Circolare della prefettura di Reggio Calabria*, 28 March 1868.

10 *Circolare della prefettura di Reggio Calabria*, 18 March 1870.

induce the municipalities to take their fate in their own hands by authoritatively planning their council meetings. Afterwards the prefecture carefully scrutinized the minutes of the meetings. Whenever mistakes, or worse, were found in the formal procedure, the deliberations were annulled: 'Many acts performed by the municipalities have been annulled, sometimes for technicalities, sometimes – one is inclined to say – for reasons of morals. There are a few administrations (in the district of Reggio Africo, Melito Porto Salvo and Rosali take the palm), which are in the habit of riding roughshod over the law, and for which repeated instructions and reproaches remain a dead letter'.[11] In the first half of 1878 93 municipal deliberations (not including the final statements) were annulled, 'a very distressing figure', the prefect wrote, 'if one takes into account that we have resorted to this rigorous measure only in the case of absolute necessity. Since in several instances, when only the form was defective and the content all right, our office has limited itself to sending back the acts for the necessary alterations'[12] In a prefectural circular of August 1878, on the eve of the autumn sessions, a baffling array of shortcomings of the municipal services were passed in review. For each of them a solution – an item of expenditure on the budget – was recommended: ramshackle municipal buildings had to be repaired, deficient archives needed new shelves and printed forms, schools had to be repaired, teachers were underpaid, existing streets were hardly maintained, there was a desperate shortage of country policemen and district doctors, the dead were still buried in churches instead of in cemeteries on the fringes of the towns, local prisons were in a state of utter decay, many communal treasurers were indebted to the municipalities, etc.[13]

The efforts of the Southern prefects to make the municipalities take care of their responsibilities were mostly fruitless. Even those who attempted to exert their task as mediators between state and society seriously were reduced to manoeuvring between sick patients and lazy doctors: on the one hand, the municipalities remained adamant in their lethargy; on the other, the state was unable to foster long-term economic development, which would enable the local administrations to profit more from their powers. In other parts of the Kingdom as well – judging from the recurrence of prefectural calls for regular sessions of the communal councils – the slow rate of economic and social change thwarted the willingness of the local representatives to perform their most elementary function: to meet periodically in order to deliberate on the most urgent administrative needs.

11 ASRC, Pref., Gab., b. 62, f. 987, report on the administrative services in the second semester of 1877, January 1878.
12 *Ibidem*, f. 988, report on the administrative services in the first semester of 1878, 29 July 1878.
13 *Circolare della prefettura di Reggio Calabria*, 15 August 1878.

3 MUNICIPAL SERVICES

Efficient control of municipal services had become possible after the unifying administrative laws of 1865. In 1867 the Ministry of the Interior sent a circular to all prefectures and subprefectures to check their implementation: 'Since in the current year 1867 communal administration has been unified in all the provinces of the Kingdom, the Ministry wishes to receive some factual information in order to get to know with a certain degree of precision whether and how the various public services entrusted to the communes function according to the regulations laid down by the new administrative laws'.[14] The Ministry wished to receive information about the maintaining of the municipal archives, the land register (*catasto*) and the attendant sources of income for the municipalities, the inventory of communal properties, the state of the communal roads, municipal regulations, the final statements, and the cemeteries. The enormous embarassment arising out of the execution of this circular in the prefectural offices, particularly Bologna and Reggio Calabria, reveals the poor knowledge of the true state of municipal administration at that time. The prefecture of Venice, perhaps still in the enterprising spirit of the recently accomplished Unification, managed to return the statistical surveys before November 1867. The Ministry had to wait until August 1868 for Bologna and until April 1869 for Reggio Calabria, before these other two submitted their final reports, and then only concerning the situation of only the districts of the provincial capitals.

The statistics collected by the prefecture of Venice showed a not too awkward situation, in particular if one takes into account that many Italian laws still had to be introduced in the Veneto. The fact that all final statements until 1866 included had been approved, was a clear indication of the relatively good start of local administration.[15] The royal commissioner and first prefect Giuseppe Pasolini had immediately taken control of the local authorities, as he explained in a letter of January 1867 to the Ministry: 'All acts concerning the various districts were requested from the royal commissioners, and the district commissioners were asked to submit elaborate reports on what had been done in the districts themselves to complete the administrative organization and to make it work uniformly in the entire province'.[16] Pasolini was undoubtedly referring to his circular of October 1866 to the district commissioners, issued shortly after his arrival in Venice. He had ordered them to draw up a detailed report, so that he could form an opinion of 'everything that was completed or started according to the new regulations' and could 'impose on the administration of the entire province the uniform and regular course that ought to be typical of it'. Moreover he urged his subordinates to 'to gear their activities in future to the principle of the control and educational action that state officials should exert under

---

14 *Circolare del Ministero dell'Interno*, 4 March 1867, no. 21.
15 ASV, Pref., Arch. Gen. (1866-71), f. 4, 1/14.
16 *Gli archivi dei regi commissari nelle province del Veneto e di Mantova 1866*, 2 vols (Rome, 1968), II, 248-249.

some circumstances'.[17] Through this initiative a straight and fruitful link was established between the existing control over municipal administration – most 'Austrian'
district commissioners remained in office – and the exigencies of the new Italian
administrative laws.

The problems in Bologna were mainly restricted to municipalities that were backward
in drawing up their final accounts of their revenues and expenditure. Nevertheless,
this negligence rendered it more difficult for the prefecture to obtain an overall
picture of the actual administrative energy of the local authorities. To judge from the
poor turnouts at the communal elections, the will to participate of even the few
entitled to vote was lacking. Or, in the words of the prefect: 'the carelessness of the
majority of communes is essentially caused by the little interest they have for the
public cause'. In a broader sense, however, the municipal services of the district of
Bologna could be regarded as fairly satisfactory.[18] This convinced the prefect that his
control was effective, and that faith in public affairs would steadily grow.

The statistics demanded by the Ministry in 1867 relating to the observance of the
communal law showed that the situation in Reggio Calabria was much worse than
in any part of the other two provinces. The list of the prefect's complaints seemed
never-ending: the communal archives were still kept according to preunitary regulations, the local secretaries were mostly incompetent, there were hardly any complete
inventories of municipal possessions, the municipal councils often failed to allocate
the obligatory expenditure on their budgets, the state of the local roads was lamentable and their classification was only slowly progressing, etc., etc. This negligence
was, of course, not surprising. It is superfluous to comment that as far as the
administrative structure was concerned Reggio, like the entire *Mezzogiorno*, had a
great deal to recuperate. Only towards the end of the first decade of the unitary state
could one say the 'era of administration' was about to start – an era that in the
province of Reggio, as we have already seen, produced its administrative fruits very
slowly.

The results of this first national inquiry into the workings of the communal services
must have come as a shock to the division of the Ministry of the Interior dealing with
local administration. Early in 1870 the division started up a second, more profound
investigation, with the intention of repeating it yearly (the report for 1869 was
expected before May 1870, whereas the reports over the years that followed had to
be submitted annually in January). The ministerial circular raised the matter discreetly: 'The principles behind the present-day administrative legislation, though reducing
the interference of central authorities in communal and provincial administration to
very small proportions, do not exempt the government from the obligation of
ascertaining that the various public services proceed with the necessary regularity
and promptness'. A form was enclosed, on which the municipalities were to fill in

---

17 *Circolare della prefettura di Venezia*, 24 October 1866, n. 33.
18 ASB, Pref., Arch. Gen. (1868), serie 1ª, cat. 25, f. 13.

figures and dates regarding population, budgets and final statements, inventories, police regulations, communal roads, elections, dissolutions, sessions of the council, and a summary of regular works of the municipal offices.[19] These elements consti-tuted the portion of the 'general interest' that had to be adopted by the municipal-ities, and were considered the fulcrum of good administration. Through control over them the Ministry could obtain an overall view of the development of municipal administration, and ascertain whether the centrally prescribed rules were correctly implemented. In other words, the administrative statistics became – in the footsteps of their Napoleonic precursors – a moment of control in order to check the degree to which the state had penetrated society.

The results of the investigations concerning 1869 were evidently so discouraging that Giovanni Lanza, minister of the Interior in those years, immediately issued another circular in September 1870, definitely more to the point than the earlier one: 'The current situation of these administrations, in particular of the municipalities (...) can be summed up as a general negligence of the communes to observe the duties and requirements imposed by law, and an excessive tolerance on the part of the govern-mental authorities towards so many infringements of the law'. The general periodic reports of the prefects had covered up the real state of affairs of the day-to-day administration. Just to give an idea of the situation Lanza thought it expedient to summarize the results. First, out of more than 8200 municipalities only 3544 had submitted their budgets in time, while 6078 final statements waited to be drawn up. These great delays provoked a downward spiral in communal administration: without final statements the budgets could not be made up regularly; without budgets the levying of taxes fell into arrears, because the level of the additional taxes could not be fixed; and, finally, without knowledge of their financial situation the municipalities could hardly pursue a satisfactory local policy. Second, 2088 munici-palities lacked inventories of their communal properties, and in the existing ones all sorts of shortcomings were found. Likewise, there were no police regulations in 5087 municipalities, and many of the existing ones were incomplete. Moreover, 740 municipalities were short of lists of communal roads; 3066 never sent the summary of their regular duties to the prefecture; and in 3224 municipalities the electoral rolls were approved only after much delay. In sum, it was high time that this lamentable chain reaction was brought to a halt. The prefects were urged to do everything they could, 'guided by the consciousness that they are responsible to both the government and the administered'.[20]

Despite these severe words the administrative statistics for 1870 showed that the situation had only slightly improved, and actually worsened over the number of approved budgets and final statements. Hence, again a ministerial warning: 'It is necessary that the administrators of communes and provinces come to realize that they

19 *Circolare del Ministero dell'Interno*, 9 March 1870, n. 18801.
20 *Circolare del Ministero dell'Interno* (confidential), 28 September 1870, n. 18801.

carry great responsibility; and, in order to add weight to this awareness, that incitements be surely followed by the disciplinary steps authorized by law'.[21] These incitements seemed to pay off in the years that followed. The report for 1872 (8389 municipalities), including for the first time the province of Rome, showed the gradual improvement since 1870.

Table 3 National report on administrative services (1872)

	budgets in order	final statements in arrears	electoral rolls not approved in time
1870	2913	6968	2607
1871	3796	6970	1362
1872	4774	5216	590

The number of lacking lists of communal roads, inventories and police regulations had also come down.[22] With slight variations in the questionnaire the Ministry of the Interior continued to ask for statistical information on the course of administrative services until the early 1880s.[23] The results referring to 1874 confirmed the positive trend: 7695 budgets were approved in time, 3309 final statements remained to be drawn up, and more and more municipalities submitted police regulations for formal approval. The author of this report, the head of the third division of the Ministry Luigi Pavolini, entered at some length into the question of local police regulations. Interestingly enough, he argued that some municipalities, especially the rural ones, insisted on including more severe provisions, e.g. for the retail sale of food, than existing legislation demanded, which invariably led to the annulment of

---

21 *Circolare del Ministero del Interno*, 16 May 1871, n. 18400.

22 'Relazione a S.M., fatta da S.E. il ministro dell'Interno, in udienza del 10 giugno 1873, sull'andamento dei servizi amministrativi nell'anno 1872', *Gazzetta Ufficiale del Regno d'Italia*, 26 June 1873, n. 175.

23 The separate reports on administrative services seem to have petered out after 1881. In a circular of 24 June 1883, n. 18400, the Ministry of the Interior made a rather belated request for the usual information on the functioning of the municipal services in 1881. After this the Ministry lost interest in the matter. An undated note found in the archives of the prefecture of Venice mentioned that the report for 1882 had been forwarded to the Ministry, and that the material for reports for 1883, 1884 and 1885 were ready to be used; but that, since the Ministry had not replied at all, the prefecture had laid the matter to rest, cf. ASV, Pref., Arch. Gen. (1882-1886), f. 2, 46/54. In the early 1890s Nicotera revived the report on administrative services for the purpose of an account to Parliament, cf. *circolare del Ministero dell'Interno*, 26 August 1891. Although his successor at the Interior, Giolitti, issued one circular to the prefects, asking for a report on the provincial and communal public services, the comprehensive statistics taken by the prefectures fell subsequently into disuse, cf. *circolare del Ministero dell'Interno*, 25 May 1893, n. 15800-5.

the regulations.[24] Paradoxically, in this example the infringement on local autonomy was intended to impose economic liberty.

Giovanni Nicotera, minister of the Interior in 1876-77 and 1891-92, took the inquiries into the public services falling under his Ministry very seriously. During both his terms of office he presented an exhaustive report to Parliament (by the second time the drawing up of long statistical reports by the prefectures had long since passed into disuse). The reports not only included information on communal and provincial administration, but also treated personnel, public order, and prisons. Perhaps the most salient conclusion from the reports of 1877 and 1891, as far as the administrative services were concerned, is that the conditions of communal administration remained critical. Although the number of administrative duties in arrears had decreased in the 1890s, the economic depression and the chronic incapacity of many municipal employees held down the performances of the municipalities.[25]

Whereas the national administrative statistics limited themselves necessarily to a bird's eye view, the statistics taken at the provincial level, which remained unpublished, gave detailed information as to how the municipalities discharged their administrative responsibilities. These provincial statistics also illustrate, for those who tend to limit their focus to the political activities of the prefects, the energy invested in collecting the raw material, and the great commitment to regular administration. From 1876 the tables were accompanied by a report on the causes of the administrative flaws that the figures brought to light.[26] The results of these inquiries were partly used in the reports many prefects presented to the provincial council at the beginning of their autumn session. Some prefects expanded these reports to extensive provincial statistics.[27] These contain mines of quantitative information on the geographic, social, and economic condition of the province, and can only be compared with the 'general statistics of France', drawn up in observance of Chaptal's circular of 15 Germinal of the year IX.[28] The comparison is not accidental. Following Chaptal in his comparison with 1789, Luigi Sormani Moretti made a comparative analysis of the preunitary period in his statistical description of the province of Venice. Sormani

24 'Relazione a S.E. il signor Minstro dell'Interno sui servizi amministrativi dei comuni e delle provincie nell'anno 1874 (il direttore capo della 3ª divisione L. Pavolini)', *Gazzetta Ufficiale del Regno d'Italia*, 19 August 1875, n. 193.

25 AP, CD, legisl. XIII, sess. 1876-77, Documenti, no. 23, 'Relazione sull'andamento dei servizi dipendenti dal ministero dell'interno dal 1° aprile al 31 ottobre 1877, presentata dal ministro dell'Interno (Nicotera) nella tornata del 22 novembre 1877'; AP, CD, legisl. XVII, 1ª sess. 1890-91, Documenti, no. 26, 'Relazione sull'andamento dei servizi dipendenti dal Ministero dell'Interno dal 9 febbraio al 30 settembre 1891, presentata dal ministro dell'Interno (Nicotera) nella tornata 25 november 1891'.

26 *Circolare del Ministero dell'Interno*, 3 February 1876, n. 18400.

27 L. Gambi, 'Le di un prefetto del Regno', *Quaderni Storici* 15 (1980), n. 45, 828.

28 F. Sofia, 'La statistica come scienza politica e dell'amministrazione', in: *L'amministrazione nella storia moderna (Archivio ISAP*, n.s. 3, Milan, 1985), I, 587; S.J. Woolf, 'Towards the History of the Origins of Statistics: France 1789-1815', in: J.-C. Perrot & S.J. Woolf, *State and Statistics in France 1789-1815*, (London, 1984), 167; M.-N. Bourguet, *Déchiffrer la France. La statistique départementale à l'époque napoléonienne* (Paris, 1988).

Moretti spoke highly of the period of the first Kingdom of Italy and the department of the *Adriatico*: 'After replacing the civil code and many partial statutes, and after abolishing the privileges of the nobility and communal bodies, the original institutions, already bound to perish through the ravages of time, almost entirely disappeared, and the new institutions were stamped by the wise force that one still admires in the laws of that really regenerating period which aroused the national consciousness – the foundation of Unity achieved in our days'.[29] Luigi Torelli, earlier prefect of Venice, explicitly chose the years 1845-47 to make an economic comparison with the years 1865-67 (even if it turned out to be a negative comparison for his own period).[30] These and similar works superseded the quality of mere descriptions of the provinces in question; they were 'discoveries' of a hitherto unknown society. The prefects, not accidently the normal editors of the statistics, made thus sure that they helped to strengthen the national identity of the unitary state.

On the basis of the raw administrative statistics it is to some extent possible to follow the developments of Venice and Reggio Calabria through the 1870s. That the differences were marked is not surprising. Perhaps the best indication of the degree to which the municipalities complied with national rules was the timing and substance of the budgets and final statements. Whereas by the end of the 1870s almost all municipalities of Venice submitted their budgets and final statements within the legally prescribed deadline (the few latecomers had good excuses), the municipalities of Reggio Calabria were, due to the negligence of municipal employees and economic crisis, rather lax. The report for 1879 of the prefect of Venice shows that all budgets and all but one final statements were submitted and approved. As usual, the budget of the city of Venice was discussed in an extraordinary session of the communal council. In the period prescribed for the autumn session (September-November) most Venetian councillors spent their time on the mainland to look after their estates.[31] In

---

29 L. Sormani Moretti, *La provincia di Venezia. Monografia statistica-economica-amministrativa* (Venice, 1880-81), 337. From 1877 to 1879 Sormani Moretti published his long reports to the provincial council. He made it a point of duty to expound on all public services that were active in the province: 'In our present special condition it is necessay for the administrator of this province to expound on what he did, planned, prepared, or set himself as a target, since in an atmosphere of apathy, face to face with the negligence of many people, in the absence of unofficial periodicals and through lack of occasions in which to speak with authority and responsibility, it is good to seize the rare opportunities to deny accusations and to clarify mistakes or inaccuracies, which sometimes through ignorance, sometimes through cunning spread and get a hearing among the public', *Le condizioni economiche ed amministrative della provincia di Venezia, esposte il 12 agosto 1878 al consiglio provinicale...* (Venice, 1878), 5. Many years later he also edited a voluminous work of statistics on the province of Verona, *La provincia di Verona: monografia statistica-economica-amministrativa* (Verona, 1898).

30   L. Torelli, *Le condizioni della provincia e della città di Venezia nel 1867. Relazione alla deputazione provinciale* (Venice, 1867), 4-8. A few years later Torelli also edited an extensive statistical monograph of his province, *Statistica della provincia di Venezia* (Venice, 1870). He wrote the large chapter (p. 46-93) dedicated to the lagoon himself, convinced that 'the head of the province of Venice has to pay special attention to the lagoon, because in the good regulation of the lagoon lies the prosperity of Venice and a large part of the province' (p. VII).

31   ASV, Pref., Arch. Gen. (1877-81), f. 1, 54/2, report on the course of the administrative services in 1879, 15 February 1880.

Reggio, however, at the beginning of the year the budgets of 34 municipalities for 1880 were not yet approved, and 144 final statements (concerning 1878 and earlier years) were not drawn up or still waited approval.[32] One could further point to the fact that the summaries of regular duties for the communal offices were never drawn up in the province of Venice. Apparently, the prefect found it safe to omit the execution of this central order. In contrast with this trust in municipal administration, one could point to a circular issued by the prefecture of Reggio in 1878 containing the most basic instructions for the municipal secretariats and archives. A few empty forms were enclosed as examples, among others a table of communal affairs divided into categories and subjects, suggesting that nothing to that effect existed in the municipalities.[33]

Other important items in the reports on the municipal services were the inventories of communal properties and police regulations. 'The inventories are the key, the guide and the control of the administrations', Achille Serpieri had already noted in the enterprising beginning of his prefecture in Reggio.[34] These inventories were prescribed by the regulations accompanying the communal and provincial law of 1865, and had to revised at any change of mayor; but by the end of 1868 many municipalities had still failed to draw them up. They were important because they gave an idea of the income the municipalities could draw from their own possessions, which in turn could influence the budgets. As is easy to see, the local autonomy that was foreseen by the administrative legislation and that assumed a certain degree of self-organization was a dead letter, if the municipalities refrained from looking after their public services. Despite ongoing instructions many municipal administrations continued to neglect their affairs. The incomplete specification of municipal real estate for example suited the usurpers of these possessions very well. In many small municipalities members of the local elite benefitted from the fruits of communal property without paying rent to the community or even stealing from it.[35]

The drawing up of police regulations (concerning urban and rural police, building, and public health) was a difficult requirement for many smaller municipalities in our three core provinces. The approval of the regulations by the Ministry of the Interior was a merely formal one; the bulk of the work fell on the shoulders of the prefectural officials. It was the task of the prefects to supervise the municipalities in drawing up the regulations or changing them (many preunitary regulations had become obsolete after the promulgation of the new laws). Since the response from below was often long in coming, prefectural circulars offered general guidelines. In 1867 the prefecture

---

32   ASRC, Pref., Arch. Gen., inv. 14, f. 220, s.f. 66, statistics on the course of the administrative services in 1879, 6 March 1880.
33   *Circolare della prefettura di Reggio Calabria*, 24 August 1878, n. 12042.
34   *Circolare della prefettura di Reggio Calabria*, 17 October 1868, n. 98.
35   Such allegations can be found in the report on the administrative services cited above (see footnote 32).

of Venice presented a blueprint for regulations of public health, to be completed with articles tuned to local circumstances. It was, however, not the intention of the authorities to 'limit by this the powers which the law imposes on the municipal *giunte* for this subject, but rather to give them the elements for a more prompt execution of certain measures related to health, which are of high interest to the public service'.[36] Public health also occupied Serpieri's mind, when he urged his municipalities to build cemeteries outside the village centres. First, he stood up against the 'genteel tombs': 'one of the ways from which to infer the civilization of people is the burial of corpses, which has always been the objective of wise measures of the legislators'.[37] And a day later he defended the system of burying the dead in public cemeteries, since 'from the beginning of this century everybody felt the need to proscribe the system, supported by false religious ideas, of burying corpses in churches within the town walls'.[38] In 1869, following ministerial guidelines, he issued blueprints of regulations for public cemeteries to be filled in by the municipalities. Likewise, he gave detailed instructions for the other police regulations.[39] In spite of these instructions the municipalities had great difficulties in drawing up the various regulations. Sometimes, they were too strict (as Pavolini, a senior official of the Ministry of the Interior, argued in his report of 1875, see footnote 24). But most of the time they had to be helped by the prefecture. The province of Bologna was no exception: a considerable number of municipalities still lacked police regulations at the end of the 1870s. The prefect Faraldo firmly hoped that 'this branch of public service, which is of so much interest to the property and health of citizens, would be settled at last'.[40] But even if the municipalities, as in Reggio Calabria, finally got their police regulations approved, it was by no means certain that they also observed them. Many smaller municipalities did not have the personnel to garantee the correct execution of all requirements.[41] Hence, again we see that the failure of many municipalities to comply with the law and, in other words, to organize their administrative autonomy, meant that the prefects were required to organize it for them.

Although separate reports on the administrative services ceased to be drawn up, the prefects still had their general reports on public affairs in which to ventilate their views on municipal administration. These general observations, however, lacked the numerical basis inherent in the former statistical reports. Nevertheless, the continuation of the irregular course of local administration clearly emerges from the notes of the prefects. Their intervention in municipal administration, therefore, remained

---

36 *Circolare della prefettura di Venezia*, 6 May 1867, n. 7086.
37 *Circolare della prefettura di Reggio Calabria*, 26 June 1868, n. 28.
38 *Circolare della prefettura di Reggio Calabria*, 27 June 1868, n. 34.
39 *Circolari della prefettura di Reggio Calabria*, 15 December 1869, n. 85 (regulations of urban and rural police); 5 March 1870, n. 22 (building regulations).
40 *Circolare della prefettura di Bologna*, 4 April 1879, n. 3588.
41 See for example, ASRC, Pref., Arch. Gen., inv. 14, f. 220, s.f. 66, report on the administrative services in 1880, 6 June 1881.

necessary. As the 1880s proceeded, the enduring agrarian crisis was identified as the main cause for the bad functioning of many municipalities. According to this reasoning administrative modernization was more and more related to the economic tide, and no more considered as an automatic product of the political revolution of Unification.

4 PREFECTURAL CHECKS

The recurrent delays and shortcomings in the execution of the rules concerning municipal services were not only resolved by giving more or less gentle guidelines. The communal law of 1865 contained an important article (145), maintained in Crispi's law of 1889, enabling the prefects to verify the regularity of the services performed by the municipal offices: 'In case of inadequacy on the part of the municipalities to discharge the duties imposed on them, the prefect may dispatch a commissioner *in loco* at their expense in order to deal with the affairs in arrears'. The commissioner was usually but not necessarily an official of the prefecture. According to the law the prefect could only take this action to repair irregularities of the municipal offices, not to interfere in activitities of the communal council or the *giunta* (which was reserved to the provincial deputation, and later the *giunta provinciale amministrativa*). The opportunity to redress the communal services, which the jurisprudence reserved for special occasions only, was in practice widely seized. In all our provinces the prefect frequently decided to cut short the delays and send in a commissioner. On the other hand, the chronic manpower shortage of the prefectures put fetters on the use of this measure. The prefecture and subprefectures of Reggio Calabria, with no more than about 30 employees, could hardly cover all 107 (later 106) municipalities of the province, of which many needed regular assistance: 'A very serious obstacle to the rapid transaction of affairs, and a permanent cause for doubling or even trebling and hindering their treatment in the prefectural and subprefectural offices, is the systematic abuse prevailing in many communal offices not to perform the tasks entrusted with them except after a second or third request'. Henceforth, the circular went on, 'in case of delay or non-execution no further request will be made, but couriers or commissioners will be dispatched at the expense of the communal secretary who fails his duty'.[42] In 1878, for example, the prefect Filippo Lamponi sent as many commissioners as he could to press home his project of administrative revival. At the end of the year, however, he had to acknowledge that his initiative had not had the desired effect. First, the municipalities were far from cooperative; and second, the commissioners themselves lacked the administrative acumen to carry out their job satisfactorily. Because Lamponi did not want to release his own officials, he had to rely on others, usually ex-municipal or ex-state

---

[42] *Circolare della prefettura di Reggio Calabria*, 17 September 1874, n. 67.

employees. This rather weakened the prefect's power to act *ex officio* in order to force the municipalities onto the right track.[43] Generally speaking, the measure of sending commissioners, in so far as it was really taken, was a mere palliative. It might bring relief one year, but the next year the original non-performance could well have returned.

Another 'instrument' in the hands of the prefects to get to know the local conditions, were the general inspections of the province. These inspection tours had already been important events during the Napoleonic period. The then prefects – upon their arrival usually not familiar with their departments – seized the occasion of an inspection to inform themselves personally about their state and to get acqainted with the local elites.[44] These visitations were not just to be held initially, but in theory on an annual basis, according to their instructions. Amassing knowledge and giving instructions were their main objectives. A similar spirit permeated the inspections shortly after Unification. Initially, the Ministry of the Interior encouraged the prefects to hold regular inspections. But it gradually appeared that the financial distress of the Ministry, stemming from the retrenchments on state expenditure, imposed restraints on the special allowances the prefects were to receive.[45] The prefects thus lost a pecuniary incentive. But apart from that, by the beginning of the 1870s administrative inspections were held at random intervals: 'Sometimes too often, at other times too infrequently. If too often, they are a waste of time and loss of money; if rarely, they are a sign of lax and indolent administration. More easily inspected are the places which are accessible; seldom those without passable roads; never those to which access is difficult or dangerous'.[46] By the mid 1870s the Ministry declared that the inspections had to be limited to lightning visits to check the functioning of municipal administration. Not the prefect himself, but one of his councillors should be appointed to carry out these routine checks: 'It is essential that, not only when they suspect abuses, but regularly, at short intervals, the prefects appoint the councillor whom they think, as the case may be, is the right person to conduct an investigation into all the acts and accounts of the various services subordinate to the prefecture or

43 ASRC, Pref., Gab., b. 62, f. 988, report on the public affairs in the second semester of 1878, 11 March 1879.

44 L. Antonielli, *I prefetti dell'Italia napoleonica* (Bologna, 1983), 485.

45 The royal decree of 13 September 1863, n. 1475, laid down that the prefects, after consultation with the Ministry, could go on a tour of inspection, and received a daily allowance of 25 lire. The employee of the provincial administration that he might take with him as secretary was not entitled to such an allowance. The ministerial circular of 17 February 1869, n. 1541, tightened up the regulations, prescribing that it was absolutely necessary that the prefect first ask permission from the Ministry in order to be paid expenses.

46 V. Della Nave, 'Sulle ispezioni amministrative dei comuni', *RAR*, 23 (1872), 91. The subprefect Della Nave regularly published in administrative periodicals. In this article he proposed uniform regulations, based on the preunitary Tuscan legislation, for prefectural inspections. His views, however, were never taken up by others.

dependent offices without warning and assiduously'.[47] It is clear that the prefectural inspection by then had become a technical operation, and had lost much of its ancient prestige.

In 1866 the subprefect of Imola, Giovanni Battista Polidori, was still imbued with a 'Napoleonic' spirit insofar as related to concerned inspections. He recommended regular inspections of the municipalities in order to resolve 'the difficulties with which one is often faced in the attempt to make the municipalities accept the advantages and disadvantages imposed by the government's confidence and the provisions of the law'. It was evident for him that 'the presence of the state in the municipalities and its contact with the administered should yield rich administrative and political rewards, both through the growing confidence in the state and through the cognizance of public opinion'.[48] Polidori, who later became prefect, put his ideas into practice, and received the full support of the prefect for his journeys. Nevertheless, it took until 1875 before the then prefect Guglielmo Capitelli (a former parliamentary deputy) went on a tour of inspection through his province – the first prefect of Bologna to do so. After his journey he justified his inquiries by pointing to the close relationship that had been established between the administrators and the administered: 'As a representative of the national government I found it was my duty to investigate the progress of communal administration in this province personally, and I tried to achieve good relations and affection between the administered and myself, of which I already see the beneficial influences'.[49] His contemporaries, however, regarded Capitelli's inspection as a mere imitation of the bishop's pastoral visit.[50] Although there might have been a dispute of competence behind the inspection, the prefect acquitted himself well of his task, sending a detailed report to each municipality he had visited. He explained in precise terms where he had observed administrative shortcomings; these varied from the absence of regular inventories and ledgers to a general negligence in financial management. Furthermore the reports of his inspection contained precise descriptions of the municipalities, which could serve as sources of information for later prefects. Once the municipal *giunte* had taken note of Capitelli's observations, he authorized them to convene the councils for an extraordinary session in order to have a general discussion on the remaining points.[51]

In the province of Reggio Calabria, where communications were bad and many municipalities were difficult to reach, inspections seemed a *sine qua non* for regular administration. For the rural population, which was used to act exclusively through personal channels, the presence of the prefect was essential for acceptance of the authority of the state. After performing his administrative duties from behind his

---

47 *Circolare del Ministero dell'Interno*, 12 February 1876, n. 5015 (confidential).
48 ASB, Pref., Gab., b. 125, letter of the subprefect of Imola to the prefect, 13 March 1866.
49 *Circolare della prefettura di Bologna*, 5 February 1876, n. 250.
50 G. Venturi, *Episcopato, cattolici e comune a Bologna 1870-1904* (Imola, 1976), 82-83.
51 ASB, Sottoprefettura di Vergato, b. 99, f. 2.

desk for almost a year, Giuseppe Cornero, prefect of Reggio in the years 1862-63, clearly saw the necessity of a tour through the province. He found, however, the allowance that was given at that time (18 lire per day) too low: 'In far-away places and particularly during general visits it does not correspond with the requirements of an official in places like these, where the necessities of life are scarce and at the moment all normal communications are blocked; nor does it account for the fact that a visitation like the one I am now preparing would not be possible without a certain decorum and a servant to accompany me'. Moreover he thought it impossible to go on a tour of inspection without a certain amount of money for subsidies.[52] The preconditions of a sensible inspection were succinctly spelled out: a decent allowance, a certain dignity, and money to satisfy the most urgent needs of the population.

Nevertheless, Cornero was transferred before he could actually carry out his tour of inspection. The only prefect – in the first decades of Unity – to visit all municipalities was Achille Serpieri. Given his ambition to reform local administration from the bottom up, he was almost in honour bound to hold regular inspections of the municipalities of his province. His aims were always rather practical: urging municipalities to take care of the roads they were obliged to maintain, solving controversies between municipalities over the financing of road building, offering assistance in administrative deadlocks, etc. He put himself out on behalf of the provincial deputation – on many inspections he was accompanied by provincial representatives – to bring together the municipalities in consortia so that they could more easily collect the necessary money for provincial road building. His visits to the municipalities were still very much influenced by the strong mission idea of the early years of Unification. He planned his journeys to 'reinforce trust in the government in communes where that is necessary, disarming ill-intentioned persons through the force of words and insistence on the interests of the population of this province, which in my view are mainly related to questions of streets and schools'.[53]

At the end of May and beginning of July 1869 he held an inspection into a number of municipalities in the districts of Reggio and Gerace. In a report to the Ministry he listed precisely his activities during his eight-day journey. His general aim was to assist the provincial administration in solving questions regarding the road that was to be built parallel to the Ionian railway. But he also brought his ideas of economic and moral development into practice. He studied a query raised by the municipality of Bianco as to a change in a stretch planned by a local consortium of municipalities. In order to benefit Bruzzano, Ferruzzano and nearby communes he tried to find a way to unite them in order to finance a road down to the coast. In Ferruzzano he visited the school, and managed to solve conflicts between local factions. In Bruzzano he assited at a meeting of the communal council (a possibility created by the communal and provincial law) in order to calm down the supporters of a recently fired

52 ASRC, Pref., Gab., b. 110, letter of the prefect to the Ministry of the Interior, 12 March 1863.
53 ASRC, Pref., Gab., b. 110, letter of the prefect to the Ministry of the Interior, 3 May 1869.

mayor, and to bring back the degenerating municipal administration on the right track again. In Siderno he gave advice for the construction of a new municipal office. In Roccella he interviewed the mayor and some state officials, warning both parties to act more prudently. In Gioiosa, Grotteria and Mammola he settled some problems related to the building of a road planned by a local consortium. In these communes he also visited the schools, and in Grotteria he urged the authorities at last to submit their accounts to the prefecture. He established an agreement between Martino and San Giovanni di Gerace to build a road together. In Gerace he laid out a plan to organize the town's schools in accordance with its position as district capital. In Cannitello he gave instructions to the local police, so that not much later a notorious fugitive was arrested. In Bagnara he settled some conflicts which had upset the population for some time. In Villa San Giovanni, Campo, Fiumara and San Roberto he occupied himself once more with the planning of a road (in the last place he also tried to find out why several murder cases had remained unsolved).[54]

The prefect's job during such intensive inspections was primarily that of mediating between local interests. The most difficult part of Serpieri's journeys was to seek agreements between communes. Most of them were poor, and had *nolens volens* cultivated their isolation for centuries. Immediate success, therefore, was unlikely. The initiatives from above needed continual repetition. Serpieri was one of the prefects who, within the limits of his term of office, persevered with what he had started up. Precisely in those years the Ministry of the Interior was hardening its terms for reimbursement of daily expenses. But even that could not distract Serpieri from his promise to visit many other municipalities. On one occasion he preferred paying the expenses out of his own pocket rather than simply giving up his plans.[55]

In every prefecture there were usually one or two prefects who in the first two decades of Unification went on an extensive tour of inspection. Sormani Moretti's comprehensive statistical description of Venice published in 1881 was the result of regular investigations into every part of his province. In 1877, a year after his appointment, he undertook an exhaustive tour of inspection, not only in order to check technicalities (as the Ministry had ordered) but also to weigh the pros and cons of one decade of Unity for the Venetian municipalities. He did not refrain from critically expounding on the state of the province. First, the size of the province did not match the importance of its capital. Although Venice was reduced to a mere provincial capital, it had not lost all its ancient prestige. The prefecture, though equipped for the provincial administration only, had taken over some of the old 'regional' administrative functions. Second, a special complaint concerned the maritime interests of the province being looked after by no less than 6 offices of the

54 ASRC, Pref., Gab., 110, f. 2464, report of the prefect to the Ministry of the Interior, 2 September 1869.
55 *Ibidem*, letter of the prefect to the Ministry, 2 October 1869. It was known at the time that the Ministry had cut off funds for Serpieri's inspections, cf. L. Franchetti, *Condizioni economiche e amministrative delle provincie napoletane. Appunti di viaggio. Diario del viaggio*, edited by A. Jannazzo (Rome, 1985), 251.

civil engineers corps – a remnant of former Austrian dominance. Apart from these matters of provincial interest, Sormani also discussed his programme of improving municipal administration. He meticulously described the natural and economic conditions and needs of each municipality. Furthermore he listed about 15 particular problems facing communal and provincial administration, which could be partly resolved by governmental intervention. He even dared to challenge his superiors to take his points seriously, asking 'the government to pay attention to the observations and proposals that the prefecture, in all conscience and well acquainted with the local needs, does not hesitate to submit to the competent ministries'.[56]

Sormani, no career official but an ex-parliamentarian, was clearly not inclined to submit himself uncritically to orders arriving from the political centre. He set himself up as defender of local interests, notably those connected with the lagoon. In his regular reports on public affairs he was always prepared to call for governmental aid for specific projects. He paid a great deal of attention to the item 'needs of the province', a usually rather neglected part of the regular reports. The ministries he addressed himself to, however, seemed not too interested in his requests. Repeatedly, Sormani lamented the lack of unity in the executive chain between ministries and prefectures. He found his role considerably weakened by the fact that the prefect's surveillance of all public administrations in the province was not taken seriously: each office was in close contact with its superior ministry, which created chaos and envy. In a report forwarded at the beginning of 1879 he said: 'I shall never cease to protest about these things, not so much for myself (I consider myself in a rather precarious position in this office) but in the interest of good administration and of the efficiency stemming from the hierarchical chain of orders, without which one gradually falls from disorder into anarchy'.[57] A year later, however, Sormani left the prefecture of Venice, officially for family reasons. It was not until 1888 that he returned to the prefectural ranks, but never again was he put in command of an important prefecture.

5 CONCLUSION

Administrative thinking in the first half of the nineteenth century had already consolidated the idea that the communes were responsible for their own sphere of interests. Whereas a certain degree of control from above through representatives of the state (intendants, prefects, *legati*, etc.) was shared by each preunitary state, the practice of this very rudimentary form of self-government differed from state to state. The differences not only depended on the peculiarities of the administrative systems,

---

56   ASV, Pref., Gab. (1877-81), cat. 5, 5/8, 'Relazione sulle risultanze della visita a tutti i comuni della provincia'.

57   *Ibidem*, cat. 19, 1/1, report on the public affairs of the province in the second half of 1878, 25 February 1879.

but also on the social and economic development. The great innovation of united Italy was the reinforcement of the representative bodies at municipal level. On the other hand, what remained was the control over the powers and duties conferred to the local authorities. The legislator had laid down a number of prerequisites for orderly municipal self-government: elections had to be held according to a precisely prescribed sequence of acts (drawing up of the electoral rolls, sending them to the prefecture for approval, announcement of the polling-day, and a regular functioning of the voting itself), budgets and final statements were to be submitted in time, police regulations and inventories of communal possessions had to be drawn up, and the municipal offices (especially, the Registry Office) were expected to function smoothly. Control of these requirements was exerted in the name of rationality and progress. The first generation of prefects conscientiously performed their task guided by these principles. Their interference was a corollary of the risorgimental spirit of the newly accomplished unity. They were, however, well aware that in large parts of the country the existing administrative traditions and the pace of economic development were fetters on the unfolding of the programme of 'good administration'.

The municipalities that fulfilled the legal requirements – most larger cities did – had nothing to fear from the prefectural offices. The governing elites of these cities could pursue their own policy without being closely watched. The vast number of small communes, however, was followed with suspicion. The first moment of control were the instructions for the two obligatory sessions of the communal council, in spring and in autumn. The avalanche of prefectural circulars, continuing into the 1890s, calling for regular meetings and the deliberation of a few core administrative subjects (electoral rolls, budgets and final statements) shows that even this seemingly uncomplicated condition of self-government created serious embarassment in many municipalities. Hence, while public and parliamentary debates on decentralization appeared to suggest that the Italian administrative system rapidly became antiquated, the state of the 'administrative reality' shows that it was not so much the system that was wrong but rather the capacity on the part of the civil society that was deficient.

The evident failure of many municipalities to perform their basic right, i.e. to initiate their own administrative programme, was but the tip of an iceberg of deadlocks occurring in communal administration. From the statistics on the municipal services drawn up from 1869 onwards emerges a picture of dramatic delays in all sectors of administration. These statistics started to be collected by the Ministry of the Interior, when it appeared that the communal and provincial law of 1865 was being haphazardly implemented. In the province of Reggio Calabria the arrears were particularly vast and enduring; but the provinces of Venice and Bologna also had their problematic zones, such as the district of Chioggia and that of Vergato. For some prefects these statistics were the basis for more profound statistical descriptions of their provinces. We have found such monograhs for Venice (one edited by Torelli in 1870 and another by Sormani Moretti in 1880-81) and Reggio Calabria (written by Serpieri). These works were perhaps the clearest manifestations of the responsibility some prefects felt to 'administer with the facts' as well as to find a wider, especially ministerial and parliamentary audience for the specific problems of their provinces. It is certainly significant that these mongraphs were not promoted from above; the initiative came from the prefects themselves.

The instruments at the disposal of the prefects to repair the situation proved insufficient. In cases of extreme maladministration the prefects could opt for the dissolution of the communal council and the dispatch of a special agent to take over the municipal executive. The dubious success of this measure has been discussed in the previous chapter. In case of more straightforward refusals of the municipalities to comply with legal requirements – usually due to the negligence of municipal employees – the prefects could send a commissioner to take care of the particular act in arrears. Like the dissolution of the council and temporary administration by a special agent, the sending of a commissionar brought only provisional relief. Furthermore, because prefectural employees had to be released from their normal duties, the measure tended to be counterproductive for municipal administration as a whole.

The presence of the state could be effectively emphasized by prefectural inspections. The personal appearance of the prefect – under peaceful conditions – underlined the commitment of the state to the development of the periphery. In the first ten to fifteen years of Unity, when administration and politics were equally involved in the unitary programme, prefects and politicians could both set themselves up as local representatives. The inspections of Serpieri, Capitelli, and Sormani Moretti, who perhaps not accidentally all had a political background, were clearly intended to voice and to meet the wishes coming to the surface in their provinces. Although some prefects continued to regard a personal visit to the farthest corners of their province as a valuable means to amass knowledge, to give instructions, and to establish their authority, the prefectural inspections never became institutionalized. Worse still, allegedly for budgetary reasons, the Ministry of the Interior tended to discourage them, or limit them to short visits aimed at immediate administrative investigations. But probably, as the system of *trasformismo* gained momentum, the government was gradually more persuaded, as far as local interests were concerned, by the particular wishes of local deputies than by the more detached opinions of the prefects.

The political centre thus withdraw from the direct interests of civil society. This was visible in other aspects of municipal administration as well. The reports on the deliberations made during the spring sessions of the communal councils were abolished in 1878; the statistical reports on administrative services became obsolete at the beginning of the 1880s. Consequently, the role of the prefects tended to assume a more unilateral direction: less time was devoted to mobilizing activities, and more emphasis was laid on the strict observance of the law. In one sense, this loss of standing by the prefects was a 'natural' process. In the first decades, despite many enduring shortcomings, municipal administration made great steps forward. This gradually gave prefectural interference a more straightforward character, directing it towards the expansion of established structures. In other words, administration was driven back to its 'original' task, that is a primarily technical one.[58] The pinnacle of this slow and hardly visible change was the new administrative legislation of Crispi passed in the years 1888-90. From then on it was clear that the prefectural offices were to play a better defined, but more subordinate and strictly executive role, in particular because of the accumulation of functions in the field of public health and poor relief.[59] Hierarchical control over the municipalities was entrusted with the new *Giunta Provinciale Amministrativa*, consisting of members of the prefectural and provincial administration. On the other hand, the prefects also fell victim to the unfolding of the peculiarities of the Italian political system, in which their voice was less and less listened to. These developments are the subjects of the two chapters that follow.

---

[58] A similar (though preconstitutional) development in the role of administration has been recognized by R. Koselleck, *Preußen zwischen Reform und Revolution. Allgemeines Landrecht, Verwaltung und soziale Beweging von 1791 bis 1848* (Stuttgart, 1967), 400. He labelled the retreat of Prussia's public administration after the initiatives of the first decades of the nineteenth century a return to 'Technizität'.

[59] See the articles on the prefectures of Milan, Mantua, Brescia, Rome, Siracuse and Catania, edited by P. Aimo, 'Le prefetture', in: *Le riforme crispine*, I, *Amministrazione statale* (Archivio ISAP, n.s. 6, Milan, 1990), 623-895; and S. Sepe, 'L'esercito del controllo in applicazione della legge 17 luglio 1890, n. 6972', in: Idem, IV, *Amministrazione sociale*, 149-228.

Chapter 6

The checking of local finances: control and modernizing initiatives

1 INTRODUCTION

At first sight, the prefect's figure seems to stand aloof from the financial management of communes and provinces. The existence of the *intendenze di finanza*, established in 1869 in each province, reinforces this impression. The intendant, receiving his orders from the Ministry of Finances, was entrusted with the tax administration in his province, i.e. with the indirect taxes that were to flow into the Treasury. If the prefect is connected at all with the vicissitudes of local finances, it is usually his role as police official in repressing tax riots that comes to mind. However, through the checking of budgets (*bilanci preventivi*) and final statements (*conti consuntivi*) of communes and provinces the prefects and the provincial authorities were able, first, to foster a certain degree of development in the local infrastructure; second, to keep a close watch on local taxation.[1]

The focus of this chapter, although it relies to some extent on statistical evidence, is first and foremost on the moment and purpose of control; in other words, the interference of prefects and provincial administrations in the municipal and, to a lesser extent, provincial economy is our central concern (it is to be noted in advance that prefects and provincial authorities were both involved in auditing municipal accounts).[2] In this connection the following central questions will be discussed: to what extent could the state impose so-called obligatory expenditure and reduce the expenditure freely determined by the communal and provincial councils? Did the prefects (or rather the prefectural councils) see to it that funds allocated on the budgets were actually implemented? Were there, consequently, significant differences between budgets and final statements? Did the division of tasks between prefectural and provincial officials work out? Could one uphold the view that the interference of

---

1 There is hardly any literature available on the subject, see R. Romanelli, 'Il problema del potere locale dopo il 1865', now in Id., *Il comando impossibile. Stato e società nell'Italia liberale* (Bologna, 1988), 57-62.; F. Rugge, 'Introduzione' [alla sezione "Profili speciali"], in: *Le riforme crispine*, 4 vols (ISAP Archivio, n.s. 6, Milan, 1990), III, *Amministrazione locale*, 783.

2 The methodology proposed by Porro for making a quantitative study of local finances based on communal budgets or final statements has, to my knowledge, never been put into practice, see A. Porro, 'I problemi dell'amministrazione pubblica in un discorso di Giuseppe Saredo (riflessioni e proposte per una ricerca di storia quantitativa)', *RTDP*, 25 (1975), 872-898.

the prefectural and provincial authorities was directed towards economic and 'moral' development, as the advocates of the administrative system claimed? To what degree was the interference succesful at all? Was there any difference between the financial policy towards large cities and the policy towards the majority of smaller municipalities, and how different were our three core provinces?

The prefects were vested with considerable legal power to control local finances. They had to validate formally every communal deliberation, hence every expenditure, with a *visto*.[3] More important still was the auditing of budgets and final statements. In their autumn session the communal councils drew up their budget, an elaborate account of the communes' planned expenditure and of the revenues to cover them. The communal and provincial law of 1865 did not say precisely which agency should approve the budgets. In principle, a *visto* by the prefect or subprefect was sufficient but through the years a growing number of checks involved the 'tutelary authority', i.e. the provincial deputation, presided over by the prefect.[4] Many sorts of expenditure for public services, for example, were imposed by law. It was the weighty job of the provincial deputation to ensure that the communes paid. In addition to this, laws subsequent to the communal and provincial law of 1865 vested the provincial deputation with powers to check the municipal tax rates. An inquiry conducted in 1888, shortly before the new communal and provincial law came into effect, brought to light that by the end of March of that year 7971 budgets were presented: 2808 had been or were to be approved by the prefect, 4540 by the provincial deputation, 623 by Parliament (in 1886 a law had transferred the approval of some of the budgets from the provincial deputation to Parliament) and 286 had not been presented at all.[5] The approval of the final statements, a more technical operation, rested with the prefectural council. The abolition of the administrative jurisdiction in 1865 stripped the prefectural council of much of its ancient prestige, leaving it with a rather vague advisory function and the approval of the final statements.[6] Because the final statements were often submitted rather late (the above-mentioned inquiry found that only 20% were presented before the legally prescribed deadline) and hence the true state of municipal finances remained obscure, it was customary for many prefects to

---

3 P. Gallone, *Il vademecum del contabile municipale contenente i precetti per la compilazione, revisione e approvazione dei bilanci e conti comunali...* (Turin, 1880), 9; G.B. Cereseto, *Il comune nel diritto tributario. Commento alle leggi sulle imposte comunali con un'appendice sulle imposte provinciali*, 3 vols (Turin, 1885-1891), I (1885), 86-87.

4 With the subsequent law of 1889 the new *Giunta Provinciale Amministrativa*, consisting of prefectural and provincial councillors and presided over by the prefect, assumed the power to approve the budgets.

5 MAIC, *Bilanci comunali per l'anno 1886* (Rome, 1888), 254.

6 P. Sabbatini, *Della tutela amministrativa* (Modena, 1885) 174-176; also AP, CD, legisl. XIII, sess. 1876-77, Documenti, no. 33A, report of the commission (spokesman A. Marazio) on the bill of Nicotera for a reform of the communal and provincial law, *all*. E. For a positive criticism of the councils of the prefecture, see 'Sui consigli di prefettura. Ragionamento del consigliere signor Giov. Ant. Intriglia', *RAR* 6 (1865), 98-110.

keep a watchful eye on the monthly check, to be carried out by the mayor, of the municipal cashier's office.[7]

The procedure of approving budgets and final statements was open to different interpretations. In fact, the communal and provincial law of 1865 avoided the matter, whereas its successor of 1889 merely laid down that the final statements were to be examined first by the prefectural accountant (*ragioniere*) – an operation that had already been in use, despite the absence of precise regulations.[8] A ministerial circular of 1874, following the distinction introduced a few years earlier between 'normal' personnel and accountants, gave instructions for the accountant's offices of the prefectures: one of their tasks was the checking of budgets and final statements before they were submitted to the provincial deputation for final approval.[9] It is rather telling that Astengo's comment on the communal and provincial law of 1889, updated with the latest jurisdiction, extensively cited the financial instructions issued by the Piedmontese government in 1838.[10] These instructions had codified existing regulations (some of them dating from the eighteenth-century Kingdom of Sardinia).[11] They included guidelines for managing the communal economy, which remained valid throughout the century. In drawing up their budgets, the communal councils were to pay attention to the ordinary and strictly necessary expenditure. Extraordinary expenditure was only allowed for the benefit of public utility or of increasing municipal wealth. If the community was running into deficit, the municipal government should not throw itself into blind retrenchment; it should, on the contrary, pursue a policy of prudent expenditure, in order to effect the growth of industry, agriculture and commerce.[12] Astengo stressed the emancipatory elements in the instructions, without, surprisingly, mentioning the passages where municipalities were exhorted to economize – by the end of the 1880s it was generally accepted that the communes spent far too much.

Although this chapter is not intended to be a history of public finances, it would not be complete without a sketch of the financial climate in which the prefectural officials and the provincial deputies were required to work. To begin with, in this context it

7   See on this topic the inside view of a prefectural book-keeper (*computista*), V. Caruso, *Manualetto teorico pratico per le verifiche delle casse comunali* (Potenza, 1880).

8   *Guida amministrativa ossia commento della legge comunale e provinciale (Testo Unico 10 febbraio 1889, n. 5921)...*, edited by C. Astengo et al. (Rome, 1889), 1589. Also Sabbatini, 178. Basically, the instructions for the drawing up of budgets, issued on 25 August 1865, and of final statements, issued on 21 January 1867, kept their validity until after the promulgation of the communal and provincial law of 1889; they were both published, for example, in Astengo's guide of 1889 and in C. Testera, *Amministrazione patrimoniale e contabilità dei comuni, delle provincie e delle istituzioni di beneficenza...* (Turin, 1897).

9   *Circolare del Ministero dell'Interno*, 29 September 1874, n. 15988. In a subsequent circular (19 February 1875) the Ministry asked the prefectures for a copy of the internal regulations for the accountant's offices.

10   At the end of the 1860s the Piedmontese instructions of 1 April 1838 had been reprinted and advertised by the Milanese publisher Pirola, as an advertising brochure found in the prefectural archives of Venice shows, ASV, Pref., Gab. (1866-71), f. 15, 1/1.

11   A. Petracchi, *Le origini dell'ordinamento comunale e provinciale italiano*, 3 vols (Venice, 1962), I, 83.

12   Astengo, 743-44.

is hardly possible to think of a more confusing term than the 'liberal state'. Even if up to the last quarter of the nineteenth century, compared to present day standards, the state sought to give free play to market forces, it would be misleading to disregard its role. The dutiful 'night-watchman' – a familiar but rather unfortunate label of the nineteenth-century state – had a strenuous job: defence, public order, education, etc. put high demands on their custodian. Moreover, liberals were keen to expand the state's radius of action, if they felt it served the purpose of progress.[13] Apart from these general considerations, the Unification of Italy rendered, at least initially, strong intervention unavoidable. Seven states with totally different monetary, banking and fiscal systems had to be made one. Priority was given to the costly building of a railway network, one of the hallmarks of the *Destra Storica*. On top of that, despite clear signs of *laissez faire* on the part of the state (e.g. the sale of demesnes of various nature), the tempestuous years between 1860 and 1870 called for huge public spending. The double transfer of the Capital and the wars of 1866 and 1870 are a clear indication of this. Nevertheless, the goal assiduously pursued by the various finance ministers of the *Destra* (notably Quintino Sella) was to balance the books.[14] The myth of balancing the books – the aim was officially reached in 1876 – strongly influenced the discussions on public finance.[15] It led the state to gradually increase the number of taxes. As a result, the tax burden, measured in relation to GNP, almost doubled between 1860 and 1880, and continued to rise, at a slower rate, afterwards.[16]

The atmosphere of impending financial crisis had strong repercussions for the legislation concerning local finances. The tax system created in 1864-65 was relatively simple.[17] The municipalities were to obtain their revenue, apart from exploiting the

13 This idea was widespread among liberal thinkers; it is certainly present in John Stuart Mill's work, see O. Kurer, 'John Stuart Mill on Government Intervention', *History of Political Thought*, 10 (1989), 457-480. Mill's body of thought was very influential in Italy; the first Italian translation (1865) of *On Liberty* was by a civil servant, the later prefect Giuseppe Marsiaj, see my 'Gli alti funzionari del Ministero dell'Interno durante il periodo 1870-1899', *RTDP*, 39 (1989), 254.

14 On financial policy in the first fifteen years of the unitary state, see G. Marongiu, *Alle radici dell'ordinamento tributario italiano* (Padua, 1988).

15 Contemporary calculations, conducted by F.A. Repaci, demonstrate that a balance had never been attained. The national figures only show a smaller deficit in the mid 1870s, see A. Pedone, 'Il bilancio dello Stato', in: *Lo sviluppo economico in Italia. Storia dell'economia italiana negli ultimi cento anni*, edited by G. Fuà, 2nd ed., 3 vols (Milan, 1974-75), II (1974), 206.

16 R. Romanelli, *L'Italia liberale* (Bologna, 1979), 84. P. Ercolani, 'Documentazione statistica di base', in: *Lo sviluppo economico in Italia*, III (1975), 442.

17 This was acknowledged by most nineteenth-century commentators. See on the development of local finances and taxation: D. Bardari, *Sull'ordinamento finanziario dei comuni in Italia. Lettere scritte all'Avv. Giorgio Curcio* (Siracuse, 1869); V. Ellena, 'Le finanze comunali', *Archivio di Statistica*, 2 (1878), fasc. 4, 5-42; A. Magliani, 'La questione finanziaria de' comuni', *Nuova Antologia*, 13 (1878), 2nd series, vol. 11, 291-320 and 485-525; A. Salandra, 'Il riordinamento delle finanze comunali', *Nuova Antologia*, 13 (1878), 2nd series, vol. 10, 345-364 and 654-687; G. Alessio, *Saggio sul sistema tributario italiano e i suoi effetti economici e sociali*, 2 vols (Turin, 1883-87); G.B. Cereseto, *op. cit.*; C. Carassai, *Il sistema tributario dei comuni e delle provincie: studio* (Pollenza, 1893); P. Lacava, *La finanza locale in Italia* (Turin, 1896); G. Merla, *Appunti e considerazioni*

little property they had, from three sources: additional levies on the direct national taxes, communal excises and a few local taxes.[18] The Italian legislators of these first years of Unity may have had too much confidence in the future. They were anyway not capable, a perspicacious commentator wrote, of preserving the system they had established or, leaving the foundations intact, of applying temporary measures and of waiting for better times.[19] Between 1866 and 1874, in order to lower the pressure on its own budget, the state restricted the freedom of the communes to raise additional taxes. Through these measures the state wanted to protect its own major resources against over-taxation. In this connection, it must also be remembered that the provincial administrations drew their revenues from additional duties on the national land-tax, thus saddling the landed interests with another burden. Sella's *omnibus* of 1870 abolished the additional levy on personal property (*ricchezza mobile*); instead, it added 'new' local taxes of doubtful productivity to the ones that had already been introduced earlier. These local taxes, dug up amongst the wide variety of abolished preunitary taxes, proved to be difficult to levy in those regions where they had not existed before, and, compared to the other revenues, they hardly yielded any returns.[20] An additional cause of the problematic levying lay in the vagueness of the relative laws, which left the drawing up of the tax-regulations to the communes themselves. In short, the initial tendency towards rationalization was superseded by a rather chaotic accumulation of taxes, which recalled the preunitary diversity, or, as someone put it: 'All systems, all schools contribute to arrange the bouquet, certainly not of flowers, which is presented to the tax-payer'.[21] The law of 1870, further complicating the tax system, laid down that communes were only authorized – the authorization had to come from the provincial deputation – to exceed a certain limit imposed on the additional levies, if they had implemented the

---

sul riordinamento finanziario dei comuni e delle provincie (Rome, 1896); C. Conigliani, *La riforma delle leggi sui tributi locali* (Modena, 1898); G. Ricca Salerno, 'Finanze locali', in: *Primo trattato completo di diritto amministrativo italiano*, edited by V.E. Orlando, IX (Milan, 1902), 687-899; I. Bonomi, *La finanza locale e i suoi problemi* (Palermo, 1903).

18 Commissione pel riordinamento triburario dei comuni e delle provincie (sen. Diodato Pallieri presidente), *Progetto di legge sulle tasse dirette comunali e sulle quote di concorso a favore delle provincie*, 2nd ed. (Rome, 1876), 7-8.

19 Conigliani, 147.

20 F. Volpi, *Le finanze dei comuni e delle provincie del Regno d'Italia, 1860-1890* (Torino, 1962), 38-39. The special local taxes included levies on draught animals and beasts of burden (*bestie da tiro e da soma*), rateable value (*valore locativo*), livestock (*bestiame*), the pursuance of a profession (except salaried work) and resale (*esercizio e rivendita*), licenses (*licenza*), coaches and household staff (*vetture e domestici*), photographs, and a family tax (or *focatico*).

21 P. Manfrin, *Il comune e l'individuo in Italia. Studio* (Rome, 1879), 145. See also, on the diversity of local taxes, the Pallieri report (1876), 14ff. The reintroduction of old taxes was not the only link with the past. Until 1875 some provinces in Calabria and the Abruzzi imposed so-called *ratizzi* on their communes to sustain royal colleges and *licei* in Avellino, Catanzaro, Monteleone, Reggio Calabria and Teramo. These *ratizzi*, definitively abolished by a law of 1 June 1882, n. 794, had been levied in the Kingdom of Naples and in the small states of Modena and Parma, see Merla, 194.

excises on consumer goods and most special local taxes. Further restrictions in this field came with the law of 14 June 1874 n. 1961, which represented, as we shall see, an important moment in the relationship between state and communes.

By the time the rule of the *Destra* ended, the foundations of a complex local fiscal system had been laid. In general, despite raised hopes, the *Sinistra* did not increase the funds available to the communes. On the contrary, in 1886 the state tightened its control over the levying of additional taxes by prescribing parliamentary approval for those municipalities that wished to go beyond a fixed limit. A law of 1894, however, abolished the requirement of a special law and returned the approval to the provincial authorities. Meanwhile, the communes, trying to maximize their revenues notwithstanding the legally imposed restrictions, were relying more and more on the excises on consumer goods. As a result, by the end of the century the returns from excises had surpassed those from additional taxes. It should be noted, finally, that the tax returns were largely dependent on the communes' size and nature. The majority of small rural municipalities lived on the receipts from additional levies on the land-tax; large cities, on the other hand, drew their revenue mostly from excises on consumer goods.

Concomitant with the state's policy of centralizing revenues was its attempt to decentralize expenditure. The many governments ruling after Unification gave subsidies to projects for public works in various parts of the country, with the intention of reinforcing ties with well-disposed clienteles. Apart from these occasional subsidies the state left a great deal of initiative to the local governments. The power of the purse, however, was bound by many rules. The communal and provincial law of 1865, taking its cue from the foregoing Piedmontese legislation, prescribed a series of obligatory items of expenditure for the communes. Their budgets had to include: expenditure for administrative services, public order and justice, the preservation of communal property, ecclesiastical affairs, education, public works, poor relief, and health care. These prescripts, the *Rivista Amministrativa del Regno* wrote in 1851, 'while contributing to general welfare, do not diminish at all the well understood liberty of the commune, because that must not and cannot consist of the privilege of escaping from any public burden, but should consist of the power to provide for the improvement of its own intellectual, moral and economic conditions'.[22] The state regulation of these services was not an exclusive Piedmontese invention. It was widespread during the Napoleonic Reign, and in the Restoration all Italian states preserved essential parts of the system. After Unification the direct motive behind the requirements, imposed by the 'advancing civilization' (as it was put in risorgimental phraseology), was of course to rectify the utter lack of infrastructure in large parts of the country. Critics, on the other hand, pointed out that the state had cunningly

---

22 'Riforme dell'amministrazione comunale e provinciale e del contenzioso amministrativo', *RAR*, 2 (1851), 822.

utilized the enforcement of obligatory expenditure to transfer some of its own responsibilities, such as the material provisions for police services and jurisdiction, to the municipalities. Furthermore, harsh criticism was levelled at the uniformity of the system; the same regulations applied to large cities and villages of less than a hundred inhabitants.[23] Obligatory expenditure steadily increased until Crispi's new communal and provincial law of 1889 called a cautious halt to it. After that, the state began to reabsorb some financial burdens formerly passed on to the municipalities and provinces. At the same time, severe measures were taken to prevent communes from plunging further into debt. Statistical evidence shows a marked increase in debts incurred by local governments in the 1870s. Whereas in 1873 the municipalities were in debt for a total of 535 million lire, in 1878 the aggregate debt had risen to 787 million lire. Communal indebtedness continued to increase in the 1880s, for example in 1885 it amounted to 856 milion lire. In 1891, somewhat belying the restrictions imposed by Crispi's law, it surpassed 1.175 million lire. The number of indebted municipalities rose from 3690 in 1877 to 5445 in 1891.[24] In extenuation of these increases one could point to the gradual shift from loans from private banks to loans from the *Cassa dei Depositi e Prestiti*, which offered the communes more favourable conditions.[25]

Successive administrative laws allowed communes to allocate so-called optional expenditure in their budgets. The definition of optional expenditure was fairly loose. Street lighting, the voluntary fire brigade, maintenance of public pavements, etc. did not appear among the requirements imposed by law; as one may imagine, however, they were absolutely essential to larger, urban municipalities. The above-mentioned law of 14 June 1874, limiting the commune's optional expenditure to purposes of public utility, curbed the freedom of communes to spend as they pleased. Moreover, it forbade communes to exceed the limit on additional levies, if they were not to cover the obligatory expenditure. A ministerial circular, supporting the implementation of the law, succinctly explained the state's objectives. It started by highlighting the large expenditure of communes and provinces, intended 'to satisfy with generosity, and sometimes with haste, the new demands of political and civil life'. The circular called for levying or augmenting local taxes but, at the same time, a decrease in expenditure: 'New taxes and increments of any duty may be justly asked from the citizens, and can be more easily borne, only when it is shown that they are an

---

23 See for example the editorials of the *Economista* at the end of the 1870s, quoted in R. Gherardi, *Le autonomie locali nel liberismo italiano* (Milan, 1984), 35-41.

24 From time to time the statistics on communal indebtedness were recalculated. The figure for 1873, which varied considerably from one statistical table to another, has been taken from A. Plebano, *Storia della finanza italiana dalla costituzione del nuovo Regno alla fine del secolo XIX*, 3 vols (Turin, 1899-1902), II (1900), 106. The other figures are from MAIC, Direzione Generale della Statistica, *Bilanci comunali, tariffe daziarie dei comuni chiusi, situazioni patrimoniali dei comuni e debiti comunali e provinciali per l'anno 1895* (Roma, 1896), p. XLIX.

25 Volpi, 117.

inevitable consequence of general and local interests, and not merely the result of the generosity and improvidence of the administrators. Insofar as the nature and extension of the expenditure and additional levies of provinces and communes are concerned, with the law of 14 June the powers of the prefects and provincial deputations are widened, *with the object of reconciling the liberty of administration with the efficiency of the guarantees that are due to the administered*.[26] Hence, the law of 14 June 1874 marked the end of the adjustment of the early communal and provincial legislation in the field of finances. The local financial system established by then clearly reflected the paradox of liberalism already formulated in relation to other subjects: whereas the communes were relatively free to deliberate expenditure and to contract debts, they were simultaneously required to allocate specific expenditure on their budgets, and their decisions were checked by superior authorities for their legality.

2 THE SIGNIFICANCE OF STATISTICS ON LOCAL FINANCE

Many nineteenth-century publicists stressed the discretionary powers of the state towards local government, particularly in financial matters. They regarded the defective autonomy of the communes as the main obstacle to a solution of the crisis of local finances. To put it more sharply, they considered the state's authority as the sword of Damocles above the liberty of the municipalities. From a careful assessment of the ways in which financial control was exerted at the peripheral level, the opposite appears: the 'liberty' granted by the administrative laws posed greater problems to local financial management than the 'authority' with which these laws were implemented. A first impression of legal control over local finances can be obtained from the national statistics on communal revenues and expenditure (see table 4).

If the figures tell us anything, it is the evident failure of control over local finances.[27]

---

26 *Circolare del Ministero dell'Interno*, 8 July 1874, n. 15982 (my italics).

27 I have almost entirely followed the classification made by Volpi, i.e. omitting the allocations for *contabilità speciali* (funds only in trust with the municipalities) and *movimento dei capitali* (purchase and sale of communal property, instalments). On the whole, however, there are considerable shortcomings attached to the official statistics. The first and foremost (albeit inevitable) drawback is that they are based on the budgets (the submission of final statements being too unpredictable). Frequently, it was acknowledged that the budgets gave far from trustworthy forecasts of real revenues and expenditure. The outstanding credits (*residui attivi*) were usually put on the budgets to increase the revenues, whereas in reality it was almost certain that they could never be liquidated; hence, the communal deficit was often larger than it seemed, see Astengo (1889), 742. There is some evidence that the final statements indeed offered another picture of local finances. The aggregate final statements of Bologna and Reggio Calabria for 1877 (no other aggregate statistics have been found), drawn up in answer to the ministerial circular of 22 February 1879, widely diverged from the budgets: in Bologna total expenditure and receipts were both estimated at 9,951,182 lire; the revenues on the final statements amounted to 11,124,781, the expenditure to 9,330,271; in Reggio the budgets estimated 4,796,708 for revenues, and 4,794,671 for expenditure; only 3,583,676 and 3,257,937

Table 4 Communal revenues and expenditure (in millions of lire)
Kingdom of Italy (1871-1895)

Communal revenues - Kingdom of Italy[28]

	1871	1876	1881	1886	1891	1895
Ordinary revenues:						
Patrimonial revenue	21.5	41.3	43.2	44.3	44.6	48.9
Additional taxes	78.5	101.6	114.1	119.4	122.3	130.0
Local taxes	27.3	36.5	45.6	52.8	62.7	60.9
Excises	71.6	85.6	98.3	122.7	145.9	152.1
Miscellaneous revenues	11.0	6.3	7.0	8.6	10.5	12.4
Extraordinary revenues	15.4	32.1	27.3	25.7	33.5	22.4
Outstanding credits		16.6	15.0	16.0	17.9	18.1
Total real revenues	249.5	320.0	350.5	389.6	437.3	444.7

Communal expenditure - Kingdom of Italy[29]

	1871	1876	1881	1886	1891	1895
Obligatory						
ordinary expenditure	221.4	206.4	228.6	254.0	298.4	320.0
extraordinary expenditure	67.7	72.0	76.2	97.3	95.6	68.9
Optional expenditure		58.8	56.6	75.6	74.3	53.4
Unspent budgeted expenditure				2.5	10.7	6.4
Total real expenditure	289.1	337.2	360.4	429.3	479.0	448.7

The steady increase in expenditure, particularly in the first decades, and the unsatisfactory distribution of taxes show that the laws and circulars aiming at repairing the damage were largely ineffective. The effective expenditure was structurally higher than the effective receipts, in particular when one considers that most outstanding credits could not be exacted. Expenditure continued to rise; only towards the end of the 1880s did the government manage to cut down extraordinary and optional expenditure. Pro-capita receipts came to a standstill in the first years of the 1890s,

figured on the final statements, ASB, Pref, Arch. Gen. (1879), Serie 1ª, cat. 25, f. 13; ASRC, Pref., Arch. Gen., inv. 14, f. 78, s.f. 77.

28 Sources: Volpi, and the official statistics on communal and provincial budgets, edited by the directorate of statistics at the Ministry of Agriculture, Commerce and Industry. Since there are no statistics available for 1896, I have opted for those of 1895. Industrial revenues have been excluded from the patrimonial revenues; the local taxes include the communal fees (*diritti*); the extraordinary revenues are without the so-called movement of capital. The term *residui attivi* has been translated 'outstanding credits; *residui passivi* 'unspent budgeted expenditure'.

29 Before 1875 the official published statistics did not distinguish optional and obligatory expenditure. The obligatory ordinary expenditure is without the *contabilità speciale*; movement of capital is not included in the extraordinary obligatory expenditure.

and pro-capita expenditure decreased.[30] This trend was to some extent due to the stricter control from above, but it can certainly not be separated from the economic crisis that afflicted the country in those years.

Public opinion insistently protested against the chronic crisis of local finance. Even the much acclaimed balancing of the state's budget in the mid 1870s did not stop a leading politician from describing the situation as a 'laughing mask on a crying face'.[31] At the same time prestigious learned journals, such as the *Nuova Antologia*, the *Economista* and the *Giornale degli Economisti*, dedicated many articles to the question of local finances. Antonio Salandra regarded the provincial deputation as utterly unsuited, because of the prevalence of local cabals, for financial control of smaller municipalities. Conversely, larger municipalities, mostly provincial capitals, were, according to Salandra, not controlled at all. He reasoned that controllers and controlled came from the same electorate, and shared opinions and interests. What is more, they sometimes were simply the same men. Nevertheless, Salandra endorsed the necessity of some restraints on the communes' spending, especially, as he put it, 'when the situation is such that grave damage is seen to derive from the abuse, not from the lack of liberty'.[32]

Many publicists, thus, did not hesitate to put the blaim, at least partly, on the controlling agencies. A diligent communal secretary, sympathetic towards the threatening destiny of local finances, denounced the negligence and compliance of the provincial deputations. He pointed to the collapse of the commune of Florence, apparently not foreseen or prevented by any controlling authority. The subsequent crises of other big cities, such as Naples and Rome, complete this gloomy picture.[33] It has been demonstrated, however, that other cities were able to pursue equally considerable but less ruinous expenditure, without intervention by the provincial deputation. In the 1880s, for example, the city of Pisa could freely attain the highest pro-capita debt of all major cities.[34] The city of Bologna, trying to create a modern urban organization, was not at all curbed in the development of its infrastructure.[35] The Roman administration remained unchecked until the financial scandals of the early 1890s.[36]

30 Pro-capita receipts were 9.3 lire in 1871, 12.3 in 1881, 14.4 in 1891, and 14.3 in 1895; pro-capita expenditure moved from 10.8 lire in 1871, to 12.7 in 1881, 15.8 in 1891, and 14.5 in 1895.

31 Pepoli, quoted in T. Grassi, *Le finanze dei comuni. considerazioni e proposte di riforme* (Recanati, 1880), 24.

32 Salandra, 659.

33 See on the finances of big cities A. Errera, *Le finanze dei grandi comuni. riforme ai prestiti e ai dazi di consumo in Italia* (Florence, 1882) and, more recently, G. Carocci, *Agostino Depretis e la politica interna italiana dal 1876 al 1887* (Turin, 1956), 465-469.

34 A. Polsi, 'Le amministrazioni locali post-unitarie fra accentramento e autonomia: il caso del comune di Pisa (1860-1885)', *Società e Storia* (1983), n. 22, 862.

35 A. Alaimo, *L'organizzazione della città. Amministrazione e politica urbana a Bologna dopo l'unità (1859-1889)* (Bologna, 1990).

36 M. Guercio, 'La prefettura di Roma', in: *Le riforme crispine*, III, 813-814.

Table 5 Communal revenues and expenditure (in thousands of lire) - Venice, Bologna,
Reggio Calabria (1871-1895)

Province of Venice - communal revenues[37]

	1871	1876	1881	1886	1891	1895
Ordinary revenues:						
Patrimonial revenue	113.3	93.2	100.1	129.8	146.5	307.5
Additional taxes	2080.1	2276.9	2382.5	2303.6	1920.6	2065.6
Local taxes	561.2	473.7	603.5	677.0	614.8	560.1
Excises	1993.2	2295.4	2260.0	2680.6	3683.8	3771.0
Miscellaneous revenues	338.0	141.5	249.6	104.3	127.6	175.6
Extraordinary revenues	84.9	186.7	174.5	56.4	72.4	125.7
Outstanding credits	139.6	82.5	61.8	167.9	269.1	156.7
Total real revenues	5310.4	5549.9	5832.0	6119.6	6834.8	7162.3

Province of Venice - communal expenditure

	1871	1876	1881	1886	1891	1895
Obligatory						
ordinary expenditure	4637.5	3752.3	4028.3	3484.6	4471.0	4924.1
extraordinary expenditure	751.7	411.0	684.6	633.7	484.3	808.7
Optional expenditure		1032.7	972.7	1367.0	1529.8	1293.6
Unspent budgeted expenditure				30.0	10.8	14.2
Total real expenditure	5389.2	5196.0	5685.6	5515.3	6485.0	7040.7

Province of Bologna - communal revenues[38]

	1871	1876	1881	1886	1891	1895
Ordinary revenues:						
Patrimonial revenue	166.0	351.9	391.3	303.1	306.5	414.0
Additional taxes	2287.3	2418.5	2616.3	2719.8	2727.0	2852.7
Local taxes	1159.3	1454.2	1636.8	1852.2	2041.0	2087.0
Excises	1145.7	1420.0	1517.0	1933.2	2209.9	2523.3
Miscellaneous revenues	239.0	170.3	213.6	160.1	168.3	219.5
Extraordinary revenues	127.2	197.0	266.1	193.6	267.8	147.4
Outstanding credits	81.6	167.7	155.3	110.5	74.0	362.1
Total real revenues	5206.1	6179.8	6796.4	7272.5	7793.6	8605.9

37 For sources, see footnote 27.
38 In 1885 3 municipalities were added to the province of Bologna.

Province of Bologna - communal expenditure

	1871	1876	1881	1886	1891	1895
Obligatory						
ordinary expenditure	4623.1	4316.1	4727.5	4932.0	5506.4	5956.0
extraordinary expenditure	505.7	689.7	824.7	798.6	1154.7	981.2
Optional expenditure		955.6	1126.0	1292.3	1483.0	1079.6
Unspent budgeted expenditure				25.1	30.5	27.4
Total real expenditure	5128.7	5961.4	6678.2	7047.9	8174.6	8044.2

Province of Reggio Calabria - communal revenues

	1871	1876	1881	1886	1891	1895
Ordinary revenues:						
Patrimonial revenue	365.9	455.9	452.6	472.6	485.3	521.1
Additional taxes	367.9	602.2	980.5	889.3	827.6	851.1
Local taxes	200.3	248.3	406.0	322.3	404.2	410.2
Excises	702.4	818.5	1059.6	1100.2	1325.3	1330.8
Miscellaneous revenues	46.8	15.3	27.2	48.9	62.9	49.1
Extraordinary revenues	155.5	798.8	498.9	322.1	295.3	257.0
Outstanding credits	288.0	333.6	268.0	239.6	170.2	227.7
Total real revenues	2126.8	3272.5	3692.8	3394.8	3570.7	3647.1

Province of Reggio Calabria - communal expenditure

	1871	1876	1881	1886	1891	1895
Obligatory						
ordinary expenditure	1401.9	1431.4	1804.5	2044.1	2225.7	2409.2
extraordinary expenditure	1163.3	1406.8	2128.6	1095.3	996.8	863.4
Optional expenditure		585.3	204.2	377.1	512.7	310.8
Unspent budgeted expenditure				14.9	5.6	26.9
Total real expenditure	2565.2	3423.5	4137.4	3531.5	3743.7	3610.3

Maurizio Ceccato, secretary at the Ministry of the Interior at the time of writing his book on communal finances, denounced the squandering of the communes and the concomitant growth of additional taxes. He regretted the slack implementation of the law of 14 June 1874, for which he blamed not only the provincial deputations but also the prefects. The prefects, he said, did not usually bother to annul the deliberations of the communal councils, which, in the course of the year, voted additional expenditure.[39] The prefects, however, were certainly not unaware of the dismal conditions of local finance. In their periodic reports they informed the Ministry of the Interior, long before the official statistics were put to print, about the weal and woe of 'their' communes. Sometimes they did not limit themselves to a description of the situation but advised the Ministry as to how the system could be reformed. For example, in 1888 Giacinto Scelsi, a highly experienced prefect, exposed the pitiful state of the local economy in parts of his province (Bologna).[40] 'Convinced that it is not possible to pursue a good administration, if finances are not good and orderly', he rhetorically started his analysis. He went on to ascribe the lack of initiative on the part of the municipalities – according to him the root cause of the problem – first, to the 'minor attitude' of the local administrators and, second, to the lack of means. This in turn had its origin in the increase of expenditure, in particular of municipal salaries; in the unexpectedly high expenditure, exceeding the special fund for this purpose, for obligatory roads; and in the continuously high expenditure for poor relief and public health. 'Forced by these impelling requirements and various other services that the law imposes on the communes, all taxes had to be increased, and the additional levies had to be raised to so high a level that any other increase would not only be unbearable but also dangerous'. There was hardly any space for optional expenditure, 'insofar as it was required by modern standards and public health'. Taxes on rateable value and on theatres made no sense for large parts of the country, because no taxable goods existed. A solution, Scelsi concluded, could be sought in the reduction of pressure on provincial budgets (through a shift of items of expenditure to the state budget), which in its turn would bring the draining of the municipal resources by the provinces to an end.[41] These observations not only reflected Scelsi's long experience in public administration, but also echoed endless complaints made by other prefects during the preceding decades. On the whole, as will be shown in the following, neither the state nor the communal and provincial administrations found a way out of the enduring crisis of local finance. The aggregate communal budgets of our three core provinces illustrate in greater detail the deficiences of financial control (see table 5).

---

39 M. Ceccato, *Sulle spese obbligatorie e facoltative delle provincie e dei comuni. Note agli art. 2, 3, 4 della legge 14 giugno 1874* (Rome, 1883), 17. Ceccato pursued his career in the peripheral administration, and was appointed prefect (first acting prefect) of Reggio Calabria in 1899.

40 On Scelsi, L. Gambi, 'Le statistiche di un prefetto del Regno', *Quaderni Storici* 15 (1980), 823-866.

41 ACS, Ministero dell'Interno, Gab., Rapporti dei prefetti, b. 5, f. 11, s.f. 5, Report on the second half year of 1887, 15 February 1888.

The figures should be handled with care. It has already been noted that the reliability of the budgets, as reflections of actual spending and receiving, is fairly low. Furthermore, the statistics include only effective receipts and expenditure; the categories of outstanding credits and unspent budgeted expenditure play a subordinate role in the official statistics, whereas in reality they were always said to distort the system of local finances considerably; the budgets of the provincial capitals weigh heavily on the overall picture. Hence, the figures should not be treated as straightforward accurate indicators of the local economy. Nevertheless, they do give some idea of the structural differences between the provinces and of the limited possibilities of altering the course of the communal finances from above. The pro-capita communal revenue in the provinces of Venice and Bologna rose steadily; the revenue of the former from 15.7 in 1871 to 18.6 lire in 1895, of the latter from 12.8 to 17.5. The pro-capita communal revenue in the province of Reggio Calabria was 6.0 in 1871, increased to 9.9 in 1881, but declined afterwards, fluctuating around 9 lire. This decline in Reggio undoubtedly had its root in the enduring agrarian crisis of Calabria, beginning in the early 1880s as international competition on the agrarian markets increased.[42] Pro-capita expenditure increased gradually in Bologna, from 12.6 in 1871 to 16.9 in 1891, losing something in 1895 (when it was 16.4); in Venice it fluctuated between 16.0 in 1871, 15.1 in 1876, 15.9 in 1881, 14.9 in 1886, 17.2 in 1891, and 18.3 in 1895. In Reggio pro-capita expenditure was 7.3 lire in 1871, reached 11.1 in 1881, but subsequently sank to a level of a little more than 9.0 lire.

In Reggio and Venice local taxes never attained the share in communal revenues that was hoped for. In Bologna their share was somewhat higher, particularly because of the larger revenues from the family tax and the tax on livestock. In all three provinces the additional levies on land and houses, on the other hand, continued to burden the propertied class, despite attempts to curb these taxes. Optional expenditure, somewhat belying the government's claims, had a relatively small share in total effective expenditure, especially in Reggio.

3 THE ROLE OF THE PROVINCIAL DEPUTATION

Although the tasks of the provincial deputation were not limited to financial affairs only, a discussion of its role seems to be in order.[43] Generally speaking, our understanding of the provincial deputation's role has been somewhat blurred by the fixation on the prefect being its president. Throughout the years following the promulgation of the communal and provincial law in 1865 the prefect's presidency

---

42   L. Izzo, 'Agricoltura e classi rurali in Calabria dall'Unità al Fascismo', *Cahiers Internationaux d'Histoire Economique et Sociale*, 3 (1974), 39ff.

43   A. Polsi, 'Comuni e controlli: il ruolo e la funzione delle deputazioni provinciali dalla legge comunale del 1865 alla riforma crispina', in: *Istituzioni e borghesie locali nell'Italia liberale*, edited by M. Bigaran (Milan, 1986), 112-124.

had been subject to discussions often marked by abstract reasoning. The system of control at the provincial level was partly inherited from the Belgian example, in which the counterpart to the deputation was an elected and salaried prefectural council. Until the reform of 1889 the provincial deputation exerted a double function; it was the executive organ of the provincial council, and, second, it controlled a number of administrative activities of the municipalities, notably the budgets and the electoral rolls. With Crispi's reforms the two functions were divided between the *giunta provinciale amministrativa*, which became the controlling body and was presided over by the prefect, and the provincial deputation, which concentrated solely on the provincial administration and chose its own president. Until 1889, certainly from a juridical point of view, the prefect, uniting in himself governmental and provincial functions, occupied an ambiguous position.[44] This was frequently taken as a clear indication of rigid centralization. A penetrating inquiry, taking into account the various administrative realities in the periphery, was conducted by the Minister of the Interior Cantelli in 1869. One of his questions concerned the position of the prefect in relation to the provincial deputation. The majority of prefects and provincial deputations tended to prefer the eligibility of the president.[45] They were, on the other hand, quite convinced of the utility of the prefect's interfering role. The provincial deputies were not always interested in the fastidious checking of budgets and electoral rolls. They lacked the know-how or simply did not have the time to attend the weekly sessions. Conversely, through his services within the realm of the provincial administration the prefect could discreetly mediate between centre and periphery. In replying to the questionnaire most prefects, in fact, expressed their sense of mission towards the communes.[46] Their interpretation could differ considerably. Luigi Torelli, at the time prefect of Venice, considered the eligibility of the deputation's president an erosion of the prefect's job.[47] Achille Serpieri, prefect of Reggio Calabria, who did certainly not shun his responsibilities towards his province, represented the extreme viewpoint that the prefect's presence within the provincial council should be entirely voluntary.[48] On the other hand, as president of the deputation, the prefect, Serpieri stated elsewhere, 'has a wide range of action for the benefit of the province and it would perhaps be opportune, here and in other places, to let more time pass before carrying through reforms, even when they seem right'.[49] From Bologna, Cesare Bardesono di Rigras reproached the deputation for

44   S. Romano, entry 'Deputazione Provinciale', in: *Digesto Italiano*, IX, parte 2ª (Turin, 1898), 167.
45   A summary of the answers to the circular of Cantelli has been given in: AP, CD, legisl. XIII, sess. 1876-77, Documenti, no. 33A, report of the commission (spokesman A. Marazio) on the bill of Nicotera for a reform of the communal and provincial law, *all*. H.
46   R. Romanelli, 'Tra autonomia e ingerenza: un'indagine del 1869', in: Id., *Il comando impossibile. Stato e società nell'Italia liberale* (Bologna, 1988), 130-145.
47   Romanelli, 'Tra autonomia e ingerenza', 143.
48   *Ibidem*, 143.
49   ASRC, Pref., Gab., b. 62, f.977, report of the prefect to the Ministry on the conditions of the province, 5 March 1869.

slowness and lack of coherence. He would have preferred to deprive it of its controlling powers.[50]

The prefects of Bologna were always, from Unification onwards, slightly suspicious of the activities of the provincial deputation. From the beginning the provincial deputation took a rather autonomous stance. In August 1862 a fierce conflict threatened to break out between the municipality of Bologna and the deputation. The latter took the provisions of the communal and provincial law of 1859 (at that time still in force) literally, and criticized conscientiously but perhaps incautiously the deliberations of the municipal council. The communal *giunta*, at any rate, was immediately up in arms and urged the prefect to intervene. The acting prefect, the *consigliere delegato* Carlo Balboni, managed to pour oil on the troubled waters.[51] Yet in December 1862 he urged the Ministry to 'settle the executive part of the powers which the new laws on the communes and the charitable institutions entrust to the provincial deputation in consultation with the prefect'.[52] In the years that followed the deputation seems to have pursued its independent course. It had its own quarters in the vast *Palazzo d'Accursio*, which also housed the prefecture and the municipality.[53] It had its own staff auditing the communal budgets. The attendance lists of its 62 meetings in 1877 (a summary of the decisions were published in the *Bollettino della Prefettura*) shows that the prefect only attended 11, and that the other 51 were presided over by a high prefectural official. The half-yearly reports of the prefects mentioned, during the 1870s, only cursorily and always approvingly the progress of the provincial administration. Giovanni Mussi, who held the office of prefect from December 1880 to September 1882, also praised the accuracy of the deputation's work, even though it sometimes led to serious delays. Interestingly enough, he still made one small criticism of the deputation, namely 'a certain autonomous character which is not in the current legislation and is not common in the rest of the Kingdom': all its correspondence passed without the prefect's signature, it received its mail directly, it signed contracts, assigned on its own account the drawing up of reports to its members, and watched over the provincial offices. No prefect before him, he went on, had dared to allude to this phenomenon, particularly because the administration had not suffered at all from the determination of the provincial deputation. For the moment Mussi refrained from taking steps, in expectation of a reform of the communal and provincial law.[54] He had probably set his hopes on Depretis' bill, presented to Parliament in May 1880. Like its precursors, however, the bill did not

50   ASB, Pref., Gab., b. 164, f. 6, report of the prefect to the Ministry of the Interior, 24 February 1869, 'Modificazioni alla legge comunale e provinciale'.
51   ASB, Intendenza Generale, Archivio riservato, b. 14, correspondence between the municipality of Bologna and the prefect, 12, 24 and 30 August 1862.
52   *Ibidem*, b. 13, letter of the prefect to the Ministry, 21 December 1862.
53   N. Randeraad, 'The State in the Provinces: the Prefecture as a Palace after Unification', in: *The Power of Imagery. Essays on Rome, Italy and Imagination*, edited by P. van Kessel (Rome, 1993), 98-108.
54   ASB, Pref., Gab., cat. IX (1884), report on the public spirit in the first half of 1881, 1 July 1881.

finish its *iter*. In his report on the first half of 1883 Efisio Salaris, Mussi's successor, repeated the observations on the workings of the provincial deputation, and added that there was not even a prefectural secretary present at the meetings.[55] Its independence is further demonstrated by a letter to the prefect, reminding him that it was rather urgent to have the municipalities pay strict attention to the law of 1874. The provincial administration anticipated further levies on real estate, and, therefore, in order to prevent the landed interests from being overtaxed, wanted the communes to restrict their expenditure.[56] The prefect promptly replied with a circular to that effect directed to the mayors.[57] Not long before Crispi's administrative reform took place, Giacinto Scelsi pointed again to the particular situation of Bologna's provincial administration. Though praising the deputation for its conscientious and impartial work, he noted that, in contrast with his own experience in other provinces, it functioned somewhat outside beaten tracks. Its meetings were not held in the prefectural offices but in a room of the provincial administration. The prefectural staff, therefore, had no say in the decisions. The provincial deputies themselves, instead of the prefect, shared out the work to be done.[58]

The Bolognese prefects never expanded upon the question as to where this veiled 'self-government' of the provincial administration stemmed from. It is, however, tempting to go back to a papal edict of 1831, which reinforced decision-making at the provincial level. To some extent the province had by then (and all the more so with another edict of 1850) become a local body, partly elected from below.[59] Furthermore, in the period of annexation (1859-60) the provincial authorities wanted to secure their primacy over the surrounding communes. For under the papal regime Bologna had never occupied the position of a regional capital.[60] After Unification the energetic local elite of Bologna, represented in the provincial council, tried to maintain a certain independence, not only by keeping a vigilant eye over the municipalities of the province, but also by withstanding the legal supremacy of the prefect. It is perhaps no coincidence that in 1861 Marco Minghetti, after the unsuccessful outcome of his decentralization bill, returned to Bologna to become president of the provincial council (a post he had to leave when he assumed the direction of another ministry in 1863). A man of his stature might well have been capable of counterbalancing the prefect and laying the foundations of a sanctuary for the provincial administration. Moreover, from 1877 to his death in 1886, the years in which the

---

55   ASC, Min. Int., Gab., Rapporti dei prefetti, b. 5, f. 11, s.f. 1, report on the first half of 1883, 30 July 1883.

56   ASB, Pref., Arch. gen. (1883), Serie 1ª, cat. 25, f. 13, letter of the provincial deputation to the prefect, 25 October 1883.

57   *Circolare della prefettura di Bologna*, 7 October 1883, n. 11422.

58   *Ibidem* (1888), cat. 9/1, report on the public spirit in the first half of 1887, 20 September 1887.

59   E. Rotelli, 'Gli ordinamenti locali preunitari', Id, *L'alternativa delle autonomie. Istituzioni locali e tendenze politiche dell'Italia moderna* (Milan, 1978), 96-117.

60   I. Zanni Rosiello, *L'unificazione politica e amministrativa nelle 'provincie dell'Emilia' (1859-60)* (Milan, 1965), 91.

autonomy of the province clearly manifested itself, Minghetti again occupied the presidency of the provincial council.

That the deputations in other provinces were often spoon-fed by the prefectures (as Scelsi more or less suggested), is proven in the case of Reggio Calabria. Shortly after the promulgation of the communal and provincial law in 1865 the Ministry and the prefect tried to convince the provincial administration to take on at least six employees. The deputation, despite these suggestions from above, refused to take on more than three, thus restricting its scope a priori.[61] In 1878 the Ministry of the Interior issued a circular with questions about the secretarial support of the provincial deputation.[62] The prefect of Reggio replied that his officials were rendering such a service, and that he wished to continue this practice: 'My experience has convinced me that the provincial deputations, except for affairs related to the province, do not worry themselves about the control of the municipalities; hence the prefectures are compelled not only to expound on all affairs, besides those connected with the electoral rolls and the elections, but also to formulate a sketch of the purview of the deliberations; otherwise the affairs fall into oblivion'.[63]

Political conflicts within the provincial council could contaminate the workings of the deputation. This was precisely the main objection lodged by contemporary observers. Earlier, we have touched upon Salandra's criticism; likewise Pio Sabbatini, professor of administrative law at the University of Modena, disliked the system of control by the deputation. In his opinion the prefect, always trying to maintain peace, was not in the best position to supervise the proceedings.[64] In the course of 1877 the prefect of Venice, count Luigi Sormani Moretti, was confronted with such a situation. In his report on the second half of 1877 he wrote that a conflict over the dissolution of charitable institutions (a highly inflammable matter in Venice) had caused a division within the deputation. Until a few years earlier it had worked rather autonomously, dispatching its own correspondence and making use of its own civil servants. The regulations for the Venetian provincial deputation, approved on 18 March 1869, explicitly laid down that an executive deputy (*dirigente*) was to be appointed, with the following tasks: dividing the business among the members, sending back those documents that could not be taken into consideration, putting a signature on all correspondence, and supervising the offices and civil servants of the provincial administration.[65] The prefect's job was thus considerably reduced. Sormani's predecessor, in his last year of office, had begun to take back some of his legally prescribed responsibilities. Sormani had continued this line, because, as he reasoned, too much

61 ASRC, Pref., Gab., b. 176, letter of the Ministry to the prefect, 9 June 1865, and reply, 30 June 1865.

62 *Circolare del Ministero dell'Interno*, 2 September 1878, n. 15900-2.

63 ASRC, Pref., Gab., b. 176, f. 5968, letter of the prefect (Lamponi) to the Ministry, 10 September 1878.

64 Sabbatini, 145-149.

65 ASV, Pref., Arch. Gen. (1867-71), f. 4, 28/41, 'Regolamento interno della Deputazione Provinciale di Venezia'.

depended on the work of one assiduous deputy. The crisis over charity, which turned out also to be one over state interference, put him in the right. Several members of the deputation were forced to resign, and a period of inactivity set in, which in turn prevented cooperation between the prefect and the provincial administration.[66]

4 THE ABORTIVE START OF THE SYSTEM OF LOCAL FINANCE

In order to assess the activities of the prefects and the provincial authorities, it helps to differentiate between various periods in the decades under consideration: the formative years from Unification to the completion of the legal framework of local taxation (1874); the next fifteen years, beset with economic difficulties for the local administrations, until Crispi's reform; and the period until the turn of the century, marked by stricter control and the shift to a different relationship between the state and local government (the move towards municipalization, which will only be touched upon).

The transition to the unitary state and the coming into force of the new legislation put financial management of the local administrations severely to the test. The communes acquired a greater degree of freedom in their spending, but they had a lot of red tape to cut through: new forms and formalities, a more complex way of drawing up budgets and final statements, new regulations and inventories, etc. Especially in the non-Piedmontese states a period of adaptation had to be reckoned with. Furthermore, between 1860 and 1865 the provincial and communal law, taken over from the Kingdom of Sardinia, was not implemented with strict observance of its rules, since many expected rapid and substantial reforms. After the promulgation in 1865 of the new law, which did not fulfil its expectations, another period of uncertainty followed. The government, hounded by the wish to balance the books, continued to issue adjustments of the tax system, but ended up throwing the municipalities into a state of constant turmoil. The *Rivista Amministrativa del Regno* tried to lend its full support by publishing, for educational purposes, the 'events of a communal final statement' sent back and forth between the communal council and the council of the prefecture.[67] The first nationwide inquiries into the working of the administrative services brought to light, among other things, that many communal budgets and final statements were years in arrears, not to mention, for example, inventories of communal properties.[68] The situation only gradually improved: in 1870 6968 final statements were in arrears, in 1871 6970, in 1872 5216; in 1870 2913

---

66   ASV, Pref., Gab. (1877-81), cat. 19, 1/1, report on the second half of 1877, forwarded on 4 February 1878.

67   *RAR*, 21 (1870), 553-570; also published in C. Beltrami, *La nuova guida per gli uffizi comunali*, 2 vols (Turin, 1871-73), II, 145-154.

68   N. Randeraad, 'L'amministrazione periferica nell'Italia liberale: una ricerca in corso', *RTDP*, 40 (1990), 1216-1218.

communes had regularly drawn up their budgets, in 1871 3796, in 1872 4774. Many prefects pointed to the lack of personnel, which imposed fetters upon the revision of budgets and final statements. The Ministry of the Interior tried to provide a remedy by setting up a distinct class of prefectural accountants (by royal decree of 20 June 1871). They were immediately overloaded with work. The accountant of the Venetian prefecture overtly complained about the wide variety of activities he had to oversee with only two subordinates attached to his office (control of budgets and final statements of municipalities, *fabbricerie* or vestry-boards, and consortiums, management of transactions for the pay-desk of the police and the prisons, custody of deposits).[69] Allegedly, the Ministry had acknowledged the importance of budgetary control, but there were no funds available to establish an efficient accounting service in the prefectures: 'the checking of budgets and final statements of municipalities and provinces demands varied and difficult study, for which the sole ability of the book-keeper is far from sufficient; the expertise of an experienced administrator is required, pariculary in order to suggest measures to restore the economic management of municipalities that are in trouble, and for many others to try to find the means to provide to some extent for the school, the nursery school, public health, roads and all other examples of civilization'.[70]

In the opening years of the unitary state, not surprisingly, numerous cases of administrative disorder occurred, which usually included some form of financial misconduct. The commune of Castel San Pietro in the province of Bologna (district of Imola) was dissolved late in 1860 (the formal annexation of Emilia to the Kingdom of Sardinia had taken place in March). Earlier that year Carlo Mayr, the *intendente generale* (the forerunner of the prefect), and the subintendant of Imola had already corresponded with each other about the rather unreliable municipal employees, hostile to the new order. An inspector of the intendency was sent to the town, who affirmed that there was great reluctance in accepting and running the new institutions, and that the communal revenues were treated light-heartedly. Even the general-intendant himself paid a visit to the municipality, in order to check accusations of changes in the tax rolls after their official approval. In a letter to the Ministry of the Interior Mayr pointed out that little had changed in Castel San Pietro since the fall of the papal regime. The old municipal employees had kept their posts and continued to exercise influence. In the past, due to their benevolence towards the clerical government, they had acquired a status of impunity, which manifested itself in a sort of selfgovernment: existing laws and regulations were interpreted to the liking of the local officials. The final statements of the commune were in great arrears. The budgets for 1860 and 1861, therefore, were pure conjecture. The drop that made the cup run over was the tampering with the tax rolls. After the prefect's

69 ASV, Pref., Gab. (1872-76), cat. 19, 1/1, report on the course of the province's administrative services in the first semester of 1875 with regard to the accountant's office, 28 June 1875.

70 'Relazione a S.M., fatta da S.E. il Ministro dell'Interno, in udienza del 10 giugno 1873, sull'andamento dei servizi amministrativi nell'anno 1872', *Gazzetta Ufficiale del Regno d'Italia*, 26 June 1873, n. 175.

visit the municipality decided to suspend the communal employees in question. The dissolution that followed had the desired effect; new councillors were elected and the special delegate, who temporarily administered the commune, set up a better organization.[71]

Throughout the 1860s the prefects of Reggio Calabria continued to complain about cases of faulty administration in their province. They noted, among other things, deep discontent with indirect taxation. The municipalities shrank from levying taxes, thus harming themselves and the state. Obligatory expenditure was generally neglected. Many public services, therefore, did not get off the ground. At the beginning of his period of office, Cesare Bardesono, prefect from 1865 to 1868, promised to stage an incessant battle against the administrative defects. It seems, however, that when his successor Achille Serpieri took up his office, little had changed. In one of his first periodical reports to the Ministry Serpieri recorded that the arrears in final statements for many communes ran up to five years. He established an extraordinary section, consisting of a prefectural councillor, a secretary and a clerk, to devote itself entirely to the communal accounts. Moreover, he exhorted the municipal accountants to submit the overdue final statements within a month, under penalty of a fine of 200 lire.[72] In a circular to the mayors he elaborately explained the advantages of regular accounting. It was his firm intention, he wrote, to close the preceding financial years, and to calculate precisely the outstanding credits and the accounts payable, which sometimes had been outstanding for decades. The settlement of their accounts was intended to give fresh impetus to the local administration; 'honest' men were incited to take part in the communal government, in order to win over the population: 'It is my firm intention to make sure that a diligent and honest administration realizes a relationship based on mutual trust between administrators and administered, and makes a start with a period of recovery, in which it is not permitted to make malicious insinuations and to rail against those who dedicate themselves to the public cause, nor to pursue the bad habit of trading upon the way in which acts concerning the most vital vital interests of the tax-payers are handled. (...) One of the most common causes of the bad state of some municipal administrations is the absenteeism of intelligent and conscientious men, who are afraid of getting involved in irregularities and turmoil, which might compromise their peace and quiet and their reputation. Under the auspices of the liberal institutions a commune may rise to its mission, in which there is a sincere ambition to participate in the public service and to do one's best for the benefit of fellow-citizens. But this cannot be expected in places where public expenditure is handled haphazardly; spending can never meet public requirements without a very precise knowledge of the use and management of public resources'.[73]

71 ASB, Intendenza Generale, Archivio riservato, b. 7.
72 ASRC, Pref., Gab., b. 62, report of the prefect to the Ministry, 20 June 1868.
73 *Circolare della prefettura di Reggio Calabria*, 21 May 1868, n. 15.

In this way, not limiting himself to financial matters, Serpieri summarized the aims of his office. His efforts, as far as the accounts were concerned, proved a success; in June and July 1868 about 150 of them were approved by the prefectural council, which reduced the arrears (up to and including 1866) to less than 100.[74] Nevertheless, it took until 1870 for the situation to be reasonably normalized.

In the general report of 1870 Serpieri, who retained his office in Reggio Calabria until October 1871, lamented the necessity of continual warnings. That local administration was somnolent did not appear only from the budgets, but even more from the final statements, which had now been approved, 'and showed a tremendous and almost insuperable inertia intended to deceive the prefectural and provincial authorities'. He considered his third year in the Calabrese capital his most painstaking. Without wasting words he listed the prefecture's incessant activities in financial matters: imposing sanctions on communes that were unwilling to submit their final statements; *ex officio* allocations in the budgets of expenditure for road building, public education and cemeteries; sending of commissioners to obtain the required inventories; the intervention of the provincial deputation to secure the implementation of local taxes; constant directives for the drawing up of municipal regulations; rigorous measures to check the handling of the communal treasury and the settlement of old accounts; frequent instructions for the organization of the charitable institutions.[75]

The vicissitudes of financial management in Melito Porto Salvo serve to illustrate the administrative zeal displayed by Serpieri; at the same time, they show that counter-forces, sometimes going back to preunitary times, were stronger than the instruments in the prefects' hands. The final statements of Melito over the years 1863-66 were approved shortly after each other in the summer of 1868, during the massive catching up programme launched by Serpieri. For each one the prefectural council had to issue a so-called 'doubts sheet' (*foglio di dubbi*), in which questions were asked about items in the accounts under consideration. For example, the doubts sheet concerning the final statement over 1865 listed a variety of irregularities: many procedural mistakes had been made; quite a lot of funds had been spent without the official approval of the communal *giunta* or the communal council; and on many accounts documentation was lacking.[76] The final statement for 1867 induced the prefect to order a judicial enquiry. Apart from 'immense irregularities', it was found that neither the communal auditors nor the *giunta* nor the council had laid eyes on the final statement before it was forwarded to the prefecture.[77] From the approval of the final statements over the following years we learn that the number of ex-cashiers in debt to the municipality for appropriation of cash balances was increasing. Furthermore, each year large sums were allocated in the budgets and final statements as

74   ASRC., Pref., Gab., b. 62, report of the prefect to the Ministry, 12 August 1868.
75   *Ibidem*, report of the prefect to the Ministry, 15 April 1871.
76   ASRC, Pref., Arch. Gen., inv. 32/2, f. 44, final statement of the municipality of Melito Porto Salvo (1865).
77   *Ibidem*, inv. 32/3, f. 10, final statement over 1867.

outstanding credits and unspent budgeted expenditure. On the basis of the final statement for 1874 Emidio Tomasini, an official of the provincial administration charged with the settlement of the old accounts until 1873, calculated that of a total of 34,794 lire credits merely 13,317 lire were exactable. Only the latter sum, therefore, to which the prefecture later added 3,000 lire, should figure on the budget. On the other hand, from the outstanding credits, amounting to 40,000 lire, only 1,723 lire ought to be added to those of 1874.[78]

These brief notes suffice to demonstrate that the financial management of Melito's administrators left much to be desired. Frequently, adjustments from above were necessary (and not only, as we have seen in earlier chapters, to find a solution to the bleak financial prospects). The special delegate Temistocle Tannarelli, temporarily administering Melito in 1875, accused the various communal governments of wasting public monies for their own benefit. Tannarelli explained that all communal councillors were in some way involved in municipal contracts. Moreover, he could not find any documents or registers to check the real assets and liabilities of the municipality.[79] In 1878 an inspection held by the prefectural councillor Giacomo Maglieri showed that the state of Melito's finances was still disastrous. Since 1866 there had hardly been one cashier not indebted to the municipal treasury. Maglieri calculated that Melito's deficit ran up to about 66,000 lire, and that its credit of 15,000 was probably uncollectable. The municipality, unable to pay the people it hired, issued payment orders (*mandati*), which subsequently changed hands at a considerable loss to the first holder. He gave the example of a contractor who could not cash his payment order of 320 lire, and sold it to a villager for 250 lire. That man (who, through an ironic twist, by the time of the inspection had become alderman) exploited a communal plot of land; he tried to use the municipality's obligation as instrument of payment for his rent. The municipality refused, got involved in a lawsuit, lost, and was fined 300 lire expenses. In like manner all creditors seized as much of the municipality's income as possible.[80] Even the municipal employees eventually resorted to these methods; they appropriated, through a third party, the revenue of a communal excise, since the communal treasury had no money to pay their salaries.[81]

A potential source of revenue for Melito was the proceeds of the dissolution of the 'promiscuous' use of ex-feudal and church lands (*scioglimento di promiscuità dei beni ex feudali ed eccesiastici*). Since the abolition of feudalism in 1806 and the attendant regulations of 1811 on the division of the demesnes (the so-called Masci Ordinance)

---

78 *Ibidem*, final statements over 1873 and 1874. That these sums were conspicuous can be inferred from, e.g., the communal receipts over 1874, which amounted to 19,866 lire. Tomasini's assistance was called in during the period of dissolution of the communal council in 1875.

79 ASRC, Pref., Gab., b. 20, f. 86, report of the special delegate Tannarelli to the prefect, 29 September 1875.

80 *Ibidem*, report of the prefectural councillor Maglieri to the prefect, 3 April 1878.

81 *Ibidem*, report of the prefect to the Ministry of the Interior, 10 April 1880.

a definitive settlement for the plots of land in question had never been found. On the one hand, the villagers continued to exert their old rights of grazing and gathering wood, which was allowed by the Napoleonic laws; on the other, some of the ex-feudal plots were sold, and the new owners, notably the marquises Ramirez, claimed full possession of them. This, of course, gave rise to continual conflicts between the local peasants and the Ramirez family (residing in Reggio). Throughout the Restoration period the former managed to defend their 'civil rights' (*usi civici*); this brought them into conflict with the municipality, which – at least in theory – could benefit greatly from the sale of the rest of the lands. With Unification a new decree (1 January 1861) was promulgated, prescribing the total dissolution of all existing 'promiscuities'. The prefect Giuseppe Cornero, in his capacity as commissioner for demesnes, thus ordered this dissolution, reserving a quarter of the lands that were nearest to the village centre for communal use. The Ramirez family immediately appealed, but the case was never brought to a satisfactory conclusion. In 1868 the law on the *Asse ecclesiastico* gave a quarter of the Church lands in question to the community. Under the prefect Achille Serpieri the municipality and Vincenzo Ramirez reached an agreement, but for the next twenty years the lands of Antonio Ramirez and some others remained a source of conflict. During the agrarian crisis of the 1880s the division of lands among smallholders to bring them under cultivation would have been desirable. Moreover, since 1884 the municipality paid the land tax on the lands attributed to itself but not yet effectively capitalized. The non-implementation of the assignment of quotas was a recurrent phenomenon in the province in these years. The prefects frequently complained in their semestral reports about the apathy of the communes in this matter. Often, the communes could not pay the administrative costs in advance or pay state officials for the demesne operations (*agenti demaniali*); on occasion, the prefecture had to coerce them to allocate the required sums in the budgets. On the other hand, if the state agents were found to neglect their job, appropriate measures were taken against them. In 1887 the prefect Paternostro took care of a sweeping purge of the personnel in question.[82] In Melito gradually, after extensive verification, a few remaining plots were divided, until in 1894 the royal commissioner for demesnes drew up a final project of assignment of quotas in the spirit of the Cornero Ordinance of 1863.[83] This finally closed the matter.

All in all, the municipality was long deprived of income that it could rightfully claim. The demesnes question, however, had another unforeseen effect. The division of property carried out in the 1860s and early 1870s did not produce, as the government had hoped, a new class of landowners among the poorer peasants. The prefect Lamponi noted in 1880 that the peasants who had come into possession of the plots just lent their names to councillors and larger landowners, who in reality had divided

---

82 Report on the second half year of 1887, 13 March 1888, in: Borzomati, 185.
83 N. Del Pozzo, *Scioglimento di promiscuità dei beni ex feudali ed ecclesiastici del Marchese Ramirez sig. Antonio* (Reggio Calabria, 1894).

the demesnes among themselves.[84] Thus, a perennial conflict of interests had been brought into a communal council already torn by the usual internal strife of a small community. As we have seen, this led to various dissolutions without a real solution ever being reached.

One of the most urgent problems in Calabria – and in the South of Italy in general – was the construction of a communication network. On the eve of Unification the total length of practicable roads in the province of Reggio amounted to only 180 km: the national road (73 km) from Rosarno to Villa San Giovanni, 67 km of provincial roads and 40 km of communal roads.[85] But even the roads that existed were frequently blocked by fierce torrents or landslides. In winter it was impossible to travel over land. In the savage uplands of *Aspromonte* a traveller could only venture at his peril, even after the suppression of brigandage. Most villages of the district of Gerace, strongholds of isolation, were high up in the mountains, and the descent of the populations towards the seaside came about very slowly. It took until 1934, before the lower town of Locri (Gerace Marina) took over the administration from the higher and more inland Gerace.

The state immediately assumed responsibility for the continuation of the national road of the Calabrias, from Rosarno through to Reggio, and the building of the Ionian railway. A great deal of initiative, however, was left to the provincial and communal governments. With the laws of 1868 and 1869 their autonomy in this field was partly abandoned; communes and provinces were asked to allocate funds to a considerable building programme, subsidized by the state (eventually, the communes could be compelled to do so). The prefecture was charged with the organization of the preparatory work, such as the (laborious) collection of the classification lists of communal roads.[86] Serpieri acquitted himself conscientiously of his task, calling on the municipalities in a unremitting stream of circulars not only to draw up the required lists, but also to reserve money and to organize themselves in consortiums. He evidently took the matter to heart, because, as he himself put it, 'in its completion lies the key to many if not all interests, as good administration is almost impossible without roads'[87]; and, taking his reasoning even further, 'the lifeblood of liberal institutions can run only through roads'.[88] But, as in other parts of his administrative project, convincing local administrators to cooperate was a strenuous job. It was,

---

84 ASRC, Pref., Gab., report of the prefect to the Ministry of the Interior, 10 April 1880.

85 A. Serpieri, *Relazione sulle condizioni amministrative, economiche e morali della provincia di Reggio di Calabria, letta al consiglio provinciale inaugurando la sua sessione ordinaria 1870* (Reggio Calabria, 1870), all. I.

86 It appeared, a year after the promulgation of the law of 30 August 1868, that some communes had not drawn up the classifications (which then had to be enacted by prefectural decree). Furthermore, it was foreseen that many communes were unwilling or unable to set aside a special fund, to be paid out of the revenues of additional land taxation, cf. Provincia di Reggio Calabria [but written by A. Serpieri], *Relazione sulle condizioni e bisogni della viabilità* (Reggio Calabria, 1869).

87 *Circolare della prefettura di Reggio Calabria*, 2 December 1868, n. 126.

88 ASRC, Pref., Gab., b. 62, f. 977, report of the prefect to the Ministry, 22 May 1869.

in fact, the main reason for his regular inspections *in loco*. 'To boost the many road building projects in progress (...), to solve problems, (...) to encourage the communes that most need obligatory roads', Serpieri declared, was the motive behind his journeys in the province, which – precisely because the connections were so bad – entailed long periods of absence from Reggio.[89]

In 1863 Giuseppe Antonio Pasquale, in his astute description of the province, had already pinpointed the causes of the slow development and inconsistency of communal road building up to that time: 'The municipal struggles, egoism, the hatred among municipalities, as well as among citizens, can be told from the layout of communal roads, which even where they exist is never guided by the united objective of neighbouring communes to bring about connections with each other; what is worse, one commune, trying to frustrate another, starts to build roads parallel to the sea, which subsequently remain unconnected and abandoned at an early stage, as dead ends which are never used'.[90] In these circumstances it was not easy to burden the communal budgets with the conspicuous sums that were necessary for further development. As the years went by and the financial position of the communes grew worse, the unity between and within the municipalities, insofar it had ever existed, gradually vanished. Hence, a large part of the ambitious road building project, designed in the late 1860s, could not be executed. When in 1877 the prefect Filippo Lamponi was transferred from Potenza to Reggio, he was forced by bad weather to take a detour via Naples, thereby doubling the length of his journey.[91] In 1906 only 212 km of provincial roads had been realized of a total of 638 km projected in the laws of 1869, 1875 and 1881 (164 km were under construction).[92] The situation of the communal roads was not much better. By 1889 243 km had been built, but many road-sections were not connected to each other or to the trunk roads.[93] It took years to settle controversies over expropriation. What was worse, many communes could not come up with the resources needed for maintenance. In 1880 the prefect Lamponi informed the Ministry that 'the obligatory communal roads, which have cost so much sacrifice, will be absolutely useless in a couple of years, since the communes, after the completion of a few sections of roads, do not maintain them at all and let them fall into decay'.[94]

Achille Serpieri also put himself out, on behalf of the provincial administration, to organize favourable loans. At the end of the 1860s the provincial government was

89 *Ibidem*, b. 110, f. 2464, letter of the prefect to the Ministry, 3 May 1869.
90 G.A. Pasquale, 'Relazione sullo stato fisico-economico-agrario della prima Calabria ulteriore', *Atti del R. Istituto d'Incoraggiamento alle scienze naturali di Napoli* (1863), tomo XI, 64.
91 ASRC, Pref., Gab., b. 110, f. 2471, expense claim of Lamponi, 6 November 1877.
92 Ministero dei Lavori Pubblici, Direzione Generale dei Servizi Speciali, *Le opere pubbliche in Calabria. Prima relazione sull'applicazione delle leggi speciali dal 30 giugno 1906 al 30 giugno 1913* (Bergamo, 1913), 43.
93 G. Cingari, *Storia della Calabria dall'Unità a oggi* (Bari, 1982), 402.
94 ASRC, Pref., Gab., b. 63, f. 990, report of the prefect on public affairs in the first semester of 1880, 26 August 1880.

willing to invest large sums of money in road and railway building and in the construction of a new harbour. When, in 1870, the preparations for a loan of six million lire had reached an advanced stage, the Franco-Prussian War and the attendant period of uncertainty on the financial markets queered the province's pitch. Serpieri, who together with the members of the provincial deputation had earlier invoked the help of a local member of Parliament, requested the Ministries of Public Works and of the Interior, and the president of the *Cassa di Risparmio*, senator Alessandro Porro, to help find a way out of the impasse. Again, Serpieri's mediation rendered but temporary relief. A loan of six million lire was eventually negotiated with the banking house Weill-Schott in Florence, but disputes over the exact conditions delayed the actual payment until 1872. The works in the meantime had started, which forced the provincial administration to some *ad hoc* measures, burdening its budget further. In addition to that, many unexpected expenses enlarged the province's deficit. Hence, after a few years, the financial position of the provincial administration was not only weakened by the long-term loan, but it also suffered from bad planning.[95] The consequences for the municipalities were grave: the province continued to increase their additional taxes, thereby narrowing the space of the municipalities to levy them. Evidently, the problems surrounding the provincial infrastructure superseded the powers of one enterprising prefect.

The engagement of individual prefects, such as Serpieri, could not prevent a growing disparity, when it came to the building of provincial and communal roads, between Calabria and other parts of the peninsula (not only in the North!).[96] The local elite of Reggio, nevertheless, did not lightly forget the extraordinary effort put in by Serpieri. From a letter of the ex-prefect to the mayor of Reggio, Fabrizio Plutino, we learn that Serpieri, having exchanged his public office for the practice of law in Rome, had been asked to defend the city against the government's refusal to give a subsidy for road building.[97] To some extent, the widening of the economic gap was not only due to the growing inadequacy of state investments, but paradoxically also had its roots in the relative autonomy enjoyed by local government. First, with the deepening of the crisis of local finances, it became more and more difficult for the municipalities to raise the required funds, and independence without resources is a cruel delight. Second, the participation of communes in provincial projects or even in consortiums on a smaller scale was not self-evident. Rivalry between different family groups, to which the division of the demesnes had greatly contributed, inhibited a uniform course of action; the time-honoured isolation of many villages was not the best breeding ground for the spirit of free association, badly needed for financing a road network in their mutual interest. In addition to these obstacles, it must of course be remembered that the landscape of Calabria was particularly hostile, and presented

---

95 'Relazione generale della Deputazione Provinciale della Provincia di Reggio Calabria per l'anno 1875', *Atti del Consiglio Provinciale di Reggio Calabria* (1875), 3-20.

96 Cingari, 54.

97 ASRC, Deposito Plutino, b. 6, f. 373, letter of A. Serpieri to F. Plutino, 28 May 1880.

many problems for road engineering. Few roads existed at the moment of Unification. The building of bridges and embankments pushed up the costs of projects, and
high demands were made for maintenance. This overall backwardness, in order to be
countered, required unremitting initiatives from the state, the prefects, and the local
authorities – something that, in the context of Italian liberalism, was hardly realizable.
The second prefect of Venice, Luigi Torelli, who held his office from 1867 to 1872,
was determined, like his colleagues in Reggio, to improve the economic position of
la Serenissima. Under the Austrian regime the city's splendid isolation had gradually
become rather inglorious. Particularly after the unfortunate events of 1848, Venice
suffered from an enduring economic recession. Shortly after his arrival Torelli
published a report on the adverse circumstances. He compared the province's
condition of 1845-47 with that of 1865-67 and came to the conclusion, on the basis of
some statistical evidence, that financial and economic activity had declined, and that
the poor rate had gone up – strong indices of crisis. With this report he addressed
himself to the provincial council, to gain support for investments into the public
sector. The state, for its budget deficit, was not capable of taking the lead in develop-
ing infrastructure. Therefore, Torelli said, 'the most important contribution has to
come from one's own strength, from the use of the freedom of action which our laws
allow in order to pursue all kinds of activities'. Just as in Reggio, although the actual
starting points were wide apart, schools and communications figured high among the
priorities set by the prefect.[98] Torelli sent a circular to the prefects of other Venetian
provinces, in which he tried to interest them in a regular shipping line between
Venice and Alexandria (Egypt). The opening of the Brenner, he argued, could make
Venice a major transit port, to the benefit of the entire region and to the detriment of
Austrian Trieste.[99] His idea of the future, however, clashed with the conservatism of
the local elites, represented in the provincial and communal councils. For other
projects, therefore, he tried to get round the local authorities and personally laboured
for gifts of rich citizens and state subsidies. In his unpublished memoirs he relates
the stories of his efforts for the *bacino Orseolo*, the restoration of the theatre and the
crypt of the San Marco, the museum of Torcello, and the *ospizio marino* on the
Lido.[100]
Attempts to direct local investments were, in the first 10 to 15 years of the Unifica-

98 L. Torelli, *Le condizioni della provincia e della città di Venezia nel 1867. Relazione alla deputazione
provinciale* (Venice, 1867). The citation is from p. 10. This report has been discussed by G. Romanelli
(*Venezia Ottocento. L'architettura, l'urbanistica*, 2nd ed., Venice, 1988, 368-373), who has critized rather
vehemently a minor aspect of Torelli's project, that of urban renewal.

99 *Circolare della prefettura di Venezia*, 4 July 1867, n. 1502. On the 11th of July Torelli addressed the
provincial council of Venice concerning the same subject. On other occasions he continued to show his
interest in the transport route to the east, cf. his *L'istmo di Suez e l'Italia* (Milan, 1867); *Descrizione di Porto
Said del canale marittimo e di Suez* (Venice, 1869); *Dieci paralelli fra il progresso dei lavori della Galleria del Cenisio
e quelli del Canal di Suez a partire dal 31 maggio 1867 al 15 novembre 1869* (Venice, 1870-71).

100 Istituto per la Storia del Risorgimento Italiano, Manoscritti, n. 1093, *Memorie autobiografiche di Luigi
Torelli* (typewritten copy), 299-358.

tion, recurrent. The provincial deputations, through their control of the communal budgets, had a large share in this activity. In 1872 the Ministry of the Interior, on behalf of a parliamentary commission, issued a circular which asked for statistical information on the activities of the provincial deputations during the period 1866-1871. It also demanded an examination of the economic conditions of the municipalities, 'because it is evident that, apart from the many reasons that could have had an influence on their present condition, the directives coming from the provincial deputations have also been of great importance'.[101] It seems that the results of this inquiry have never been published, but in the prefectural archives of Venice and Reggio Calabria minutes of the answers have been preserved. Alessandro Bonafini, prefectural councillor in Venice, pointed to the differences in control from above between the Austrian and the current system.[102] Before, the district's commissioners virtually led the smaller communes by the hand: they were present at the gatherings of the communal councils, looked after their registers, and kept their archives. More important matters were subject to 'governmental tutelage', i.e. auditing by the provincial or the central congregation. The more thriving economy of that time, he argued, could not be attributed so much to the stricter control, but more to the higher level of expenditure that was now imposed on the communes in the public interest. In the years between 1866 and 1871 221 requests (relating to 51 communes) to exceed the legal limit of the land tax had been treated by the provincial deputation, for a total of about 3.5 million lire. Furthermore, there had been 20 requests for authorization of lawsuits (only 1 had been rejected), and 28 *ex officio* allocations (for obligatory expenses) on the communal budgets. The statistics drawn up by the prefecture of Reggio Calabria showed a markedly different picture. In the quinquennium, 95 requests (for 106 communes) for additional levies had been presented, for the sum of little more than 300.000 lire. The number of lawsuits requested by the communes, on the other hand, was 64. The most striking difference, however, was the number of allocations imposed by the deputation: 603 times it changed a communal budget, usually for the benefit of schoolteachers' salaries, the building and maintenance of roads, the planning of new cemeteries, etc. In the district of Gerace especially the budgets revealed enormous gaps, forcing the deputation, sometimes year after year, to leave its imprint on the municipal administration.[103] In its general report for 1873 the provincial deputation of Reggio registered a decline in the *ex officio* allocations, ascribing this to the 'moral power' that the law had begun to acquire. Conversely, the approval of electoral rolls – also a task of the provincial deputation – had become more wearisome. This development was evidence, on the one hand, of the 'awakening' of municipal life; on the other, it filled the observers with despair, because the appeals were mostly made out of pure self-interest.[104]

101   *Circolare del Ministero dell'Interno*, 26 May 1872, n. 16400-4.
102   ASV, Pref. A.G. (1872-76), f. 12, 1/8, report to the Ministry of the Interior, 20 December 1872, 'Dati statistici sui lavori della Deputazione Provinciale'.
103   ASRC, Pref., A.G., Serie 1ª, cat. 13, (inv. 14), f. 76, s.f. 44.
104   'Relazione generale della Deputazione Provinciale di Calabria Ultra 1ª per l'anno 1873', *Atti del*

The reluctance of the communes to allocate the obligatory expenditures to their budgets underlined the great distance between the aims of the liberal project and the level of economic, cultural and administrative development in the periphery. The smaller rural communes especially – the vast majority in nineteenth-century Italy – perceived no relation at all between the increasing tax burden and the benefits that were promised. The district commissioner of Mestre (Venice) reported the widespread discontent with the state and communal taxes, and regretted that it was impossible for the municipalities 'to develop their administrative life corresponding to the autonomy they have acquired'.[105]

In a circular of 27 October 1873 the Ministry of the Interior inquired into the nature of the optional expenditure. At that time the national statistics did not yet specify optional and obligatory expenditure, but the Ministry feared that the steady increase in communal expenditure was due to the uncontrolled growth in optional expenditure. Although the law of 14 June 1874 imposed restraints on the optional expenditure, its actual share in total expenditure was marginal (it turned out to be 17% in 1874).[106] The prefecture of Venice, in its answer to the ministerial circular, calculated that optional expenditure took up a mere 7% of all communal expenditure in the province. Furthermore, the prefecture had to acknowledge that 'much of it is acquiring a sort of obligation, particularly in large cities, where it is imposed by today's progress, by a more demanding public opinion, and by the atmosphere of imitation and emulation which is prevalent in large cities, and makes itself felt more than in the past in poorer villages as well'. Examples were the expenditure for the voluntary fire brigade, for the purchase of books and notebooks for students at the elementary schools, for gratuities to schoolteachers, for free places at the training schools, etc. Some optional expenditure, in the eyes of the prefecture, could be well left out, in particular if it was connected with the church. He took as an example the annual building of a bridge over the Grand Canal to connect the *sestiere* San Marco with the church of Santa Maria della Salute – up to the present day a regular custom on the saint's day.[107]

5 THE ENDURING CRISIS

As recorded repeatedly above, the law of 14 June 1874 on obligatory and optional expenditure marked the temporary end to a period of frantic search for a satisfactory tax system. Whereas the law seemed to satiate the government's hunger for further meddling, local finances had by no means found a just equilibrium. The state's

---

Consiglio Provinciale di Reggio Calabria (1873), all. C, 236.

105 ASV, Pref., Gab. (1872-76), cat. 19, 1/1, report of the district's commissionar of Mestre to the prefect, 16 April 1872.

106 Calculated on the basis of the figures given by Volpi, 197.

107 ASV, Pref., Arch. Gen. (1872-76), f. 12, 1/51, report to the Ministry, 8 December 1873.

preoccupation with its own revenues gradually gave way to an awareness that the existing legislation was inadequately implemented and that the problem was in need of serious attention. The prime minister Agostino Depretis presented in 1882 a bill on the optional expenditure of communes and provinces. His motivation was the poor execution of the law of 1874. He claimed that the provincial deputations, from province to province, were applying double standards, and that the definition of optional expenditure was fairly vague. Some communes, therefore, were free to spend as much as they wanted, whereas others were subject to the full rigour of the law. The reform proposals of Depretis, however, did not reach the Chamber for discussion.[108] There were other voices, from within the state administration, that called for a more accurate execution of the official rules and regulations. Writing in 1883, Ceccato, who knew the Interior administration intimately, defended the intrinsic justice and even rationality of the law of 1874. He claimed that full observance of the law, by state and local administrators alike, would considerably enhance the communes' economic position. Almost ten years after its promulgation – which unequivocally underlined the discrepancy between law and administrative reality – Ceccato observed that hopefully in the not too distant future, 'when knowledge of the law of 14 June 1874 has spread more, and everybody has understood the importance of its provisions, the beneficial effects will not be long coming'.[109]

In fact, the implementation of the law presented municipalities and state officials with serious difficulties. The subprefect of Imola, Giorgio Manolesso-Ferro, reported in 1875 the doubts of some communes as to what to regard as optional expenditure. They were faced with bans on a number of expenses that they could hardly do without, such as acts of charity required by extraordinary circumstances or prior engagements, and provisions for public decorum imposed by 'progress' and bourgeois aspirations. The subprefect, agreeing with the prefect that on principle the communes should not be given a free hand, explained that denying expenditure could give rise to serious discontent: 'Since there are sometimes circumstances in which the apparent generosity of the councils can only be understood as a greater local opportunity, I take the liberty of asking Your Honour for instructions, also for the practical reason to avoid increasing the moral malaise that is growing among the communes based on the erroneous assumption that the government only regards the communal administration as a simple cash office for the benefit of the national treasury'.[110] A few months later Manolesso complained about being unable to prevent 'certain legal offences which in the fullness of their powers the communes sometimes commit by making donations that are more appropriate for a charitable

---

108 AP, CD, leg. XIV, sess. 1880-81, Doc., n. 319, 'Disegno di legge presentato dal presidente del Consiglio ministro dell'interno (Depretis) nella seduta del 29 maggio 1882. Sulle spese facoltative dei comuni e delle provincie'.

109 Ceccato, 19.

110 ASB, Pref., Gab., b. 256, letter of the subprefect of Imola to the prefect, 10 October 1875.

institution than for a serious administration only taking care of general interests'.[111] His successor in the subprefecture, shortly after entering upon his duties, observed that the municipalities still cleverly eluded the law. On the other hand, although they surpassed the legal limit on additional levies, 'in expectation of better harvests I think that the fiscal increase can be born without disrupting the agrarian economy which is the only sector to keep the region in satisfactory conditions'.[112] In the district of Vergato the subprefect was faced with similar problems. Carlo Flori, well-informed about his communes (he had taken up his office in 1871), described the proceedings of the communal administrations, 'which are said to be excessively tied up by their freedom and more burdened now than in the past'.[113]

Towards the end of 1884 the Ministry of the Interior again investigated the amount of optional expenditure that was still allocated in the communal budgets.[114] Unfortunately, only the results of the province of Reggio have been preserved. They show that there the optional expenditure had been virtually eradicated in municipalities with less than 1500 inhabitants. In fact, the city of Reggio accounted for almost half of all optional expenditure in the province.[115]

With the prefecture of Filippo Lamponi (starting at the end of 1877) Reggio Calabria made another full-scale attempt, after the emancipatory project launched by Achille Serpieri, to bring the municipal administrations on the right track. Lamponi's first half-yearly report was discouraging. The part on communal administration, drawn up by the prefectural secretary Pietro Ferri, listed a series of shortcomings in the financial management. All trouble, according to him, had its roots in the fictitious and unrealizable forecasts of the budgets. It seemed that the majority of the communes were only interested in imposing taxes on the proletariat and in exceeding the legal limit on additional taxes, the greater part paid by persons outside the municipality. Hence, additional levies on land tax and on some goods were extraordinary high, whereas the state excise was not charged at all, and the special local taxes were levied on the basis of low tariffs. Ferri added that the municipalities only allocated revenue from special taxes in their budgets to the satisfaction of the prefecture and the provincial deputation, but that they were just as eager to escape control from above by eventually not levying them. Other grievances were the tendency to disregard contracts and to deceive creditors, the slowness in paying schoolteachers and municipal servants, and the propensity for getting entangled in lawsuits without any hope of an advantageous settlement. Finally, the local authorities were too free in allocating optional expenditure and in incurring debts. Undoubtedly, Ferri concluded, without the unavoidable economizing towards the end of the financial

---

111 *Ibidem*, b. 434, report of the subprefect of Imola to the prefect, 8 January 1876.
112 *Ibidem*, b. 434, report of the subprefect of Imola, 4 July 1876.
113 *Ibidem*, b. 434, report of the subprefect of Vergato, 3 July 1876.
114 *Circolare del Ministero dell'Interno*, 25 November 1884, n. 15200.13-136961.
115 ASRC, Pref., Arch. Gen., inv. 15, f. 99, n. 21; the statistics were forwarded to the Ministry on 23 February 1885.

year and some control from above, all municipalities would have run into grave deficit.[116] The prefecture tried to repair the defects by providing the subprefects and the mayors with precise instructions. In September 1878 Lamponi forwarded a few circulars he had issued as examples to the Ministry of the Interior, drawing attention to the communes' neglect of public services.[117] One of them gave instructions on communal accounts, especially on the drawing up of tax rolls and cash registers; it was so detailed that it was as if the communal and provincial law of 1865 and other laws had passed entirely unnoticed.[118] After notifying the Ministry Lamponi continued to issue circulars on financial matters. He informed the municipalities further about how to draw up their budgets – it was the period of the autumn session of the council – and monthly checks of the communal cashier's office. In the report on the first semester of 1878 Ferri gave an account of the prefectural efforts. The aim of the provincial deputation in checking the budgets had been twofold: to drive back expenditure and to put into effect local taxes (on animals, on the practice of a profession, on rateable value, etc.). As it took longer to approve the budgets and the taxes could not yet be levied, the immediate consequence for some communes had been a recourse to short-term loans, in order to provide for the most urgent needs. This had deepened the financial crisis in the province. Furthermore, Ferri admitted that the increase of revenue out of local taxes was obstructed by economic backwardness; for the time being, therefore, landed property had to produce further development: 'Particularly in a province like this one, where industry is still in its infancy, capital is scarce and communications are poor and impassable, there is no hope, for the time being, that local taxes develop if not in the letter than in the spirit of the law, so that the propertied class may not have to contribute on its own towards the expenditure required for the material and moral improvement of the municipalities'.[119] In his report on public affairs in the second half of 1878 the prefect hinted at his inevitable moderation in executing the existing regulations. The communes' gap between receipts and expenditure was still too large.[120]

The prefecture's efforts did not come to an end with this guidance from above. As Serpieri had said ten years before and Lamponi now repeated, only continuing pressure could incite the local ruling elites to attend to the communal administration. In 1879, in another stream of circulars, the prefect called on the municipalities to do their duty in financial matters. He pointed again to the instructions issued in 1878, urged them to draw up their final statements, and informed them about reasonable

116   ASRC. Pref., Gab., b. 62, report on the course of the communal administrations, written by P. Ferri (January 1878), part of the general report on public affairs in the second half of 1877, 23 February 1878 forwarded to the Ministry.

117   ASRC, Pref., Gab., b. 176, letter of the prefect to the Ministry, 12 September 1878.

118   Circolare della Prefettura di Reggio Calabria, 20 August 1878, n. 12043.

119   ASRC, Pref., Gab., b. 62, f. 988, report on the course of communal administration, 29 July 1878 (written by P. Ferri, integrated in the prefectural report on the first half of 1878, 8 August 1878).

120   Ibidem, report on public affairs in the second semester of 1878, 11 March 1879.

loans offered by the *Cassa di Risparmio* of Turin.[121] He assumed the checking of the budgets and final statements himself, in stead of leaving them in the hands of his accountant. His guidelines for the 1880 budgets included, again, incitements to observe the law of 1874, i.e. eliminating expenditure that was not strictly required and applying the special local taxes. Here, Lamponi mentioned another flaw in fiscal management on the local level: there was no sense in taxing the greater part of the people but leaving the revenue in the hands of the municipal accountants, who used it for their own benefit. 'That is why it is necessary to abandon every form of consideration for relatives and friends; someone who for whatever reason gets hold of the commune's money, has to be forced by legal means to deposit it immediately in the municipal safe'.[122] Despite these exhortations the obstacles remained insuperable. It was unlikely that the communes would free themselves on their own from economic isolation. Given this limit, communal revenue could not be expected to rise much. The prefecture had no choice but to tolerate, in order to protect the tax-payers against further charges, the omission of a few items of obligatory expenditure. In observance of the law the *pro forma* allocation on the budget was enough.[123] The conclusion of the prefectural secretary Francesco Mazzei, commenting upon the municipal administration in 1880, left no doubt about the failure of external audit of the communal accounts: 'The budgets of most communes of this province are illusory; they do not represent the real state of the administrations but are a mere formality; this can be deduced from the accounts at the end of each financial year, in which the unspent budgeted expenditure accounts for almost fifty percent because the massive revenues entered up have not been collected'.[124]

Lamponi, still prefect, died on 29 March 1881 in Reggio, taking many initiatives with him in his grave. His death certificate stated that if he had conducted a less laborious life, he would have lived on for many years. His sickness had begun in the winter of 1879-80, as a consequence of his working late at the office. His travels through the province during bad weather contributed to his ill health.[125] Not a transfer, as in the case of Serpieri, but an early death brought a period of active prefectural administration to an end.

During the 1880s complaints about the communes' financial management alternated with attempts to improve the situation. In their semestral reports prefects and subprefects continued to signal defects in the system, but no structural changes were made. The burden of obligatory expenditure remained heavy. The communes

---

121 *Circolare della prefettura di Reggio Calabria*, 1 March 1879.

122 *Circolare della prefettura di Reggio Calabria*, 10 October 1879, n. 15139-929.

123 ASRC, Pref., Gab., b. 62, f. 989, report on public affairs in the second half of 1879, 15 January 1880.

124 *Ibidem*, f. 990, report of the second division to the cabinet, 9 February 1881. The passage was dutifully copied onto the report on public affairs in the second half of 1880, 10 March 1881, cf. ASRC, Deposito Plutino, b. 7, f. 394.

125 *Ibidem*, b. 110, f. 2471, medical certificate without date.

increasingly exceeded the legal limit to additional levies on government taxes. For example, information about financial anomalies in the districts of Imola and Vergato were regularly passed on to the prefecture. The subprefect of Imola Francesco Palomba coldly stated: 'Municipal life is doubtless shaky; but this problem, connected with the high demands of the state budget, cannot be solved in a more suitable way than by giving back to the municipalities their most appropriate resources, in other words, by relieving them of the accumulation of expenditure which at the moment they cannot sustain'. He showed that in order to cover the deficit of 1,079,592 lire at the end of 1881, only 63,006 lire were available from patrimonial revenue and that the rest had to come from taxes. The additional levies within legal limits amounted to 170,383, whereas those exceeding the legal limit, for which authorization from the provincial deputation was required, ran to the absurdly high sum of 270,729 lire.[126] In all three provinces the prefecture continued to try to bring local finances under control. The instructions for drawing up budgets and final statements, patiently issued each year (but sometimes with unconcealed annoyance), became such a regular custom that the municipalities let them pass by unnoticed. The ministerial guidelines of 1865 and 1875 (for the budgets) and of 1867 (for the final statements) were the usual reference points; from time to time the regulations prescibed by the law of 1874 were represented. As the times of great arrears in submitting the accounts were now over, the Ministry became more interested in the qualitative aspects. In a circular of 1883 it repeated the criticism levelled by the *Corte dei Conti* in its annual report to Parliament, and urged the prefectural councils to take their task more seriously.[127] The Ministry also reserved more money and manpower for inspections into the workings of the prefectural offices.

An inspection into the prefecture of Reggio Calabria, held in 1883, demonstrated that 'on the whole the budgets of the 106 communes of the province were more poetic [sic] than based on facts': many commitments were not realizable and, if necessary, long-outstanding accounts should be declared uncollectable. The Ministry attributed the defects partly to the negligence of the accountant's office of the prefecture.[128] The prefect then in office, Giorgio Tamajo, was already well-informed about the shortcomings. He had ordered a list to be made up of allocations that he wished to see on the budgets for 1884. Subsequently, he had the list sent to the mayors.[129] In fact, as he wrote later, he himself had requested the ministerial inspection, and he had already asked for additional personnel. Until the arrival of the new accountant the final statements had been examined and discussed by the prefectural council,

126 ASB, Pref., Gab. (1884), cat. IX, report on the second half of 1881 written by the subprefect of Imola, 5 January 1882.
127 *Circolare del Ministero dell'Interno*, 11 August 1883, n. 15200.9-112014.
128 ASRC, Pref., Arch. Gen., inv. 15, f. 99, n. 16, letter of the Ministry of the Interior (4th division), 30 September 1883.
129 ASRC, Pref., Arch. Gen., inv. 15, f. 99, n. 16; *Circolare della prefettura di Reggio Calabria*, 31 August 1883, n. 15468.

without observance of and sometimes in contradiction to the instructions in force. Hence, daily appeals were made to alter decisions. This, according to the prefect, not only damaged the authority's prestige, but it also gave rise to malevolent interpretations and rumours of favouritism. The reestablishment of the communal administrations, he went on, was not just a question of regular accounting. Much of it required a reorganization of the local secretariats, which, in turn, was severely hampered by the lack of officials within the prefecture who could be released to dedicate themselves fully to that job.[130] Another inspection into the workings of Reggio's prefecture, ordered by the Ministry of the Interior in 1888, brought to light the fact that its personnel still showed signs of inefficiency on some points: the fund for obligatory road building was not administered with appropriate care, the decisions made by the prefectural council and the provincial council were not properly recorded (which has frustrated work of historians until the present day), and there was no complete collection of communal regulations. In sum, 'control by the prefectural and provincial authorities over the municipal and provincial administration is regularly exerted, but (...) requires greater effort; in particular those persons who ought to exercise administrative control should show no slacking'.[131]

In Chioggia – the second municipality in the province of Venice – bad financial management and frequent crises in municipal government caused ever deeper trouble for the town. Chioggia lived under the constant threat of the lagoon running dry; loans were piling up, and the costly building of a railroad connection with the mainland had driven the town onto the verge of bankruptcy (state subsidies were a long time coming). Several dissolutions of the communal council during the 1870s did not effect enduring improvement in the administrative and economic situation. For fear of unpopularity the various municipal administrations shrank from taking rigorous measures. Special local taxes, such as the family tax, were not levied for years.[132] The communal council regularly but fruitlessly discussed a change in the system of excises. In spite of having more than 20,000 inhabitants, Chioggia had declared itself 'open' in 1868, because it seemed impossible to form effective toll-gates in the lagoon-area. No serious study, however, had been made, and little by little it appeared that this system caused a considerable lack of income. The special delegates governing the town in 1879 and 1882 tried to convince the most influential local rulers to declare the town 'closed', even if this necessitated immediate and large investments and burdened the population of the municipality. Matteo Maggetti, special delegate in the first months of 1882, was rather sceptical about the chances of persuading the eventual majority in the council. He evocatively depicted the course

130 Report on the public spirit in the second half of 1883 (March 1884), published by P. Borzomati, *La Calabria dal 1882 al 1892 nei rapporti dei prefetti* (Reggio Calabria, 1974), 90-91.

131 ACS, Min. Int., Div. 1ª, Arch. Gen., Affari Generali (1852-1905), b. 26, report of the general inspector Frate, 30 September 1888.

132 *Relazione letta dal cav. Pietro Pavan delegato straordinario per l'amministrazione della città di Chioggia all'atto del insediamento del consiglio comunale 18 agosto 1879* (Venice, 1879), 8.

of events as he expected it: 'If I were to bring about the resurrection [of the change in the excise levy] today, I would be doing a useless job, because as soon as I had left Chioggia poor Lazarus would crawl back to his grave'. Instead, he worked out a plan, in close collaboration with the prefecture, to consolidate the loans accumulated through the years into one large loan from the *Cassa dei depositi e prestiti*, which could offer more favourable conditions. The Ministry of the Interior, however, called in to give advice, replied that the consolidation of loans was a commendable initiative of the special delegate, but that it exceeded his competence. The matter ought to be decided by the communal council. Grudgingly, Maggetti submitted under this pressure, not without mentioning in his final report that in his view the government was too easily washing its hands of the whole affair.[133] Shortly after his departure, during the annual partial elections, differences of opinion within the council again rose to unacceptable heights, rendering unavoidable another dissolution and threatening to put financial reforms on the back burner. Once again we see that the state, leaving important decisions to the local representation, was not too keen on expanding its hold on the communal administration. Yet in situations such as that of Chioggia the local administrators were not capable of directing their responsibility to the benefit of their municipality.

6 CONCLUSION

Before concluding this chapter some notes on the development of local finance in the late 1880s and early 1890s. The first structural attempt to change the pattern of local finance came in 1886 with the law that charged Parliament with the approval of additional levies above the legally prescribed limit. In the first year the law brought about a small decline in additional levies (from 119.4 million in 1886 to 117.2 in 1887). Conigliani attributed the initial decrease to the confusion among smaller municipalities which did not present their requests to Parliament in time.[134] After they had made themselves familiar with the new procedure, the aggregate additional levies resumed their rising tendency. Since the system of parliamentary approval had little effect, it was abolished in 1894.

The new communal and provincial law of Crispi, promulgated in 1889, changed little in the composition of local receipts and expenditure. Some restraints were imposed on the loans for communes, and the approval of budgets was transferred to the new *giunta provinciale amministrativa* (GPA). The efficiency of this organ is difficult to measure before the law of 1894, which charged it with the approval of those budgets that exceeded the legal limit to additional levies. A discussion of its workings,

---

133 ASV, Pref., Gab. (1882-87), serie 2, 1, 4, report of special delegate Matteo Maggetti to the communal council of Chioggia, 4 April 1882.
134 Conigliani, 124.

therefore, is somewhat outside the scope of this research.

In 1891 the Ministry of the Interior, under Giovanni Nicotera, launched a fierce attack against the faulty drawing up of budgets. Apparently, the regulations of the new law had not yet born fruit. The prefects and the GPA were called on to distrust communes and provinces. All the old complaints about local financial management returned. Many municipalities, according to a ministerial circular, abounded in optional expenditure, such as subsidies for schools, bands, theatres, feast-days, etc. Funds for the building of roads and edifices could be useful, but were often so urgent that large sums had to be allocated in them. Moreover, the abuse of public revenue was widespread: many communes were involved in enduring lawsuits, or in ruinous financial adventures. All this had to end through promptitude of the controlling authorities, not just consisting in 'accounting technicalities' but also in investigations into the substance of the allocations.[135] The Ministry tried to contribute by presenting new forms for budgets and final statements, allegedly easier to be filled in.[136] Another circular gave precise instructions for the drawing up of the communal budgets for 1892. The municipalities were urged, among other things, to benefit fully from their properties and from fees on communal services, to pay up or to cash arrears, to curb even the obligatory expenditure, in particular for public works, etc.[137] The ministerial circulars were diligently adapted by the prefectures for their own circulars.

All in all, in the early 1890s, the state and the prefects displayed renewed vigour in order to get local finance under control. The results, however, were meagre. The upsurge of critical books and articles on the subject from the mid 1890s onwards (see n. 17) demonstrates that the initiatives coming from above had no more success than in the preceding decades.[138] Nevertheless, the political and economic elites, particularly in the large cities, demanded a larger say in urban finance. Around the turn of the century this call for more power resulted in the first steps towards the municipalization of public services. As to the first decades of the existence of the unitary state, perhaps the most salient conclusion to be drawn is that interference from above, by law or in person, fell considerably short of expectations. It seems that, although this has not specifically been a research topic here, the ups and downs of the largely agrarian economy had greater influence on the fluctuations of communal revenues and expenditure than legislation aiming at financial reform. The statistics on communal budgets, for what they are worth, show a steady development of expenditure, and a persistent shortfall of revenues, despite the continual attempts to lead them in another direction.

Optional expenditure, the bone of contention for the critics of communal freedom in spending, continued to be, until the beginning of the 1890s, a fixed share of total

135 *Circolare del Ministero dell'Interno*, 26 June 1891, n. 16600.
136 *Circolare del Ministero dell'Interno*, 1 August 1891, n. 1508.
137 *Circolare del Ministero dell'Interno*, 19 August 1891, n. 16600.
138 See also P. Frascani, 'Le entrate', in: *Le riforme crispine*, III, 893-929.

expenditure (15 to 18%). On the other hand, it is hard to grasp how this relatively small share could have had the alleged disastrous effects on communal finances. In general, the vast majority of smaller communities were burdened with obligatory expenditure to such an extent that they could hardly spend one lira as they wished. The larger cities, in comparison with the smaller municipalities, could more elastically respond to the various checks and balances imposed on local finances; therefore the cities, not least because they were less rigidly controlled, were able to spend more on what could be called urban decor and other things of their choice. On the credit side the special local taxes, frantically introduced between 1866 and 1874, never relieved the municipalities as was hoped. Furthermore, the law of 1874, linking optional expenditure to approval of exceeding the legal limit, was badly implemented: more and more communes exceeded the legal limits to additional levies on state property taxes.

Within this context of structural shortcomings of the system of local finances the prefects had a difficult job. We have cited the unrelenting activities of prefects such as Serpieri and Lamponi in the province of Reggio Calabria, but one could easily add the names of Torelli and Sormani Moretti in Venice, and those of Salaris and Scelsi in Bologna. In general, they were not blind to the needs of the communities in their provinces, especially the smaller ones, and tried to bring relief through active interference. Conversely, the larger provincial towns were almost completely entrusted to the municipal administrators. The 1860s and 1870s were filled with attempts to impart a certain degree of financial responsibility to the municipal governments. Yet even the most basic conditions for an orderly financial management – annually drawing up budgets and final statements – were only fulfilled after repeated exhortations through circulars or visits from prefectural commissioners. The obstacles facing the prefects, apart from the enduring agrarian crisis, could be listed as follows. First, as the number of municipalities exceeding the legal limit on additional levies rose, the role of the provincial deputation in checking the budgets became more important. It has been argued that the eligibility of this organ, usually strongly tied to the elite of the provincial capital, was not a secure basis for independent auditing. One should not overestimate the predominance of the prefect as president of the deputation. In Bologna, and to a lesser extent in Venice, the provincial deputation was able to pursue a virtually autonomous line. As to the prefecture's share in checking local finances, the manpower shortage seriously hindered effective control. Once the prefecture loosened its grip, the municipalities paid no heed to the laws and regulations.

Second, particularly in Reggio Calabria, economic and social backwardness imposed restraints upon the prefect's discretion. The abortive division of the demesnes denied many communes a possible source of income. Furthermore, it provoked perennial conflicts amid the various factions in the communal council. In general, the traditional alignments within the municipalities created an atmosphere of hostility towards interference from outside, especially when higher authorities pleaded for contributions to improve the provincial infrastructure. Ironically, it was the freedom of movement granted to the municipalities that most obstructed modernizing intervention from above. The majority of small rural municipalities were in no position to benefit from their budgetary rights. Having totally exhausted the tax-capacity of their inhabitants, they had to cut down expenditure, sometimes even renouncing obligatory expenditure. Hence, the prefects had great difficulty in creating schools and roads, the hallmarks of progress. On the other hand, the municipalities had to be repeatedly asked or compelled to levy local taxes. They turned to levying surtaxes on property rather than collecting unknown duties. In the main, the prefects and the provincial authorities in Reggio were mostly occupied with incitements to spend, whereas their colleagues in Bologna tended to call for retrenchment. In Venice municipalities and controlling authorities were equally convinced of the necessity of a cautious economic policy. The conservatism of local elites was not only a Southern phenomenon: the attempts of Torelli to raise support for improving the position of Venice as a transit port were nipped in the bud by unwilling local councillors.

Third, the central ministries did not eagerly lend their ear to the frequent requests made by the prefects to bring about general reforms. Rome responded to these pleas by subsidizing individual projects, rather than by enlarging the amont of state personnel in the periphery. The prefects, therefore, had to cope with a lack of know-how in their own offices and, in particular, in the municipalities.

Chapter 7

Parliamentary elections between manipulation and the construction of a representative system

1 INTRODUCTION

Nineteenth-century observers and contemporary students have often focussed on the incidence of the prefect's political interference during election campaigns. The famous saying of the Giolittean period 'sell the prefect and buy the deputy' has since led a life of its own.[1] Nasalli Rocca, an experienced prefect of the Giolittian years, bitterly complained about the power of deputies over the prefects: 'The prefect, rather than the executor of anyone's will, ought to be the executor of the law, which is superior to the minister, survives all caprices and the overbearing influence of the masses and their representatives in Parliament. In practice, many former ministers, whenever the prefect was faced with the contrary interests of deputies, have almost done away with his noble mission'.[2] The mainstream of historiography seems to have accepted the predominance of politics in the activities of the prefect.[3] In contrast to this view we set out to separate politics and administration, thus clearing the way for an extensive analysis of the prefect's administrative tasks. Bearing in mind what has been said in that connection so far, one can hardly overlook the importance of the administrative control over the powers and duties conferred upon local authorities. This is, however, not to say that the political role of the prefect should be wholly ignored from now on. On the contrary, it should be seen in the right perspective: first, within the entire range of prefectural duties and, second, in the context of the development of the representative system in liberal Italy.

The question as to what extent politics formed part of the prefect's activities is bound to lead to confusion when no clear definition of 'politics' is given. In the juridical thinking of the turn of the century the matter was easily dismissed as irrelevant, since the political character of the prefect's job was inherent in the law, and hence not

---

1 D. Bartoli, *L'Italia burocratica* (Milan, 1965), 71, who took the expression from one of Salvemini's philippics against Giolitti.

2 A. Nasalli Rocca, *I prefetti in Italia ... fino a jeri* (Città Di Castello, 1916), 5. For a similar view C. Morini, *Corruzione elettorale. Studio teorico pratico* (Milan, 1894), 50-59.

3 A recent study on the workings of the prefectures in the period of Crispi has underlined 'the central importance of the political dimension in the prefect's figure, his career and his discharge of public services', P. Aimo, 'Introduzione alla sezione "Le prefetture"', in: *Le riforme crispine*, 4 vols (ISAP Archivio n.s. 6, Milan, 1990), I, *Amministrazione statale*, 638.

problematical. Teodosio Marchi, in the authoritative manual of administrative law edited by Orlando, distilled the political function of the prefect from the supervision exerted by him over everything that was directly connected with the supreme interests of the state: 'Whoever is invested, albeit under the supervision of central government, with the function of permanently watching over the province, to whose needs he should pay particular attention, whose inclinations he should follow or adjust, whose votes he should listen to or whose prevalent passions he should mitigate, that man governs and administers at the same time'.[4]

In the classical literature on politics and administration their relationship is equally clear. Vivien put it very sharply: 'The executive is divided into two branches: politics, that is the moral management of the nation's general interests, and administration, which mainly consists in rendering public services'.[5] Herman Finer, in the theoretical part of his work, drew a clear-cut distinction between the administrative and the political process, subordinating the activities of the administrative apparatus to the political phase of government.[6]

For the historian the vexed question cannot be solved by appealing solely to doctrines and lawtexts. The worlds of politics (Parliament and government) and administration were certainly intertwined, but to regard the latter as a mere tool of the former would be a serious underestimation, at least when we take the administrative and political reality of the liberal period into consideration. It has been argued that the 'osmosis' between politics and administration was a corollary of the narrowness of the ruling class and its fundamental consensus regarding the defence of Italian unity; it should not be mistaken for an unsolicited intrusion of one upon the other.[7] Rather one should look for the factors that united them in their confrontation with society, not so much in order to 'revisit' the old distinction between the *paese reale* and the *paese legale*, but to find out to what extent the liberal project took root into various 'realities' of the unitary state. In this connection the difference between 'political' and 'administrative' prefects loses much of its explanatory force.[8] Some prefects did have a parliamentary background, but this did not necessarily entail a greater susceptibility to the wishes of the government of the day. The revolutionary experience shared with many ministers could even imbue some prefects, particularly of the first generation, with a certain sense of equality towards their superiors.[9] For

4   T. Marchi, 'Gli uffici locali dell'amministrazione generale dello Stato', in: *Primo trattato completo di diritto amministrativo italiano*, edited by V.E. Orlando, II (Milan, 1907), 191.

5   A.F.A. Vivien, *Etudes administratives*, reprint of the 3rd edition (Paris, 1974), 3-4.

6   H. Finer, *The Theory and Practice of Modern Government*, 4th ed. (London, 1965), 7.

7   G. Miglio, 'Le contraddizioni dello stato unitario', in: *Istituzioni e società nella storia d'Italia. Dagli stati preunitari d'antico regime all'unificazione*, edited by N. Raponi (Bologna, 1981), 558.

8   The distinction, frequently made in present-day historiography, had already been drawn by nineteenth-century commentators, cf. *Guida amministrativa ossia commento della legge comunale e provinciale...*, edited by C. Astengo e.a. (Rome, 1889), 88. By subsequent laws of 1860 and 1877 parliamentary deputies could not be appointed prefect at the same time. This was changed in 1887, when the two offices were rendered compatible.

9   Out of 46 prefects exercising their office between 1861 and 1895 in Venice, Bologna, and Reggio

example, Luigi Torelli, before his appointment in Venice, had been minister of Agriculture in the cabinet of La Marmora (1864-65) and, as emerges from many affectionate letters, was a close friend of Ricasoli.[10]

Although Italy had inherited a relatively liberal Constitution from the Kingdom of Sardinia, the further development of the political system brought to light a series of peculiarities, which compromised its liberalism and need to be spelled out before the position of the prefect can be fruitfully assessed. The political system of united Italy has been labelled, in a comparison with other European nations, 'the triumph of ambiguity'.[11] The moderate liberals, having accomplished unification, continued to believe that society and its political representation, if carefully guided from above, would gradually develop themselves along the lines of the much-praised 'Anglo-saxon' model. The liberals, fully identifying themselves with the state they had created, did not organize themselves in a political party; they simply made the state into their own party. Hence, they failed to establish a firm societal basis. This was partly a result of the lack of interest in national politics among the landowning notables, who, due to the restricted franchise, formed the vast majority of the electorate. Although public opinion divided Parliament into two large movements (the *Destra* and the *Sinistra*), the political scene of the 1860s and 1870s was character-ized by many, shifting parliamentary groupings. In the 1880s, under the influence of the then prime minister Agostino Depretis, this constellation gave way to the well-known phenomenon of *trasformismo*, the absorption of as many factions as possible into the government coalition. On the other hand, the more disciplined organizations of the opponents of the existing political system (republicans, catholics, and socialists) came nearer to modern party-formation. These parties, however, were virtually excluded from the scene of national politics, partly because of the restricted suffrage, partly because of voluntary absenteeism and severe persecution.

Given these broad outlines of the liberal political system, what role could one attribute to the prefect? The historiography of the past decades has come up with various anwers, but basically the debate has not progressed much since the acute reaction of Alberto Aquarone to Ernesto Ragionieri's severe judgement of the prefect's role. The latter, despite a great sensitivity towards the importance of the first

---

Calabria 14 had had a career as deputy before taking up the office of prefect; 15 were appointed senator (of whom 10 had been deputy too, and 13 simultaneously exercised the office of prefect for some time). See on the overlap between high bureaucracy and the Senate, G. Melis, 'La partecipazione dell'alta burocrazia italiana al Senato nell'epoca liberale', *Trimestre*, 21 (1988), n. 1-4, 211-236. The combination of the office of prefect and that of senator turned out to be a bitter experience for Giuseppe Pasolini: in 1864, two years before his appointment as royal commissioner in Venice, he was required, as senator, to vote for the transfer of the capital from Turin, of which he was prefect, to Florence, G. Pasolini, *Memorie raccolte da suo figlio*, 2 vols (Rome, 1915), II, 14-15.

   10   See, for the correspondence between Torelli and Ricasoli the selected letters of the latter in the still incompleted (*Carteggi di Bettino Ricasoli*, edited by M. Nobili & S. Camerani, Rome, 1939-), and A. Monti, *Il conte Luigi Torelli* (Milan, 1931).

   11   P. Pombeni, *Introduzione alla storia dei partiti politici* (Bologna, 1985), 331.

generation of prefects, emphasized the negative aspects of their job: 'It consisted of systematic control and suffocation of local political life, of assiduous and meticulous interference, which constantly and systematically transformed the representative of the state into the representative of the government, and the representative of the government, in turn, into the executor of the will of the party in power'.[12] Aquarone objected that before generalizing about the possible suffocation of local political life one should take into account its scarce consistency in many parts of the country. Following Carlo De Cesare, a well-known publicist and politician of the *Destra*, he pointed out that in many municipalities it was impossible to find someone to exercise the office of mayor; that in local elections the turnouts were often disgracefully low; and that parliamentary deputies were elected on the basis of no more than 150 votes.[13]

Subsequent historians have modelled their interpretations on these, rather schematically sketched, contrasting views. Giovanni Aliberti, focussing on the electoral activities of the Southern prefects, *grosso modo* concurred with Ragionieri. He argued that until the mid 1870s – the period of the *Destra* – the prefects were involved in a centrally coordinated campaign in favour of the 'ministerial' candidates. Under the various governments of the *Sinistra* this interference became a such an endemic aspect of the prefect's activities, that it was even possibile, according to Aliberti, to speak of a 'bureaucratization of the role of electoral agents of the government played by the prefects'.[14] A less unilateral hypothesis, closer to Aquarone's stance, has been recently put forward by Raffaele Romanelli. Basing his case on examples of electoral battles at the grass roots level he has called, among other things, for a more balanced view of the interventions of public officials in elections: they should be studied from case to case, in the light of attempts to forge a dialogue between the newly formed state and an in many ways evasive society. At the moment of Unification Italy, with the exception of the terrritory belonging to the former Kingdom of Sardinia, totally lacked an electoral tradition. Hence, 'to make the system take root, to spread it, to mobilize the electorate and to make it acquainted with the rules of the game was initially one with the establishment of the constitutional system and therefore with the battle fought by government majorities against the opposition'.[15] The electoral system, therefore, should not primarily be seen as a rigid limitation of potential

---

12   E. Ragionieri, 'Politica e amministrazione nello Stato unitario' (1961), now in: Idem, *Politica e amministrazione nella storia dell'Italia unita* (Roma, 1979), 129. A still more crude interpretation has been given by R.C. Fried, *The Italian Prefects. A Study in Administrative Politics* (New Haven and London, 1963), 122, who attributed 'the leading role in the manufacture of parliamentary majorities' to the prefects.

13   A. Aquarone , 'Accentramento e prefetti nei primi anni dell'Unità' (1967), now in: Idem, *Alla ricerca dell'Italia liberale* (Naples, 1972), 168-169.

14   G. Aliberti, 'Prefetti e società locale nel periodo unitario', in: Idem, *Potere e società locale nel Mezzogiorno dell'800* (Rome/Bari, 1987), 165.

15   R. Romanelli, 'Le regole del gioco. Note sull'impianto del sistema elettorale in Italia, *Quaderni Storici*, 23 (1988), 701. For a similar view, G. Guidi, 'Parlamento ed elezioni. Le dinamiche elettorali nel giudizio dei deputati italiani 1870-1882', *Ricerche di Storia Politica*, 4 (1989), 40.

voters, but represented the attempt to mobilize an electorate supporting the constitutional regime.[16] The political organization in the constituencies closely followed the social hierarchy dominated by notable power. The implementation of the electoral system was to a large extent an attempt to come to terms with these authoritarian and paternalistic structures. If the conduct of the elections is no longer exclusively explained as an extension of oppressive centralism, the perspective on the function of the prefect may also change: from an obedient manipulator in the service of the government to a careful mediator between the government's preferences and the demands of the electorate and of society as a whole.

2 CHECKS AND BALANCES IN THE GOVERNMENT'S ELECTORAL STRATEGY

Although it is too simple to see in the prefect an electoral agent of the government, there is much evidence that the consecutive governments, from the first national elections onwards, did exert a barely concealed pressure on the prefects to direct the vote. Illustrative was Minghetti's confidential circular of January 1861 to the governors of the provinces, calling for open support, if there were two or more contestants, for the candidate who was closest to liberal principles and the national cause. The newspaper *Il popolo d'Italia* vehemently attacked this way of interfering in the free vote. It put the circular on par with the 'Napoleonic system in France, where the elections are the exclusive work of the prefects'.[17] On the other hand, these ministerial instructions could also be explained as a defence against anti-constitutional candidates who might present themselves on the occasion of the elections for the first Italian Parliament. In the hectic period of Unification this fear was of course anything but groundless.

During the elections that followed it was quite usual for the minister of the Interior, mostly prime minister too, to warn the prefects against candidates or parties that compromised the foundations of the liberal state. On the eve of the elections of 1865 Giuseppe Natoli, minister of the Interior, called on his prefects 'to act as interpreter and executor of the government's mind, and to persuade the voters of the incommensurable evils that would arise, if many of those entered into the new Chamber who either tried to drive Italy (...) from monarchy into fatal experiments; or would like to see the restoration of governments condemned by the national will and conscience; or even abuse religiosity in order to knock down the splendid monument of Italian power and to restore the country to the degradation of the old servitude'. The enemies of the unitary state, however, were not only republicans and catholics, but

---

16 See on this theme R. Romanelli, 'Alla ricerca di un corpo elettorale. La riforma del 1882 e il problema dell'allargamento del suffragio', in: Idem, *Il comando impossibile. Stato e società nell'Italia liberale* (Bologna, 1988) 151-201.

17 *Il popolo d'Italia*, 21 January 1861, n. 20, in: A. Caracciolo, *Il parlamento nella formazione del Regno d'Italia* (Milan, 1960), 287.

also, as was underlined in the same circular, local factions. The successors of Cavour were highly preoccupied with the resurrection of local factions on the national level. Hence, Natoli stressed that the prefects should not take sides with 'regional names or factions'; they should support those who were 'resolute in fighting for those achievements of the Kingdom that, with freedom of opinion or conscience, are the most valuable property of modern society; in not striving in parliament for mere local interests but solely intent on securing the prosperity and the greatness of our country'.[18] Initially, the threat of local interests being promoted in the national Parliament was deeply felt. It contravened one of the principles of liberal belief, namely that the two be clearly separated in accordance with the difference between administrative and political rights.

From these defensive guidelines for the behaviour of the prefects it was a short step to the manipulation of the vote in favour of a ministerial candidate. In the circular just mentioned Natoli enumerated the main electoral promises of his government (led by La Marmora): to dissolve religious associations (*corporazioni religiose*), to curb state expenditure, and to complete legislative unification – evidently not a universally accepted programme. The prefects were 'to enlighten the minds', and 'to prevent them from being misled'. 'By fulfilling this high duty', Natoli continued, 'you will act as interpreter and executor of the government's mind'. The local press, heavily politicized, was always ready to rail against these alleged infringements of electoral liberty, if its candidate was handicapped. Consequently, accusations against the total corruptibility of government, including the prefects, were easily uttered.

Attempts to manipulate the vote were particularly evident during the elections of 1867 after the fall of Ricasoli's government. Various regional groups within the *Sinistra* launched a vigorous campaign against the government policy on finance and the Roman question. Ricasoli responded with a careful mobilization of potential supporters. He ordered his secretary-general at the Interior, Celestino Bianchi, to keep in touch with the prefects, in order to follow the electoral movements from day to day.[19] Furthermore the premier issued a number of circulars explaining his policy and urging the prefects to organize support among the state officials serving in the provinces. Ricasoli gave the example of a district where an anti-governmental candidate won while the majority of the registered voters were state employees: 'Keeping a watchful eye on the political conduct of their subordinates and of those belonging to the public administration, and in this connection passing on highly accurate and prompt information to this Ministry for the necessary provisions, the prefects will easily understand that not only the grave question of moral and political dignity is involved in the behaviour of state officials, but also a real guarantee for a more efficient manifestation of the national will, which will turn out to be more

18   *Circolare del Ministero dell'Interno*, 20 September 1865, n. 42.
19   See on these contacts the numerous telegrams sent by Bianchi to the prefects instructing them to pave the way for governmental candidates, ACS, Carte Bettino Ricasoli, Fondo Bastogi, sc. 2, f. 23.

sincere and solemn, in that it will be withdrawn from the underhand influence exerted by anti-governmental parties'.[20] Despite these far-reaching attempts to direct the voters the elections hardly changed the balance of the political forces in Parliament. Moreover, several prefects (in particular those of Lecce, Campobasso, Cosenza, and Napoli) had to admit that the state employees in their provinces had gravely undermined the regular (that is, pro-government) course of the elections.[21]

It is, however, far from self-evident that the electoral strategy of the various governments was as a rule cynically intended to manipulate the vote and to use the prefects for their own benefit; or that, even if the Ministry of the Interior issued straightforward instructions to support a particular candidate, the prefects implicitly obeyed. The circulars directed to the prefects at election times used to treat many subjects. On the one hand, when elections were near, the minister invariably pointed out to the prefects that perfect behaviour was expected of him, that is strictly within the bounds of the law. These instructions were usually public and published in official periodicals. On the other hand, as we have seen, the confidential circulars often went a great deal further, calling on the prefects to defend government policy vigorously.

A recurrent theme in the official circulars was the turnout. It had naturally not gone unnoticed that the number of actual voters fell considerably short of the number of persons registered in the electoral rolls. In some political elections, just as in the administrative ones, absenteeism reached dramatic levels. In 1861 the turnout at the first poll was 57.2%; it fell to 45.5% in 1870 (shortly after the taking of Rome); subsequently it rose again but remained between 55% and 60%.[22] After the marked decline in 1870 the secretary-general of the Ministry of the Interior Gaspare Cavallini made a strong appeal to the prefects to labour for heavier polls. He underlined the importance of the right to vote, 'the first and foremost right of a citizen in a free country'; the election of a deputy was all the more valid when he really represented the will of his district. 'The prefects are especially responsible for achieving that goal, because they, through the high position they occupy and being in close contact with the administered, are able better than anybody else to make them understand the great importance of the elections'.[23] In June 1876 the Ministry of the Interior urged the prefects to see to it that the mayors issued enough certificates for voters travelling by train.[24] And on the eve of the second poll of the elections of that year the Ministry send a telegram to all prefectures, calling for 'the strictest observance of the free vote (...). Someone who does not respect the right to vote of his opponents is

---

20 *Circolare del Ministero dell'Interno*, 26 February 1867, n. 1610 (confidential).
21 ACS, Carte Bettino Ricasoli, Fondo Bastogi, sc. 1, f. 15. On these events also Aquarone, 167. It has been shown that in the elections of 1867 many polls were decided by the predominance of notables, who through their clienteles managed to control the vote, cf. Romanelli, 'Le regole del gioco', 710-714..
22 P.L. Ballini, *Le elezioni nella storia d'Italia dall'Unità al fascismo. Profilo storico-statistico* (Bologna, 1988), 305-306.
23 *Circolare del Ministero dell'Interno*, 3 January 1871.
24 *Circolare del Ministero dell'Interno*, 8 June 1876, n. 3200.

unworthy of a free government'.[25] Likewise, in 1882 Depretis insisted that the new electoral law be implemented in strict observance of law and order.[26]

The call for high turnouts and a free vote, however, easily turned into a propaganda campaign of the government. In 1870 Giovanni Lanza allowed his prefects 'in those ways that are consistent with their office and authority', to develop and to elucidate government policy 'in person to all those whom they think it is good to be in touch with, in order to take away possible doubts, to overcome facile opposition and to explain the government's intentions'. The prefects were to arouse a 'peaceful electoral struggle', trying 'through newspapers and committees consisting of highly influential persons' to spark off interest for the poll.[27] Similar instructions were given in 1874. First the principal elements of the government's programme were passed in review; subsequently the prefects were called in to promote it: 'because their high office frequently puts them in contact with a large sector of the citizens, the prefects should not miss any opportunity to elucidate and explain the government's plans, dissipating those mistakes and misunderstandings to which lack of knowledge or the cunning of subversive parties could give rise'.[28] There was nothing secret about this circular: it was published in full in the *Bollettino della Prefettura* of Venice.[29]

There is, as has been shown, unmistakable evidence that the prefects were used as peripheral branches of a governmental 'party', which of course changed with each new coalition (the word 'party' is unavoidable, but it certainly does not indicate the modern, well-organized party form). In this sense the liberal ruling class indeed made the state into its own party. The governments of the *Sinistra* certainly did not differ from those of the *Destra*, which have so far served as examples.[30] The elections of 1876 are known, first, for the landslide victory of the *Sinistra* and, second, for the crude manipulation of the vote, notably through the prefects.[31] There is no need to discuss the 'parliamentary revolution', as the events of 1876 have often been summarized. The alleged interference in the conduct of the elections, however, needs closer examination. This interference has been inferred from a major transference of prefects. It has been repeatedly affirmed that between March, the fall of the Minghetti government, and November a sweeping purge took place within the higher ranks of the public administration, which, through the imperative logic of hierarchy, was felt even in the lowest layers. The replacement of high officials had been one of the demands in Crispi's famous manifesto *I doveri del Gabinetto del 25 Marzo*. Indeed, many prefects lost their post. A brief survey demonstrates that 36 prefects were

25   *Circolare del Ministero dell'Interno*, 9 November 1876, n. 4936 (telegram).
26   *Circolare del Ministero dell'Interno*, 25 October 1882, n. 7911 (telegram).
27   *Circolare del Ministero dell'Interno*, 6 November 1870, n. 962 (confidential).
28   *Circolare del Ministero dell'Interno*, 10 October 1874.
29   *Bollettino della Prefettura di Venezia* (1874), 331-335.
30   See for many examples G. Carocci, *Agostino Depretis e la politica interna italiana dal 1876 al 1887* (Turin, 1956).
31   Fried, 126.

transferred to another province, 21 were suspended (from whom 5 only temporarily) and 12 prefectures kept their leading officials.[32] Hence, only 16 prefects (less than a quarter) lost their job, and some of them had reached the age of retirement anyway. It is reasonable to assume, therefore, that it was not the political 'colour' as such of the prefects that provoked their removal (as one is led to believe). Rather one should look for the mechanisms at work. In the preceding years (in particular on the occasion of the elections of 1874) the prefects had developed strong ties with the local elites and the state officials in their provinces. Letting the same prefects organize the elections in the same provinces, letting them issue instructions and defend the government's policy, would have made their position rather dubious. That is also why Nicotera emphasized the neutrality of state officials: 'In electoral battles, which sow the seeds of further development of liberty and welfare for the nation, public officials should not use the influence their office bestows on them'.[33] Furthermore, the renewal of mayors for the three-year period 1876-78 had already taken place. Hence, new alliances at the local level were necessary to effect the desired swing in the parliamentary balance of power. In this light the redistribution of prefects formed part of a new administrative élan that the *Sinistra* tried to activate.

It is another matter whether this spirit lasted very long. As soon as the swing to the left had taken place, the same practices as under the reign of the *Destra* returned, perhaps exerted with even greater determination. In January 1882, shortly before a series of important bills was to be passed (among others the new electoral law), Depretis sent a telegram to his prefects notifying them that the presence of all deputies in Parliament was required, and that the prefect should urge especially those who supported his government to go to Rome.[34] Immediately after the elections of November 1890 Crispi ordered the prefects to send back all telegrams related to political affairs, so as not to leave any compromising traces in the prefectural offices.[35] The prefect of Bologna, Giacinto Scelsi, noted that he had already taken care of secrecy by not writing down the decodings of the telegrams in cipher.[36]

The propaganda for the government programme could also have a defensive purpose connected with the liberal reason of state. The governments of both the *Destra* and the *Sinistra* were extremely fearful of what they considered subversive parties: republicans, catholics, and later socialists. Hence the frequent requests for information on political gatherings, lectures, and associations. If prefectural or police archives

---

32 These figures have been elaborated from M. Missori, *Governi, alte cariche dello stato e prefetti del Regno d'Italia*, 3rd edition (Rome, 1990).

33 *Circolare del Ministero dell'Interno*, 4 April 1876, n. 1709.

34 *Circolare del Ministero dell'Interno*, (telegram) 8 January 1882 (confidential).

35 *Circolare del Ministero dell'Interno*, (telegram) 5 December 1890. The incessant activity of Crispi in organizing support is amply discussed, for example, in the correspondence between the prime minister and the prefect of Naples Codronchi, in Aliberti, 167; and, on the electoral caprices of the Roman prefects during Crispi's period, M. Guercio, 'La prefettura di Roma', in: *Le riforme crispine*, I, 804ff.

36 ASB, Pref., Gab. (1890), cat. 5, letter of the prefect to the Minister of the Interior, 6 December 1890 (confidential).

were used in historical research, it was often to assess these types of control. Already in the 1860s personal dossiers of the leaders of these 'extremist' parties were kept in the prefectures and, on demand, sent to the Ministry. This political policing was gradually intensified as opposition rose. It was strictly speaking a task performed by the head of police (*questore*), but the prefect bore the final responsibility. During election time the prefectures thus became the most important information channels for the government.

The various forms of electoral control demanded by the political centre were not automatically successful. First, the prefects, in particular those of the first generation, were not blind executors of commands from above. Within the higher circles of public administration the infringement of politics was dismissed with indignation. As early as 1858 the *Rivista Amministrativa del Regno*, strongly objecting to Cavour, made clear that government ought to refrain from publicly defending its candidates: once a government pushed forward its candidates, state officials (mayors, judges, tax collectors and *carabinieri*) were morally and professionally required to support them; moreover, 'it is impossible that the government restrict itself to indicating the man to be elected; after this first move circulars of intendants, manifests of mayors, precepts of judges and pressure of police officials will not be long coming'. Then politics intermingled with public administration in the province, and the end of it was that the freedom of the vote was lost.[37] In 1865 the leading administrative journal repeated its viewpoint, stating that a truly free vote was only possible, if there were no 'official' candidates.[38] Individual prefects too protested against governmental interference. Luigi Zini, prefect of various provinces during the 1860s, was known for his sharp criticism of ministerial pressure on the prefects.[39] It is hardly imaginable that a prefect like Sormani Moretti, recorded in an earlier chapter for his energetic and independant assertion of the interests of the province of Venice, became a docile servant during election time. He did not hesitate to express his indignation at the preponderance of political interests. In his view the government was too much preoccupied with party politics, and did not pay attention to the functioning of public administration: 'Close relations between ministers and prefects are rare, and sometimes do not occur for months. The proposals of the prefects sometimes remain unanswered, whereas the motions and complaints of private citizens, corporate bodies (municipalities , charitable institutions or other), even echos of partisan voices are received or listened to, without first consulting the local responsible official, who can and should give detailed explanations. Serious measures are taken by ministries intended for important local administrations without informing or warning the prefectural authorities'.[40]

---

37 *RAR*, 9 (1858), 123.
38 V. Aliberti, 'Elezioni generali politiche', *RAR*, 16 (1865), 513-526.
39 Aquarone, 165-167.
40 ASV, Pref., Gab. (1877-81), cat. 19, 1/1, regular report on public affairs in the second semester of 1879, 20 February 1880.

Second, the success of 'ministerial' candidates also required certain political skills, notably the capacity to reach compromises and to stay away from the limelight – surely not the virtues of all prefects.[41] There are many examples of prefects being replaced because they got entangled in some local scandal. Such involvement could be fatal to the government's interests when elections were due.

Third, and perhaps most importantly, the extent to which the prefect's interference could be successful was also a societal problem. Little could be done when there was no response from below. The lack of participation revealing itself in low electoral turnouts could have many causes: observance of the papal ordinance to boycott the government of the unitary state, prevalence of local interests, poor communications, etc. We shall try to expand on this when we take a closer look at the prefect's activities at the grass roots level.

3 THE REVISION OF THE ELECTORAL ROLLS

To appreciate the industriousness in the prefectures during election time, one should keep in mind that the law imposed a multitude of bureaucratic checks to be carried out by the prefect and his staff. They were required to supervise the various stages of the electoral process, from the annual revision of the rolls to the final collection of the votes to be notified to the Ministry of the Interior. The prefect's function was first and foremost one of control of the observance of the law. All ministerial circulars, irrespective of their further purposes, stressed the importance of regular elections. Especially on polling day itself the prefects were responsible for the freedom of the vote and the avoidance of public disturbances.

Behind the scenes the supervision of the revision of the electoral rolls was the most crucial activity of the prefects (this in contrast with the revision of the rolls for the administrative elections, which were checked by the provincial deputations). The Italian way of drawing up and revising electoral rolls (*titolo 2°, capo I*, electoral laws of 1848 and 1860) was a mixture of two procedures, one from below and one from above: first, the municipalities issued public announcements calling on everybody who considered himself entitled to vote, to present his qualifications; in addition to this, the communal councils could include those who were known to have the proper qualifications. Subsequently, the prefect for his part could register *ex officio* those who according to his information were still missing.[42] On top of that, he was the first authority for appeals relative to the registration of voters.

---

41 The biographical notes edited by Crispi's cabinet leave no doubt that the prefects were expected to act energetically but at the same time had to pay strict attention to the various interest groups in their provinces; any transgression of these unwritten rules could lead to transfer, see E. Gustapane, 'I prefetti dell'unificazione amministrativa nelle biografie dell'archivio di Francesco Crispi', *RTDP* 34 (1984), 1061-1101.

42 Romanelli, 'Le regole del gioco', 693.

These prefectural powers were heavily criticized. In the words of Zanardelli, commenting upon the bill and the earlier legislation: 'At present the prefect's powers are unlimited, since it is his decision to add and cross off electors; in the case of appeal as well the prefect himself, assisted by subordinate officials, acts as judge; afterwards, he simply validates the rolls on the basis of which parliamentary elections are held; thereafter appeals before the Court of Appeal or Cassation often do not result in anything but posthumous and useless sentences'.[43] The law of 1882, withdrawing these discretionary powers from the prefect, laid down that a provincial commission (presided over by the prefect and consisting further of the highest judge in the province and three provincial councillors) approve the rolls and judge appeals.

As has been repeatedly demonstrated for other aspects of the prefect's job, his activities did not start at the moment the municipalities had neatly discharged their responsibilities. Each year, including the years in which no parliamentary elections were held, the electoral rolls were to be revised by the municipal councils in their spring session. The execution of this revision left much to be desired, and hence needed the constant attention of the prefects. Shortly before the period of the spring sessions began most prefects sent a circular to the municipalities reminding them of the importance of their duties. These calls were usually a first opportunity to alert the municipalities of the desirability of high turnouts. The registration of those entitled to vote thus became a first step in the battle against absenteeism.

In March 1874, for example, the prefect of Venice issued instructions for the correct revision of the political rolls, underlining that during last year's supervision many irregularities had come to light. He therefore explained again the entire procedure, from the public notices to invite citizens to register themselves to the final check by the prefecture.[44] In a subsequent circular the prefect impressed on the municipalities the value of orderly elections; it was necessary for the municipal authorities not only to revise the rolls in time, but also 'to exert positive interference, which the law imposes on them, (...) just as they should use their moral influence to rouse the people from their apathy, and to feed and kindle the voters' mind'.[45] The pressure on the municipalities paid off: in 1866 5022 men were entitled to vote, in 1870 6088, and in 1874 7263 (a growth rate which far surpassed the relative rise in population). In his regular report on public affairs the prefect noted that these positive results were to a great extent due to *ex officio* registrations. The number of actual voters, however, remained nearly the same (2865 in 1866, 2650 in 1870 and 2927 in 1874). Faith in the liberal institutions, the prefect concluded disappointedly, lagged behind the growth of the electorate.[46]

---

43 AP, CD, Leg. XIV, sess. 1880-82, Documenti, n. 38A, 'Relazione della commissione sul disegno di legge presentato dal ministro dell'interno nella tornata del 31 maggio 1880'; cf. also A. Brunialti, *Legge elettorale politica* (Turin, 1882), 103-106.

44 *Circolare della prefettura di Venezia*, 9 March 1874, n. 2948.

45 *Circolare della prefettura di Venezia*, 28 April 1874, n. 5241.

46 ASV, Pref., Gab. (1872-76), cat. 19, 1/1, report on the public affairs in the second semester of 1874, s.d.

The prefects of Bologna and Reggio Calabria were equally persevering in urging their municipalities to fulfil what they used to call the basic liberal duty of drawing up the electoral rolls. The prefects of Reggio in particular were involved in an unremitting battle against the indolence of the municipalities. In a report on the second semester of 1877 the responsible prefectural official mentioned that the political rolls were, as usual, submitted rather late: 'Otherwise no appeals, no fury and rarely requests for registration'.[47] Apparently the parliamentary elections gave less rise to disagreement and family or faction struggles than the local elections. Later in this chapter some peculiarities of the parliamentary elections in Reggio will be more amply discussed. The supervision of the revision of the electoral rolls was part and parcel of the attempts to 'awaken' society, or at least that part of society that could broaden the basis of the constitutional monarchy. Much to the regret of both the Northern and Southern prefects society was not simply lying there waiting to benefit from the wonders of the liberal state. Despite the assiduousness of the prefects the registration of voters remained a painstaking project, while the turnouts continued to fall short in comparison to the number of registered voters.

The powers of the prefects in checking the accuracy of the rolls could be used for less noble goals as well. *Ex officio* registration became more and more a means to effect a consensus in favour of the government of the day. Until 1882 the prefect could personally add names to the rolls. He was therefore eager to mobilize reliable voters in particular. These were most likely to be found within the ranks of state employees. The control over this group (about 10% of the entire electorate) was of vital importance to the government. Admittedly, it would appear odd, if state employees (to whom the electoral law explicitly gave the right to vote) were omitted from the rolls. It frequently happened that prefects asked their colleagues in other provinces to grant leave to their employees, if their vote was required elsewhere. There is also evidence that some prefects deliberately changed the number of voters by crossing off unwanted persons and registering massively bureaucratic and military personnel (even if they had already been registered elsewhere).[48] In 1874 Mayr, prefect of Venice, somewhat exaggerated his mobilization attempts (recorded above), just as in the event of the administrative elections, by urging the chief administrators in his province to close the ranks of the liberals, and 'to use their legitimate influence in support of candidates on the government's side'.[49]

The 1880 elections in the district of the city of Reggio Calabria caused a lot of confusion. The centre-left Domenico Genoese-Zerbi (close to Nicotera's group, which had recently clashed with Depretis) lost his seat in the first ballot. Fabrizio Plutino,

47   ASRC, Pref., Gab., b. 62, f. 987, Report on the administrative services in the second semester of 1877 (P. Ferri to the cabinet), January 1878.

48   Romanelli, 'Le regole del gioco', 699, has given some examples of these practices in districts of Naples in the 1860s.

49   ASV, Pref., Gab. (1872-76), cat. 5, 1/1, confidential circulars to the district commissioners and other heads of administration, 10 September and 8 October 1874.

exponent of the *Sinistra* too and mayor of Reggio, was pushed forward, and indeed in a second ballot defeated his opponent, Francesco Saverio Melissari (deputy of Reggio between 1868 and 1875 supporting the left). Plutino, however, opted for the constituency of Palmi, which he had represented since 1873, and Melissari withdrew. From the internal struggle of the *Sinistra* a new candidate of the *Destra*, Luigi De Blasio, benefitted, defeating a new candidate from the left, the progressive democrat Pietro Foti.[50] The prefect of Reggio, Filippo Lamponi, had probably tried to prevent this outcome by registering, on orders from the Ministry of the Interior, *ex officio* about 50 persons on the electoral rolls (out of a total of 1196 registered voters), mostly policemen and civil servants stationed in Naples, Catania, Messina, and Catanzaro.[51] Shortly before polling day, however, the *Corte d'Appello* of Catanzaro overruled the prefect's registrations, which thwarted the aspirations of the governmental candidate Foti.[52]

The new electoral law of 1882, apart from widening the franchise, reduced the discretionary powers of the prefect by handing over the supervision of the drawing up of the rolls to a provincial commission. Nevertheless, the municipal administrations continued to enjoy the privilege of the first revision. Hence the opportunity to manipulate the number of voters, sometimes with the tacit consent of the provincial authorities, was not yet expelled.[53] At last, in 1894 another law was passed, dealing exclusively with the drawing up of the electoral rolls, in order to discourage the abuses still being committed. The electoral rolls were to be drawn up *ex novo* by a municipal commission consisting of the mayor and four elected members (not necessarily communal councillors). As before, a provincial commission (consisting of the president of the provincial court of law, a prefectural councillor, and three citizens appointed by the provincial council) dealt with secondary checks and appeals.[54] The results of this nationwide extraordinary revision were quite shocking: the electorate decreased from 2,934,445 to 2,120,185, that is from 9.4% (in 1892) to 6.7% of the total population, thus falling to the level of 1882.[55] The search for a new electorate, culminating in the

---

50 G. Cingari, *Reggio Calabria* (Bari, 1988), 123-124. Names of elected and non-elected candidates, the number of votes and other relevant information on the parliamentary elections have been drawn from: *Indice generale degli atti parlamentari. Storia dei collegi elettorali 1848-1897* (Rome, 1898).

51 According to a note of his successor Gilardoni the rolls of 1880 for the parliamentary elections had not been revised nor officially decreed at all, due to lack of prefectural personnel and the anticipation of a new electoral law, ASRC, Pref., Arch. Gen. (inv. 14), f. 148, s.f. 21, letter of the prefect to the Ministry of the Interior, 31 January 1882.

52 A few days before the elections the Ministry of the Interior telegraphed the prefect to notify him that it had asked the prefects in question to release the employees, so that they could take part in the ballot, ASRC, Pref., Gab., b. 66, f. 1052, telegram of 7 July 1880. Three days later the *procuratore generale* informed the prefect about the nullification of the prefectural decree, *ibidem*, b. 65, f. 1035, letter of 10 July 1880.

53 M. Saija, 'La prefettura di Catania', in: *Le riforme crispine*, I, 868.

54 C. Summonte, *Commento della legge 11 luglio 1894 n. 286 di modifica della legge elettorale politica e della legge comunale e provinciale per la parte concernente la compilazione delle liste elettorali...* (Naples, 1895).

55 P. Villani, 'Gruppi sociali e classe dirigente all'indomani dell'unità', in: *Storia d'Italia, Annali*, I, *Dal feudalesimo al capitalismo* (Turin, 1978), 924-926.

law of 1882, had thus been replaced by a more defensive strategy (from the outset it was clear that the direct political victims of the revision would be the opposition groups and parties).[56] The liberal belief in economic growth and economic progress going hand in hand with increasing participation was crudely crushed by reality.

4 POLITICAL MOBILIZATION AND CONTROL IN THE PERIPHERY

So far we have predominantly discussed the prefect's practices in the light of his official function and governmental pressure. Neither the spirit of the law nor the strategy of the government, which were not necessarily identical, had sufficient ascendancy over society to impose their will. Persisting traditional power relations, on the one hand, and the rise of strong opposition movements, on the other, impeded the quiet execution of the liberal project. The prefects, already torn between the government's diktat and the requirements imposed by law, were faced with the additional problem of bridging the gap with society. In spite of all their formal and informal powers the prefects had to deal with various forms of societal resistance. Each province, each constituency set other problems to which the prefects had to adapt themselves.

4.1 Reggio Calabria

After the withering of the initial enthusiasm (except in the capital itself the parliamentary elections of 1861 had been a victory of the moderate liberals), disappointment crept up on the prefects of Reggio Calabria. In 1863 Cornero found 'an adverse mentality, which fills the population with repugnance and makes it disobey every governmental measure; it choses with care every opportunity to oppose the local government authorities'. He was rather struck by the indifference 'that is harboured against the government and liberty, so that on feast-days, like that of the Constitution, neither enthusiasm nor interest is shown, but only indifference and coldness'.[57] In his reaction to the elections of 1865 Bardesono was not so much preoccupied with the growing strength of opposition candidates as with the personal and municipal character of the electoral struggle. People cast their vote to be of use to their municipality, not for any broader political aim.[58] All prefects after him expressed themselves in similar terms. Political parties were said not to exist, with the possible exception of a clerical party exercising an indirect but considerable influence on the chances of success of many candidates.[59] Serpieri, with his usual frankness,

---

56   Ballini, 124.

57   ASRC, Pref., Gab., b. 62, f. 971, report on public affairs to the Ministry of the Interior, 1 July 1863.

58   *Ibidem*, f. 973, quarterly report of the prefect to the Ministry on the political, moral and economic conditions of the province, 5 October 1865.

59   See for example the report on public affairs of Tamajo, March 1884, published in: P. Borzomati, *La Calabria dal 1882 al 1892 nei rapporti dei prefetti* (Reggio Calabria, 1974), 85-86.

attributed the indifference of the population ('a profound anarchy in society', as he put it) to the long tyrannical government of the Bourbons. He particularly regretted that the moderate liberals did not organize themselves into a solid party to promote the benefits of liberty in the farthest corners of the province: 'I think that the lack of a real governmental party among the population is not limited to this province, but as for this problem I must frankly say that really it does not exist and therefore will not be a motive for disorder, since (...) the crowds are ignorant about everything; the activities of a few men keeps alive hostility towards the government, and the masses continue to be confused, which retards the benefits of liberal institutions and makes them believe the most absurd things'.[60] Interestingly enough, Serpieri proposed 'administration' as a substitute for the lacking political organization: 'It is my profound conviction that everywhere, but in these provinces in particular, only with good administration is it possible to pursue good politics'.[61] He even held that public administration could help to educate the liberals in the province: 'Through diligent and efficient administration they can be helped and rendered capable of forming the nucleus of a truly monarchical-constitutional liberal party, which needs constancy and many supporters'.[62] Where everything else failed, the prefect and other state officials had to function as the link between state and society. For Serpieri it was not party politics that mattered, although he did not hide his appreciation for the Monarchy and the liberal cause; he rather considered his activities as prior to particularistic interests, as a way of clearing the field for a more mature electoral struggle and the unfolding of the parliamentary system.

Between 1861 and 1882 (according to the system of single-member constituencies) the seven constituencies of the province of Reggio Calabria frequently elected the same deputies: Bagnara Calabra remained in the hands of Saverio Vollaro, from the election of 1865 until that of 1880 included, mostly elected in the first ballot (he was also elected in 1884, 1886 and 1890 for Reggio Calabria I according to the system of list-voting); elected always in the first ballot, Agostino Plutino firmly held the seat of Melito Porto Salvo, until the new electoral law of 1882 changed the existing balance of power (Melito became part of the larger district of Reggio I). The Plutino family was prominent in the ranks of the deputies of Reggio. Antonino Plutino, Agostino's brother, who had been governor of Reggio in 1860-61, represented Cittanova from 1863 until his death in 1872. Fabrizio, Agostino's son, entered Parliament in 1873 for the constituency of Palmi and, after 1882, for Reggio Calabria II (in 1888 he was appointed prefect and therefore lost his seat).

The strong bond between voters and deputy underlined the local and highly personal nature of the parliamentary elections in Reggio.[63] Many deputies were landowners

---

60 ASRC, Pref., Gab., b. 62, f. 981, quarterly report of the prefect to the Ministry, 10 October 1870.
61 *Ibidem*, f. 977, regular report on public affairs, 14 June 1869.
62 *Ibidem*, f. 981, political report of the prefect to the Ministry, 5 July 1870.
63 On this subject V. Cappelli, 'Politica e politici', in: *Storia d'Italia. Le regioni dall'Unità a oggi. La Calabria*, edited by P. Bevilacqua & A. Placanica (Turin, 1985), 501.

of considerable wealth, which gave them a lot of prestige among the population.[64] Moreover the same names reappeared in the rolls of the provincial council and the municipal council of Reggio. Fabrizio Plutino, for example, was mayor of Reggio in 1879-82 and 1883-84, and again after the turn of the century. Under the uninominal voting system paternalistic relationships and *ad hoc* alliances determined to a high degree the outcome of the ballot. And, contrary to the aims of the legislator, the electoral law of 1882 (introducing list-voting in fewer constituencies) did not reduce the influence of local factions.[65] The structure of the clienteles were so clearly laid out that electoral results could be predicted with amazing precision. On the 13th of May 1880 the subprefect of Gerace, Filippo Errante Rampolla, made a forecast of the elections of the 16th in the two constituencies of his district. His error rate was about 10% in Gerace: the opposition candidate Luigi De Blasio got 234 votes instead of 261 in the prognosis, and Luigi Raffaele Macry received 365 votes against 375. The situation in Caulonia was more complicated, because there were three candidates. Nevertheless, Errante forecast 369 votes for Giuseppe Nanni, the current deputy tipped to win again, whereas he got 353 votes in the actual poll.[66]

In the context of this predominance of political 'dynasties' and clienteles the room for action by the prefect was limited. The elections of 1874 were, because of the strength of the incumbent deputies, a sure victory for the opposition, and the prefect could do little to change this destiny. Likewise, during the campaign for the elections of 1876 the prefect did not have to resort to backroom-activities in order to ascertain the victory of the *Sinistra*. Only in cases where the candidacy was controversial could the prefect exert some influence.[67] In the first and second ballot of the elections of 1880 in the constituency of the city of Reggio, already recorded for the obscure practices related to the revision of the rolls, the struggle between Fabrizio Plutino and Francesco Saverio Melissari was a complete deception. Plutino, pushed forward by the electorate of Reggio, openly asked his supporters to vote for his opponent, pointing to a fruitful future cooperation between himself as mayor of Reggio and Melissari.[68] A personal letter of Melissari, residing at his factory of sericulture in Montepulciano, to Plutino shows the surprise of the former to find himself in the second ballot running against a political sympathizer. He declared, under these circumstances, that

64   The turnouts in the various constituencies of Reggio were considerably higher than the national mean: they fluctuated (in the first ballot) between 53% in 1870 and 70% in 1880, MAIC, Direzione di Statistica, *Statistica elettorale politica. Elezioni generali politiche, 16-23 maggio 1880* (Rome, 1880), 36.

65   Cingari, 126.

66   ASRC, Pref., Gab., b. 65, f. 1042, letter of the subprefect of Gerace to the prefect, 13 May 1880.

67   It has been put forward that the Northern origins of most prefects rendered them insensitive to the 'the human environment of the Calabrese communities and to the local struggles', Cappelli, 511. This seems unconvincing for the case of Reggio. First, out of the 20 prefects of Reggio between 1861 and 1895 11 came from South Italy, 5 from the Centre, and only 4 from the North. Moreover, there is no evidence that the Southern prefects were more able to manipulate the clienteles.

68   Cingari, 124.

he had not the least intention of standing for Parliament again.[69] It seems that the prefect, who was responsible for the official nomination list, made a serious miscalculation in complying with the demands of the city's electorate and organizing a second ballot between the two, despite the declaration of Plutino that he remained faithful to the constituency of Palmi and the intention of Melissari to withdraw. Indeed, after the two false rivals had disappeared from the scene, an opposition candidate won the supplementary elections. In places where the local elites were so closed and their clienteles so compliant, the prefects had to employ a lot of tact in dealing with the deputies and their supporters.

4.2 Venice

The prefects of Venice, like their colleagues in Reggio, were alarmed by the indifference and apathy on the part of the electorate. The turnouts were dramatically low, reaching their nadir in 1874 with 40% in the first ballot and 38% in the second.[70] Much as in many other parts of the Kingdom the influence of local groupings was very strong. In the elections of 1870, for example, two candidates were running for the constituency of Portogruaro-San Donà. Only shortly before polling day, after many heated gatherings had the 'grand electors' of the district more or less agreed on their candidates.[71] About 700 voters were registered: 400 in Portogruaro and 300 in San Donà, of whom scarcely 50% showed up at the polling stations. The votes were sharply divided between the two main centres of the constituency: Gabriele Pecile received 150 votes in Portogruaro, Pacifico Valussi 154 in San Donà, but since a few minor candidates had got some remaining votes, a second ballot was needed. The division was now even more clear-cut: Pecile received 241 votes in Portogruaro, against 216 of his opponent in San Donà. The turnout for the second ballot was considerably higher (about 65%) – a result of the effective propaganda in the two towns. But what was most evident, was the neat division of the support emphasizing the local ties of the candidates and, apparently, the minor interest in national political issues.

The low turnouts indicated that the loyalty of the local elites was all but secure. Furthermore the catholic Church, with its strong parish organization in the region, had wide appeal among the population in the countryside. Hence, the representatives of the state had the crucial task of silencing the dissenting voices and winning the support of the bourgeoisie. Sormani Moretti, prefect between 1876 and 1880, ascribed the slumbering opposition to the lingering on of a preunitary mentality among various strata of the population used to 'the most absolute systems of government'; moreover the people did not form 'a just idea of the developments and advantages of constitutional government, nor do they know the parliamentarians and earlier

69 ASRC, Deposito Plutino, b. 7, f. 399, letter of F.S. Melissari to F. Plutino, 18 May 1880.
70 *Statistica elettorale politica. Elezioni generali politiche, 16-23 maggio 1880*, 29.
71 ASV, Pref., Gab. (1866-71), cat. 5, 1/1, letter of the district commissioner of San Donà di Piave to the prefect, 18 November 1870 (polling day was fixed on the 20th).

events in parliament'.[72] It is difficult to assess up to what point on the social ladder Sormani thought his interpretation to be applicable. His reading of the popular attitude, like that of many other prefects for that matter, certainly did not square with the more common explanation (given by contemporary supporters of decentralization and taken over by many present-day scholars) of the origins of administrative resentment: excessive centralization and its suffocating effects on communal liberty. Yet looking for the roots of the 'administrative question' only from the side of the state is undoubtedly bound to remain unsatisfactory. The opinion of the prefects, therefore, taking into account the backwardness of society is in my view worth at least as much as the other.

Nevertheless, the political culture in Venice was of a very different nature from that of Reggio Calabria. Even if in the opening years of Unification the *paese reale* and the *paese legale* were worlds apart, the sociability within the elite groups was quite high. The strongly represented nobility could indulge itself in the flourishing fine arts. The press was omnipresent in the literate circles. A wide variety of journals and periodicals were published in the city. All kinds of associations were leading an active life. Insofar as the aristocracy and the high bourgeoisie of *la Serenissima* were politically interested, they tended to conservatism, and used to support the moderate liberals in the elections. According to Manfrin the moderate 'party' consisted of 'the noble part of the Venetian society': 'rather than a political party it[s membership] had become a question of social respectability'.[73] This rather unorganized grouping dominated local politics and parliamentary elections in the first two decades after the annexation of the Veneto.[74] The first prefects, therefore, did not have to be too worried, had there not been the uncompromising catholics. Every prefect of Venice in the 1870s and 1880s recognized the unrivalled strength of the clerical party. Fortunately, they said, the catholics were only actively involved in the administrative elections, but abstained from voting in the parliamentary elections. Particularly Carlo Mayr, prefect of Venice from 1872 to 1876, considered their presence on the political front as an almost personal threat (his activities during the local elections have been discussed in chapter 3). The clerical manoeuvres behind the scenes in the local elections of 1873 had shown him that he could not fully rely on the aristocrats. First, as we have seen, he took firm action to increase the number of registered voters. Second, from April 1874 onwards (the elections were held in November) he closely scrutinized the developments in the various constituencies. In May (long before the dissolution of Parliament) he was able to inform the Ministry that the governmental candidates were most likely to win, except in Chioggia and, perhaps, in Venice (his predictions would all come true).[75]

---

72 ASV, Pref., Gab. (1872-76), cat. 19, 1/1, report on the first semester of 1876, n.d.

73 *Ibidem* (1877-81), cat. 19, 1/1, regular report on the public affairs in the second semester of 1880, 23 March 1881.

74 *Venezia*, edited by E. Franzina, (Bari, 1986), 50ff.

75 ASV, Pref., Gab. (1872-76), cat. 5, 1/1, confidential report of the prefect to the minister of the Interior, 14 May 1874.

In September and October he started to work on the district commissioners and other heads of public administrations to support the liberal cause, 'so that the sluggishness or lack of precautionary agreements about the most acceptable candidates do not give an easy victory to the opposition, which often takes advantage of absenteeism and discord among its adversaries'.[76] It is beyond doubt that Mayr's fanaticism, under the veil of liberalism, was primarily directed against the catholics.

After the political turn of 1876 the moderate liberals were followed with more scepticism. Sormani Moretti, the new prefect appointed by Nicotera, described the electoral struggle as more fervent than before (the turnout reached a peak of 55%); but the moderates had built up such a large clientele and disposed of such a potent propaganda machine that they could not be defeated.[77] Gradually, however, the moderate deputies were taken in by the amalgam of liberals supporting the government of the day (by 1886 the same deputies who earlier belonged to the *Destra* were called 'ministerials'). The various prefects in the decade after 1876 (Sormani Moretti, Manfrin, Mussi) had all been deputies before their prefectural career and were closely associated with the *Sinistra*. Yet a too overt support for the progressive liberals would have rendered their position in the Venetian society circles intolerable, in particular since the city government remained in the hands of conservative aristocrats and moderates who, on occasion, made common cause with the catholics. Hence, they were expected to act tactfully, and to use their influence with caution.

By the mid 1880s the political climate in Venice had been affected by the practices connected with the 'transformism' of Depretis. The district commissioners were urged to commit themselves fully to the electoral campaign of the ministerial candidates. They visited the municipalities under their control, studied the changing alliances, and tried to favour the incumbent deputies. In the district of Chioggia an independent candidate, Roberto Galli (later, in Crispi's second cabinet, secretary-general of the Interior), was certain to obtain a seat. His relationship with the other two candidates of the constituency, however, was fairly loose. The district commissioner, therefore, used his influence to persuade the supporters of Galli to add the names of the other, demonstrably ministerial candidates (Papadopoli and Gabelli) on their ballots. The problem was that many voters were practically illiterate and could scarcely write Galli's name, let alone the other names.[78] In this example, not untypical for the 1880s, political intrigues dominated the work of the state officials during election periods. This was only possible in a context in which the electorate was fairly malleable, without falling victim to 'anti-constitutional' parties.

---

76   *Ibidem*, confidential circular, 10 September 1874.
77   *Ibidem*, (1877-81), cat. 19, 1/1, regular report on the public affairs in the second semester of 1876, 25 January 1877.
78   *Ibidem*, (1882-87), serie 3, 3, 2, confidential letter of the district commissioner to the prefect, 17 May 1886.

4.3 Bologna

At first sight the political landscape of Bologna was dominated by the moderate group around Minghetti, closely connected with the landed elite. Its hegemony in the social, cultural and economic life of the province was unrivalled until the last decade of the century. It seemed, therefore, that the prefects could let the network of loosely organized liberal clubs and associations take its course. The regular reports on public affairs, however, show that the representatives of the state felt a constant threat from opposition movements: first of republicans and catholics (before the annexation of Rome the return of the Pope's temporal power was a vague hope of clerical circles but a serious worry of the authorities); then of socialists, internationalists and anarchists. The lurking dangers of social conflicts between large landowners and sharecroppers and, especially, the landless day labourers could always be seized on, according to the authorities, by the 'subversive' or 'anti-constitutionalist' parties, as they were invariably depicted, to increase their following. As in the other provinces – but with even lower points – the turnouts were pitiful: a little over 40% in the elections of 1861, 1865 and 1867; 28% in 1870; again 40% in 1874; and thereafter a rise to 53% in 1876 and 55% in 1880.[79] In the district of Imola, where most day labourers were concentrated, riots broke out regularly. The district was relatively small; it had only 7 municipalities but 89 parishes and hamlets (frazioni), a situation which according to one subprefect was certainly not 'favourable to communal life'.[80] The same prefect bemoaned the 'lack of political education one finds in these places, for which reason even the most legitimate matters are often discussed and commented in the strangest ways and in growing contradiction to the government's intentions'.[81] In public politicians were inclined to mitigate the political implications of the rural violence; the prefects and subprefects, on the other hand, pointed often in their confidential reports to the activities of 'sects' inciting the population. In 1871, when high officials still dared to stand up against politicians, Lucio Fiorentini, subprefect of Imola, denounced the standoffish attitude of many local deputies: 'By denying any political character to the many bloody crimes that have afflicted the cities of Romagna, they no doubt had some personal interest in mind, but this is no manner of enlightening parliament or country, nor of fulfilling the obligations which every representative of the nation should have towards his government'.[82] From the beginning the prefectural officials were very accurate in describing the various movements within the opposition. They carefully distinguished progressive liberals, democrats, republicans, internationalists and socialists, and the eventual attitudes of these groups towards the 'party of order'.

---

79 *Statistica elettorale politica* (1880), 29.
80 ASB, Pref., Gab. (1884), cat. IX, regular report on public affairs in the subprefecture of Imola in the second semester of 1881, 5 January 1882.
81 *Ibidem*, regular report on the public affairs in Imola in the second semester of 1882, 2 January 1883.
82 *Ibidem*, (1871), b. 188, f. 15, report of the subprefect of Imola to the prefect, 2 July 1871.

The prefects of Bologna relied heavily on their heads of police for information on pamphlets, journals and gatherings of the anti-liberal parties. The heads of police of large cities were usually promising officials, who could attain high offices as civil employees as well (e.g. Giovanni Bolis, *questore* of Bologna, at the end of the 1860s, became director-general of public order at the Interior); the prefects frequently forwarded, without significant alterations but under their own name, the police reports to the Ministry. Thus the prefecture, helped by its own peripheral channels and the police, became a centre of information on the various political movements in the province. This task, though part of the work of all prefects, was particularly time-consuming in Bologna, where the politically active groups were so varied.[83] The subprefect of Imola once remarked that his direct superior ought to pay special attention to administration, when ministers and deputies left him a moment of peace: 'It is a universally felt desire that you profit from the parliamentary holidays rapidly to take all those measures that are needed to restore the credit and give a more solid basis to the administration'.[84]

The popular support for the anti-liberal movements, particularly the clerical party, was often ascribed to the backwardness of the countryside. Support for the clericals was strongest in the isolated district of Vergato. The municipalities lay scattered over the mountains (even the parishes within municipal boundaries could lie wide apart); they were often difficult to get to in winter, and had few resources to rise autonomously from their underdevelopment. The moral conditions of the mountain population, as the subprefects used to write, were low. Of about 100 parish priests only 5 or 6, Vannetti noted, were trustworthy, 'the others being interested parties, ignoramuses, guzzlers and fornicators'.[85] Such imputations, of course, did not help to improve the relationship between Church and state.

In 1876 the catholic campaign, though somewhat overshadowed by the political changes on the national scene, was getting into its stride. The *Sinistra*, once in power, was quite worried by the possibility of catholic participation in the parliamentary elections (much of Nicotera's involvement in the organization of the elections had its origins in this state of preoccupation). Nevertheless, following Cavour's adage of a free Church in a free state, the Ministry of the Interior, through its secretary-general Lacava, warned the prefect of Bologna not to offend the independence of the Church. Any abuse of its religious power, however, was to be denounced: 'If people notoriously averse to the current political organization of the state try to obstruct and discredit the free unfolding of that will, you should do all you can, as long as it is legitimate, to prevent them from achieving their goal'. Hence, the prefect had to make sure that on the electoral rolls only those who were unquestionably entitled to

83   G.M. Maestri, 'Bologna tra clericalismo e radicalismo: una politica di "notabili"', in: *All'origine della 'forma partito' contemporanea. Emilia Romagna 1876-1892: un caso di studio*, edited by P. Pombeni (Bologna, 1984), 181-208.
84   ASB, Pref., Gab. (1867), b. 139, report of the subprefect of Imola to the prefect, 4 August 1867.
85   *Ibidem*, report of the subprefect of Vergato to the prefect, 2 August 1867.

vote were registered, and others who could 'effectively neutralize the actions and influence of the clericals' were not crossed off.[86] But apart from these measures the authorities could do little to obstruct the clerical organizations, which officially did not have political objectives.

Conversely the 'red' opposition met with severe repression. Their associations were regularly dissolved; their newspapers and pamphlets closely examined for inflammatory language; and their leaders screened, frequently arrested and put to jail. The widening of the franchise in 1882 constituted an unprecedented opportunity for the republicans and socialists to expand their presence on the national level. The following of Andrea Costa brought him close to a seat for Bologna II. In the city of Imola he received more votes than the influential moderate liberal Codronchi but he failed to split the paternalistic bonds in the countryside (Costa was however elected for the constituency of Ravenna).[87] The socialist associations, despite stern police surveillance, had established themselves firmly in Romagna around 1880.[88] The district of Imola, with its sharp difference between the moderate block of large landowners on the one hand and impoverished sharecroppers and artisans on the other, was one of the strongholds of the rising socialists, who gradually outnumbered the republicans. The subprefect was almost daily in touch with the prefect in Bologna to report on the movements of the opposition, which was much more tightly organized than the loose associations of the moderate liberals (and therefore more easily controllable). After the partial success in the parliamentary elections of 1882 the republican and socialist forces directed their strategy towards 'infiltration' of the local administrations, forcing a break-through after the widening of the franchise for local elections in 1889 (see chapters 3 and 4).

Although the liberal hegemony lasted for some time after 1882, the prefects of Bologna were increasingly involved in policing the various manifestations of the 'extremist' parties, as the catholic and socialist groupings continued to be called. The liberal ruling class was extremely scandalized by their demands, and did not tolerate that those who contested its rule should use the freedom existing in 'its' state to propagate subversive ideas. Some prefects were so impregnated with this bourgeois indignation that their work was seriously affected by it. Giovanni Mussi, ex-deputy and prefect of Bologna from 1880 to 1882 (before his transfer to Venice), followed the activities of the 'extralegal' parties with great suspicion. He tended to interpret the right of association and assembly – one of the most important achievements of the liberals – according to his own ethical standards: 'I must confess that I think that liberty granted to someone who does not accept our institutions not only offends the moral sense of the people, but also increases the audacity and proselytism of the

---

86 *Ibidem*, (1877), b. 290, letter of the Ministry of the Interior to the prefect, 25 April 1876.

87 R. Scaldaferri, 'L'organizzazione elettorale di Andrea Costa nel 2° collegio di Bologna nel 1882', *Rivista di Storia Contemporanea*, 12 (1983), 91-107.

88 R. Scaldaferri, 'Un laboratorio del socialismo italiano: il caso di Imola', in: *All'origine della 'forma partito' contemporanea*, 209-252.

illegal parties'.[89] Catholics and socialists, using their growing influence in local government and mobilizing their grass roots networks, were each in their own way very inventive in getting their supporters registered as voters, even if this meant that they had to take recourse to illegal methods. A reaction of the controlling authorities was bound to come: on the one hand, by supervising more thoroughly the revision of the rolls; on the other, by trying to register potentially liberal voters.

The politicization of Emilia-Romagna beyond the limits set by the liberal ruling class was a great worry to the various governments of the last decades of the century. Particularly Crispi, who won the consensus of the Bolognese liberals after the death of Depretis, left his mark on the political repression. The socialist successes in the administrative elections of 1889 clearly influenced the strategy laid out at the central level for the political elections of 1890. The maintenance of public order was often used as a disguised measure to curtail the activities of the opposition. The general revision of the electoral rolls in 1894-95 hit the socialist following more than others. Whereas Scelsi could somewhat restrain Crispi from acting too impulsively (as in the case of the nomination of a mayor in Imola in 1889) during his first cabinet, Giovanni Giura (prefect from 1894 to 1897) obediently followed the line of the Sicilian prime minister. In order to support the liberal candidate, the army general Mirri, against Costa in the constituency of Budrio (during four ballots in 1895) Giura called on the electoral committees, state officials and communal secretaries not to abstain and to vote for the liberal candidate. In the last ballot, however, Mirri's supporters did not show up and the seat went to Costa.[90]

5 CONCLUSION

Politics, meaning governmental and parliamentary interests, played a major part in the life of the prefect. But it was certainly not as predominant as many would have liked it to have been. The prefect, as the law said, was the representative of the executive power in his province, responsible to the entire cabinet for the execution of his duties but to the minister of the Interior alone for his career and most confidential orders. The ministry of the Interior, holding the virtual monopoly of centre-periphery relations, thus had an 'immense power, of which the enticements were irresistable'.[91] Hence politics undoubtedly permeated the offices of the prefecture. The basic problem to be thrashed out, however, is that of the extent to which politics can be separated from administration. I have tried to define administrative modernization broadly, so that it encompasses the prefect's political tasks. This not only entailed a scrutiny of the executive chain between Ministry and prefecture, but also required an

89 ASB, Pref., Gab. (1884), cat. IX, report on public affairs in the first semester of 1881, 1 July 1881.
90 *Ibidem*, (1895), cat. 5, various letters.
91 S. Spaventa, 'Giustizia nell'amministrazione', in: Idem. *La politica della Destra. Scritti e discorsi raccolti da B. Croce* (Bari, 1910), 94.

assessment of the relations of these two organs with society. Here the focus has been on parliamentary elections, pivot of the representative system. Were the prefect's activities related to the organization of elections merely intended to reinforce the government of the day, or did his job involve more than this auxiliary function?

The Italian political system as it evolved from the Risorgimento cannot be exclusively analyzed in terms of limited representativeness and oligarchical objectives of the ruling class. The debates on electoral reform culminating in the law of 1882 demonstrate that wealth and capacity – the main criteria of the suffrage – were regarded as means to expand the electorate, not to close its ranks. The drawing up of the electoral rolls can be seen in this perspective too. Given the yearly fluctuations in the number of registered voters (which cannot be explained by population growth or economic developments alone), the restricted franchise had considerable latitude leaving room for mobilization from above and from below. The prefects were the obvious persons to make use of the margins left by the law. This brought them in a rather ambiguous position. On the one hand, they sought to ascertain that all those entitled to vote were really registered on the rolls; on the other, they were often urged to be on the look-out for reliable (i.e. pro-government) voters, to be found among military personnel and the civil service.

Not only was there no identification between the groups of registered voters and citizens entitled to vote, which left room for the mobilization of specific groups, but there was also a gap between the number of registered voters and the actual voters at the polls: on average only 50% showed up. Here again lay a task for the prefects. They made repeated attempts to mobilize the electorate. In close contact with the social and administrative elite of their provinces they seized every opportunity to propagate the right to vote as a truly liberal duty.

The initiatives intended to increase participation were not always as virtuous as they appear. The emphasis on the free vote and other merits of liberalism could easily lapse into propaganda for the government progamme. Calls for high turnouts were often secretly accompanied by pressure on subordinate employees to support the 'government party'. These tactics were particularly used on occasions that opposition candidates threatened to gain the upper hand. In the absence of a liberal party-apparatus the ministers turned to their peripheral representatives as publicity agents for their own interests.

Prefectural mobilization campaigns sometimes had the direct aim of frustrating opposition movements, which were just as keen on registering their supporters as the government. The defenders of the liberal *raison d'Etat*, however, could not abide parties that were considered dangerous to the Constitution. Hence the associations, meetings and periodicals of catholics, republicans and socialists were followed with suspicion. In their regular reports on public affairs the prefects used to pay disproportionate attention to these activities. In the province of Bologna especially the opposition movements enjoyed considerable appeal: clericals prevailed in Vergato, radical democrats and republicans had important foremen in the city of Bologna, and socialists gradually gained ground in Imola. Although the parliamentary seats used to go to the liberals, the prefects paid much attention to the screening of 'subversive' actions of different persuasion. Likewise, the prefects of Venice showed great worry over the strength of the clericals. Through the ramified parish organization they had a strong hold on the countryside. In Reggio Calabria, despite higher turnouts, the lack of interest in national politics was seen as the main obstacle to the unfolding of the parliamentary system as the liberals had devised it. Supported by ancient family bonds and clienteles, the same deputies reigned for decades in their constituencies. In these cases the prefects could do little more than adapt themselves to the circumstances, trying not to get entangled in situations that they could not control.

In all three provinces the main task of the prefects, when elections came near, was to make sure that the law was implemented. This was not as obvious as it seems. The municipalities were extremely lax in carrying out the administrative requirements connected with the electoral operations. As for many other aspects of prefectural control the prefect's task was predominantly corrective. First, the revision of the electoral rolls left much to be desired, which necessitated special measures such as the dispatch of a prefectural commissioner. Then there was a sequence of administrative acts to be performed: the announcement of the elections, the layout of the polling stations, and the organization of the ballot itself (the composition of the presidency of the electoral office, etc), which had to be checked through the minutes sent to the prefecture. Finally, the prefects had to keep the police forces on standby in order to avoid disturbances before, during and after the elections.

Centrally led electoral campaigns, involving the prefects in supporting governmental candidates, were mounted from the first elections of the unitary state (and before in the Kingdom of Sardinia). The susceptibility of the prefects to influences from above differed from case to case. Their involvement, on their own initiative or on that of others, was not clearly separable from the construction of the parliamentary system. To install the system was a herculean task. The largest part of Italy did not have any parliamentary experience. The horizon of the elites did not reach much further than local interests. Whereas the deputies remained committed to their local backgrounds, the prefects saw themselves as the true representatives of national interests. Gradually, however, the relationship between politics and administration changed. To put it simply, administration was superseded by politics. To some extent this was a logical consequence of the maturing of the political system, though not along the lines of liberal hopes. The rise of opposition movements together with the tactics stemming from the 'transformism' of Depretis rendered the prefect more and more an instrument of the government's particular interests. Simultaneously, as we have found in earlier chapters, the prefects tended to lose their function of privileged link between centre and periphery. Deputies and local interest groups found their own channels through to the corridors of Rome, putting the prefects on the sidelines.

Conclusion

In 1894 the ex-prefect of Venice Pietro Manfrin critically looked at the development of Italian public administration. He even went as far as to prefer the Napoleonic organization, which he otherwise considered unsuited for liberal governments, compared to the situation of his own days: 'The Napoleonic institutions, come down to us through the first Italian Kingdom, had a subtle coordination, which reveals the sharp mind of their initiator. (...) Only shrewd writers and wise statesmen noted the intricate coordination which actually constituted the strength of the Napoleonic institutions; empiricists did not see beyond a despot who was in command and the people who obeyed'. It is interesting to see that a man who knew the Interior administration intimately looked back to Napoleonic rule with so much admiration. He saw in the dispersion of state services the main impediment to the proper functioning of the prefect, the fulcrum of the administrative system. Each ministry preferred to act through its own channels in the periphery rather than through the sole intermediary of the prefecture. This not only often led to contradictory orders but also threw the people into such confusion that they took refuge with political representatives – an even greater evil, according to Manfrin.[1]

These allegations were among the more nuanced expressions of criticism levelled at the public administration in the 1890s. They were part and parcel of the general feeling of crisis about the workings of the political and administrative system. The *fin de siècle* crisis deeply marked the prefectural corps, which within a couple of years was transformed from a prestigious administrative elite, rooted in the very heart of the Risorgimento tradition, into the repository of rival political groups.[2] At the same time, public administration definitively broke away from its nineteenth-century dimensions. Towards the turn of the century and in particular during Giolitti's rule the development of social legislation burdened administration with many new functions, putting the existing organization under great pressure and demanding greater professionalism. The growing incidence of 'technicalities' in public administration went hand in hand with a more independent, albeit clearly subordinate

---

1 P. Manfrin, *Dell'arbitrio amministrativo in Italia. Memoria* (Rome, 1894), 35-37 (the citation is from p. 35).

2 The tempestuous career of Angelo Annaratone, prefect of, among other provinces, Bari, Livorno, Florence and Rome, was characteristic of this period of frantic political conflicts, see V.G. Pacifici, *Angelo Annaratone (1844-1922). La condizione dei prefetti nell'Italia liberale* (Rome, 1990).

position in relation to politics.[3] To a certain extent this new phase in administration had already been called into existence by Crispi's reforms in the years 1889-1891 (although these did not immediately lead to an increase in administrative personnel).[4] With Orlando administrative law extricated itself from other branches of law, thus giving way to a more specific legal culture of administration. The state was rigidly defined as a public juridical person. This notion reduced the organization and activities of the executive to mere juridical phenomena, thereby excluding private law and extra-legal interests from interfering with public administration.[5]

Within the realm of local administration the municipalization act of 1903, placing certain public services under the direct control of the communes, represented the temporary settlement of the debate on local autonomy. The reform had been preceded by a reconsideration of the commune's place in the polity. Many theorists became aware that the commune was more suitable than the state for fulfilling certain social needs.[6] The trend towards more decentralization also found expression in special laws for the *Mezzogiorno* and other underdeveloped areas (Sicily 1896, Naples and Basilicata 1904, Sardinia 1907), creating regional commissariats with attendant powers. Concomitantly, the system of control was tightened up. For example, an act of municipalization required approval from the Corps of Civil Engineers, the *Giunta Provinciale Amministrativa* and a royal commission. Despite the growing bureaucratic control the prefecture increasingly lost its position as sole reference point in the province. Again, Crispi's laws of 1889-1891 constituted a decisive moment in this development. The *Giunte Provinciali Amministrative* were created to keep a closer watch on the various local administrations; within the field of public health a new directorate at the ministerial level was put in command of a network of provincial doctors; the establishment of the Ministry of Postal and Telegraph Services generated another network parallel to that of the Interior administration. In general, the distance between centre and periphery began to shorten through a more complex state bureaucracy, but the prefects were gradually removed from the core of centre-periphery relations.

The developments, both in public administration as a whole and in local administration, had profound consequences for the position of the prefect. Clearly, in comparison with other administrative bodies and officials, his office was robbed of a large part of its strength; he enjoyed less freedom of action, and was more defenceless

---

3 The emergence of a more 'technical' administration has been amply analyzed by G. Melis, 'Amministrazione e mediazione degli interessi: le origini delle amministrazioni parallele', in: *L'amministrazione nella storia moderna* (Archivio ISAP, n.s. 3, Milan, 1985), II, 1429-1511; Id., *Due modelli di amministrazione tra liberalismo e fascismo. Burocrazie tradizionali e nuovi apparati* (Rome, 1988).

4 S. Cassese & G. Melis,'Lo sviluppo dell'amministrazione italiana', *RTDP* 40 (1990), 333-357.

5 G. Rebuffa, 'Trasformazione delle funzioni dell'amministrazione e cultura dei giuristi', in: *L'amministrazione nella storia moderna*, II, 1101-1170.

6 F. Rugge, 'Alla periferia del Rechtsstaat. Autonomia e municipalizzazione nell'Italia di inizio secolo', *Quaderni Sardi di Storia* (1983-84), n. 4, 159-178; Id., 'Trasformazioni delle funzioni dell'amministrazione e cultura della municipalizzazione', in: *L'amministrazione nella storia moderna*, II, 1233-1288.

against political interference. The main body of this study, however, deals with the period prior to the one characterized by the erosion of the prefect's job. In the first decades of Unification the government was primarily concerned with legitimizing itself and creating a consensus large enough to guarantee the development of the national liberal state. In this process of nation-building the prefects stood in the front line and identified themselves fully with the project of administrative modernization. If they had a collective ideology, it was certainly that of moulding local administration to their own image and likeness. In this light it was not surprising that Giuseppe Sensales (1831-1902), a powerful prefect who has not made his appearance in the preceding chapters, bequeathed a sum of 1,200,000 lire to a new literary foundation and to 'poor students' in the provinces where he had been prefect: Catanzaro, Ascoli, Agrigento, Messina, Pisa, Ravenna and Palermo.[7]

Several aspects from within the wide array of their tasks have been passed in review. Seemingly the least problematic of the prefect's duties was the legal control of acts performed by lower administrations. However what had been devised as mere formal control turned into a massive interference into the workings of local government, simply because many municipalities were mostly indifferent towards the powers conferred upon them. Thus, instead of merely verifying whether the deliberations of the communal councils complied with legal prescripts, the prefects were perforce more concerned with getting the municipalities to make the deliberations, whatever their contents. The majority of smaller municipalities found great difficulty in drawing up the elementary requirements of good administration: electoral rolls, budgets and final statements, police regulations, etc. Financial management in particular proved to be a real struggle for many local administrators. Lack of skill and responsibility drove the municipalities into the arms of the prefecture, which was hardly equipped to take over such an essential part of communal administration.

The prefect's discretion seems almost absolute in the appointment of mayors (although, of course, the nomination as such had to receive royal assent). In practice, however, the limited availability of suitable candidates left the prefects, who were responsible for the final proposal, with little to go on. To nominate a mayor against the will of the communal council was ill-advised, since the council could employ several tricks to obstruct the exercise of the mayor's duties, and thereby derail municipal administration. Local politics were a hotbed of family and faction strife, which required all the prefect's tact. His primary objective was pacification rather than overt support for a particular group. Mediation and arbitration were his key activitities.

The subject that has attracted most historiographical attention is the prefect's involvement in parliamentary elections. By placing the prefect's role against the background

---

7 *Corriere della Sera*, 1-3 June 1902. Apparently, his testament caused quite a stir; it was mentioned in *La Nazione*, 1-2 June 1902, in the *Rivista della Beneficenza Pubblica*, 30 (1902), 495-497, and no doubt in other journals.

of the difficult birth of the representative system in Italy, I have tried to argue that his primary concern was the mobilization of the voters, to begin with by urging them to register on the electoral rolls and subsequently by persuading them to use their electoral right. With the gradual democratization, or at least increasingly unlimited 'electoralization' of politics the central political elite began to use the prefects as protectors of narrowly defined government interests.[8] But in order to rate their activities at their true value it is necessary to take the circumstances in the constituencies into account.

The administrative instruments at his disposal to control and guide the municipalities were doubtless inadequate for difficult cases – and these were legion in the first decades after Unification. Circulars did not cut much ice; general inspections of the province were rare; prefectural commissioners brought only provisional relief; and dissolution of the communal council, the most drastic measure, often proved to be equally unavailing, if it had to be ordered more than once within a short period. There were, furthermore, several structural obstacles to the project of administrative modernization. First, the economic crisis that characterized a large part of our period turned the system of local finance upside down. The bulk of the smaller municipalities, largely dependent on the strained agricultural sector, could hardly bear the obligatory expenditure. It was unthinkable that they could profit from the freedom to spend, tax and incur debts as they wished.

Second, centralized administrative organization could only bear fruit if the local elites, to whom the restricted franchise gave unrivalled power, lent their support. One of the prefect's most important tasks, therefore, was to further a consensus for the main goals of the government. This entailed not only passing on orders, but also listening to the demands of society and, possibly, defending them at the central level. Although many prefects dedicated themselves zealously to this task and set themselves up as mediators for the benefit of the administered, they often clashed with unwilling exponents of authoritarian and paternalistic traditions, who refused to give up their old privileged position in the local power network. As Carlo Alfieri put it in 1867 (but his observations remained valid for years to come): 'The Interior administration, the heart of the nation, is still that of the old regimes, since unfortunately blatant ignorance and poor civil and political education linger on among the people (relatively equally among all classes, since with us, beneath very small buds of liberalism taken over from foreign legislation, the mentality and the customs of despotic, so-called paternal regimes continue to exist)'.[9] Equally, emerging middle classes, such as those who obtained possession of the demesnes and church lands in Calabria, could thwart the prefect's pursuit of pacification. Precisely the freedom of action granted to local elites who, for many reasons, were unable to cooperate in the

---

8 I have borrowed the term from E.J. Hobsbawm, *Nations and Nationalism since 1780. Programme, Myth, Reality* (Cambridge, 1990), 83.

9 C. Alfieri, *La dottrina liberale nella quistione amministrativa* (Florence, 1867), 24.

communal council turned out to be a tenacious impediment to the successful implementation of the administrative project. The continuity of notable power from the preunitary era right into the liberal period is a subject that requires further study, especially in terms of the possibilities the state administration possessed to tighten its grip on local life. We know too little of the workings of administration in the years between 1815 and 1860 to measure the weight of tradional power relations at the local level. It is safe to say that the all-embracing administrative project set in motion by the Napoleonic conquest and partly continued by the Restoration regimes had not yet reached full maturity at the moment of Unification. Hence in many parts of Italy the administrative revolution to be carried out by the prefects entailed a major change in social relations – a task that lay beyond the reach of one generation.

Third, after the massive initiatives of the first generation of prefects the continuation of their work was considerably compromised by the lack of professional preparation of the lower ranks of the prefectural, provincial and municipal administrations. The examinations were, at all levels, utterly insufficient, and there were no attempts to establish, as in France, a special school for the higher education of public officials.[10] The prefects thus remained isolated, and their actions were bound to die away in the ignorance of the executive chain subordinate to them. In the long run, through the logic of hierarchy, this deficiency even reached the level of the highest officials. The communal and provincial legislation of the unitary state, designed to bring about uniformity in administration, was in reality incapable of fulfilling the intention of its makers. Admittedly, the procedures were all equal, all municipalities great and small had the same organization and were subject to the same controlling authorities; but that did not alter the fact that there were plenty of regional differences: in social and economic conditions, in administrative traditions, and consequently in the ways in which the prefects dealt with the problems they were faced with in day-to-day administration. This study has only taken into account three provinces, and a lot of material may emerge from research in other areas. This is not the place to go deeper into the obvious different levels of development in Venice, Bologna and Reggio Calabria. To a certain extent, the initial difficulties were surprisingly similar. In all three provinces the first prefects were much concerned with the overthrow of traditional notable power, trying to replace it with the alleged benefits of the representative system. Yet everywhere the dialogue between the old and the new was conflict-ridden, and certainly did not come to an end with the total victory of the latter. Problems connected with land use and landownership, often going back to preunitary times, were fetters on the unfolding of good administration: the old fishing and grazing rights of peasants and fishermen in Chioggia, the *partecipanza* of Medicina and the question of the demesnes in Calabria kept the prefects busy for decades. After the first hectic days of Unification were over, the different practices

---

10 E. Gustapane, 'L'introduzione nell'ordinamento amministrativo italiano del principio del merito per l'accesso agli impieghi pubblici: il caso del Ministero dell'interno', *RTDP* 37 (1987), 449-466.

of administration in the various provinces came to light. A glance at the various *Bollettini della prefettura* suffices to note the differences in administrative culture. In the second half of the 1860s the bulletins of Venice, Bologna and Reggio Calabria were all filled with basic instructions for regular administration. Whereas these instructions soon tended to become obsolete in Venice and Bologna, they continued to be issued on a regular basis in Reggio. In the South the educational part of the prefect's job was more prominent, and clearly left its mark on those prefects who devoted themselves entirely to the liberal project. Their attempts to win over the elites and to penetrate society necessarily generated more discontent than in other parts of Italy where the state could entrust representative bodies with the further development of public administration. Differences in political organization at the local level left a clear mark on the prefect's actions and on the way these were judged by contemporaries. The strength of the bonds between deputies and their clienteles in Calabria often rendered the prefect's intervention fruitless. This practical powerlessness contrasted sharply with the criticism levelled by political commentators. Paradoxically, control seems to have been greater and more efficient in Bologna and Venice (at least until the 1890s) in holding the so-called subversive parties in check.

The comparisons do not have to remain restricted to various regions in Italy. Napoleon's attempt to integrate and modernize Europe – the starting point of our analysis – had lasting effects in many countries. The administrative systems of most European states were modelled on the Napoleonic organization. It would, therefore, be highly interesting to compare the mechanisms of administrative modernization, and to see how the dialectics between state and society worked out from country to country. The activities of state officials in the periphery, such as the Italian and French prefects, the German *Landräte*, the Belgian governors and the Dutch commissioners of the King, who were perhaps the most privileged links between state and society, offer good opportunities to study the interaction. In the Netherlands, for example, the tradition of unity, the gradually increasing identification between dynasty and people, the correspondence of interests between local elites and the state engendered far less resistance to centralized administration than in Italy. The Dutch communal and provincial laws, promulgated in 1850-51, were inspired by the Belgian example of 1836, which in its turn had greatly influenced the Piedmontese and, later, Italian legislation. The administrative practices, however, were strikingly different. It is not unusual to find Italian supporters of decentralization praising local administration in the Low Countries, whereas the principles were just the same. Such comparisons of theory and practice may also serve to dispel certain examples of historical short-sightedness or common misunderstandings, such as those related to the sources of inspiration of Thorbecke, the author of the Dutch Constitution and communal and provincial laws. Clearly, his thinking on the polity was not only influenced by the German Historical Law School, as Dutch historiography never fails to mention, but has to be seen against the wider background of administrative modernization in post-Napoleonic Europe.

The comparative approach in administrative history I propose here does not start from the administrative structure as such (though the similarities between most European countries are striking). It rather seeks to single out the significance of the interaction between administration and society in each country. It deals with checks and balances imposed by societal forces on state intervention. Towards the end of the nineteenth century administrative action was of course less concerned with such problems as the foundation of a representative system, the basics of financial responsibility and the conditions of efficient self-government – aspects of general administration that have been amply discussed in this book. By then, the most pressing challenge facing public administration in a large part of Europe was how to control industrializing society.

Bibliography

Only archival sources and literature cited in the text, and some general works on the subject have been included. For the primary sources I have given only the years consulted, whenever this was appropriate.

UNPUBLISHED PRIMARY SOURCES

Archivio Centrale dello Stato
Ministero dell'Interno
- Gabinetto, Circolari (1863, 1865-66, 1868-1895)
- Gabinetto, Rapporti dei prefetti (1882-1894)
- Divisione prima, Archivio generale, Affari generali (1852-1905)
- Direzione generale degli affari generali e del personale, Divisione del personale, Fascicoli personali
- Direzione generale degli affari generali e del personale, Atti amministrativi
- Direzione generale dell'amministrazione civile, Divisione per le amministrazioni comunali e provinciali, Comuni (1868-1904)
Carte Francesco Crispi, Roma
Carte Bettino Ricasoli, Fondo Bastogi

Archivio di Stato di Bologna
Intendenza Generale
- Archivio riservato (1859-1862)
Prefettura
- Gabinetto (1860-1895)
- Atti generali (1861-1866)
- Archivio generale: Serie 1ª, Affari generali; Serie 2ª, Affari speciali dei comuni, della provincia, delle opere pie (1867-1895)
- Sottoprefettura di Vergato (1860-1890)

Archivio di Stato di Reggio Calabria
Prefettura
- Gabinetto (1860-1895)
- Archivio generale: Serie 1ª, Affari generali (1860-1895)
Deposito Plutino

Archivio di Stato di Venezia
Prefettura
– Gabinetto (1866-1887)
– Archivio generale (1866-1893)
Biblioteca legislativa, Dono Bonafini

Istituto per la Storia del Risorgimento, Rome
Manoscritti, n. 1093, Memorie autobiografiche di Luigi Torelli

Ministero dell'Interno, Rome
Matricole del personale

PUBLISHED PRIMARY SOURCES

Official documents
Atti parlamentari. Camera dei Deputati. Senato (1848-1900)
Atti del Consiglio Comunale di Venezia (1866-1890)
Atti del Consiglio Provinciale di Reggio Calabria (Calabria Ulteriore Prima) (1861-1890)
Atti del Consiglio Provinciale di Venezia (1867-1890)
Commissione pel riordinamento tribunario dei comuni e delle provincie (sen. Diodato Pallieri presidente), *Progetto di legge sulle tasse dirette comunali e sulle quote di concorso a favore delle provincie*, 2nd ed. (Rome, 1876)
Gazzetta Ufficiale del Regno d'Italia (1870-1875)
MAIC, Direzione di Statistica, *Debiti comunali e provinciali al 31 dicembre 1877* (Rome, 1879)
MAIC, Direzione di Statistica, *Statistica elettorale politica. Elezioni generali politiche, 16-23 maggio 1880* (Rome, 1880)
MAIC, Direzione Generale della Statistica, *Bilanci comunali. Anni XVIII e XIX, 1880 e 1881* (Rome, 1882)
MAIC, Direzione Generale della Statistica, *Bilanci comunali per l'anno 1886* (Rome, 1888)
MAIC, Direzione Generale della Statistica, *Bilanci comunali per l'anno 1891* (Rome, 1892)
MAIC, Direzione Generale della Statistica, *Bilanci comunali, tariffe daziarie dei comuni chiusi, situazioni patrimoniali dei comuni e debiti comunali e provinciali per l'anno 1895* (Rome, 1896)
MAIC, Direzione Generale della Statistica, *Statistica dei debiti comunali al 1° gennaio 1879* (Rome, 1880)
MAIC, Direzione Generale della Statistica, *Statistica dei debiti comunali e provinciali per mutui al 31 dicembre dell'anno 1885* (Rome, 1888)
MAIC, Direzione Generale della Statistica, *Statistica elettorale amministrativa. Composizione del corpo elettorale amministrativo secondo le liste definitivamente approvate per*

l'anno 1887 e numero dei votanti nelle elezioni comunali avvenute nello stesso anno (Rome, 1888)

MAIC, Direzione Generale della Statistica, *Statistica delle tasse comunali applicate negli anni 1881-84* (Rome, 1886)

MAIC, Divisione di Statistica, *Bilanci comunali 1875-76* (Rome, 1877)

Ministero dei Lavori Pubblici, Direzione Generale dei Servizi Speciali, *Le opere pubbliche in Calabria. Prima relazione sull'applicazione delle leggi speciali dal 30 giugno 1906 al 30 giugno 1913* (Bergamo, 1913)

Statistica degli elettori amministrativi e degli elettori politici secondo le liste definitivamente approvate per l'anno 1883 (Rome, 1885)

Statistica del Regno. Amministrazione pubblica. Bilanci comunali (anno 1866). Bilanci provinciali (anni 1866-67-68) (Florence, 1868)

Statistica del Regno d'Italia. Amministrazione pubblica. Bilanci comunali. Anni 1871 e 1872 (Rome, 1874)

Statistica del Regno d'Italia. Elezioni politiche e amministrative. Anni 1865-66 (Florence, 1867)

Periodicals

Bollettino della Prefettura di Bologna (1866-1876); thereafter *Foglio Periodico della R. Prefettura di Bologna. Bollettino* (1877-1892)

Bollettino della Prefettura di Reggio Calabria (Calabria Ulteriore Prima) (1867-1896)

Bollettino Ufficiale della Prefettura di Venezia (1866-1876); thereafter *Foglio Periodico della Prefettura di Venezia* (1877-1896)

Calendario Generale del Regno (1861-1895)

Manuale (Il) degli amministratori comunali, provinciali e delle opere pie (1862-1900)

Rivista Amministrativa del Regno (1850-1895)

Contemporary monographs and articles

Accame, F., *Del diritto comunale*, 2nd ed. (Genoa, 1853)

Acossato, S., *Manuale dell'elettore amministrativo* (Turin, 1889)

Alasia, G., *Lettere sul decentramento* (Florence, 1871)

Alessio, G., *Saggio sul sistema tributario italiano e i suoi effetti economici e sociali*, 2 vols (Turin, 1883-87)

Alfieri, C., *La dottrina liberale nella quistione amministrativa* (Florence, 1867)

Arabia, T. & M. Adorni, *La legge comunale e provinciale del Regno d'Italia commentata* (Florence, 1865)

Astengo, C., *Relazione del regio delegato straordinario al consiglio comunale di Venezia, letta nella seduta d'insediamento del 21 febbraio 1883* (Venice, 1883)

Bardari, D., *Sull'ordinamento finanziario dei comuni in Italia. Lettere scritte all'Avv. Giorgio Curcio* (Siracuse, 1869)

Baschirotto, A., *Vademecum per l'elettore amministrativo* (Padua, 1875)

Béchard, F., *Essai sur la centralisation administrative*, 2 vols (Paris/Marseille, 1836-37)

Beltrami, C., *La nuova guida per gli uffizi comunali*, 2 vols (Turin, 1871-73)

Block, M., *Dictionnaire de l'administration française*, 3ʳᵈ edition (Paris, 1862)

Boggio, P.C. & A. Caucino, *Legge provinciale e comunale. Commento* (Turin, 1860)

Bolla, G., *Relazione letta dal cav. avv. G.B. R. Delegato straordinario per il Municipio di Bologna nell'atto che il giorno 7 novembre 1868 insediava il nuovo consiglio comunale*, Bologna, n.d.

Bonnin, J.Ch., *Principii di amministrazione pubblica*, Italian translation of the third French edition, edited by A. De Crescenzi & M. Saffioti, (Naples, 1824)

Bonomi, I., *La finanza locale e i suoi problemi* (Palermo, 1903)

Brunialti, A., *Legge elettorale politica* (Turin, 1882)

Capitani, G., entry 'Scioglimento del consiglio comunale e del consiglio provinciale', in: *Digesto Italiano*, XXI, parte 1ª (Turin, 1891), 804-807

Caramelli, G., *Elettorato ed eleggibilità amministrativa e governo locale: osservazioni pratiche* (Bologna, 1887)

Carassai, C., *Il sistema tributario dei comuni e delle provincie: studio* (Pollenza, 1893)

Caruso, V., *Manualetto teorico pratico per le verifiche delle casse comunali* (Potenza, 1880)

Cavour, Camillo. Tutti gli scritti di, edited by P. Pischedda e G. Talamo, 4 vols (Turin, 1976-78)

Ceccato, M., *Sulle spese obbligatorie e facoltative delle provincie e dei comuni. Note agli art. 2, 3, 4 della legge 14 giugno 1874* (Rome, 1883)

Cereseto, G.B., *Il comune nel diritto tributario. Commento alle leggi sulle imposte comunali con un'appendice sulle imposte provinciali*, 3 vols (Turin, 1885-1891)

Civardi, A., *Manuale dell'elettore amministrativo* (Chiavari, 1883)

Colajanni, N., *Le istituzioni municipali. Cenni ed osservazioni* (Piazza Armerina, 1883)

Conigliani, C., *La riforma delle leggi sui tributi locali* (Modena, 1898)

Conti, V., *Il sindaco nel diritto amministrativo italiano. Studi di legislazione e di giurisprudenza* (Naples, 1875)

D'Ambrosio, G., 'Lo scioglimento dei consigli comunali e provinciali', *Il Filangieri*, 28 (1903), 566-597

Del Pozzo, N., *Scioglimento di promiscuità dei beni ex feudali ed ecclesiastici del Marchese Ramirez sig. Antonio* (Reggio Calabria, 1894)

De Sterlich, A., *Annotazioni alla legge sull'amministrazione comunale e provinciale del 20 marzo 1865* (Naples, 1865)

Dizionario di diritto amministrativo, edited by L. Vigna & V. Aliberti, 6 vols (Turin, 1840-1857)

Drago, R., *Lo scioglimento dei consigli comunali e i delegati straordinari* (Genoa, 1886)

Id., *Manuale dell'elettore amministrativo* (Genoa, 1889)

Ellena, V., 'Le finanze comunali', *Archivio di Statistica*, 2 (1878), fasc. 4, 5-42

Errera, A., *Le finanze dei grandi comuni. riforme ai prestiti e ai dazi di consumo in Italia* (Florence, 1882)

Falconcini, E., *Cinque mesi di prefettura in Sicilia* (Florence, 1863)

Foucart, E.V., *Eléments de droit public et adminstratif, ou exposition méthodique des principes du droit public positif, avec l'indication des lois à l'appui, suivis d'un appendice contenant le texte des principales lois de droit public*, 2 vols (Paris/Poitiers, 1834-35)

Franchetti, L., *Condizioni economiche e amministrative delle provincie napoletane. Appunti di viaggio. Diario del viaggio*, edited by A. Jannazzo (Rome, 1985)

Frezzini, L., 'Prefetto e sottoprefetto', in: *Digesto Italiano*, XIX, parte 1ª (Turin, 1909-1912), 308-367

Id., entry 'Sindaco', *Digesto Italiano*, XXI, parte 3ª, sezione 1ª (Turin, 1895-1902), 459-460

Gallone, P., *Il vademecum del contabile municipale contenente i precetti per la compilazione, revisione e approvazione dei bilanci e conti comunali...* (Turin, 1880)

Gérando, J.M. de, *Institutes du droit administratif français ou éléments du code administratif*, 4 vols (Paris, 1829-30)

Grassi, T., *Le finanze dei comuni. considerazioni e proposte di riforme* (Recanati, 1880)

Grizzuti, C., *Scioglimento dei consigli, secondo la nuova legge comunale e provinciale...* (Portici, 1890)

Guida amministrativa ossia commentario della legge comunale e provinciale del 20 marzo 1865..., edited by C. Astengo e.a., 3rd ed. (Milan, 1865)

Guida amministrativa ossia commento della legge comunale e provinciale (Testo unico 10 febbraio 1889)..., edited by C. Astengo e.a. (Rome, 1889)

Lacava, P., *La finanza locale in Italia* (Turin, 1896)

Laurin, F., *Relazione fatta al consiglio comunale di Venezia dal regio delegato straordinario nella seduta 10 dicembre 1868* (Venice, 1868)

Liberatore, P., *Instituzioni della legislazione amministrativa vigente nel Regno delle Due Sicilie dettate nel suo privato studio di diritto*, 4 vols (Naples, 1836-38)

Magliani, A., 'La questione finanziaria de' comuni', *Nuova Antologia*, 13 (1878), 2nd series, vol. 11, 291-320 and 485-525

Magni, E., *Gli ufficî elettorali amministrativi: guida teorico-pratica* (Venice, 1891)

Malgarini, A., 'Del modo di nominare il capo del comune secondo la legislazione comparata', *Archivio Giuridico*, 30 (1883), 347-412

Manfrin, P., *L'avvenire di Venezia. Studio* (Treviso, 1877)

Id., *Il comune e l'individuo in Italia. Studio* (Rome, 1879)

Id., *Dell'arbitrio amministrativo in Italia. Memoria* (Rome, 1894)

Manna, G., *Partizioni teoretiche del diritto amministrativo ossia introduzione alla scienza ed alle leggi dell'amministrazione pubblica*, 2nd ed. (Naples, 1860)

Marchi, T., 'Gli uffici locali dell'amministrazione generale dello Stato', in: *Primo trattato completo di diritto amministrativo italiano*, edited by V.E. Orlando, II (Milan, 1907), V-XII, 3-494

Merla, G., *Appunti e considerazioni sul riordinamento finanziario dei comuni e delle provincie* (Rome, 1896)

Messedaglia, A., *Della necessità di un insegnamento speciale politico-amministrativo e del suo ordinamento scientifico* (Milan, 1851)

Minghetti, M., *I partiti politici e l'ingerenza loro nella giustizia e nell'amministrazione* (1881), now in: Id. *Scritti politici*, edited by R. Gherardi (Rome, 1986)

Moerdes, 'Loi sur l'organisation et l'administration des communes dans le grand duché de Bade, en date du 31 décembre 1831', *Revue étrangère et française de législation et d'économie politique*, 2 (1835), 1-31

Monterumici, D., *Raccolta di alcune notizie statistiche sul cholera nella provincia di Venezia e nel distretto di Chioggia (invasioni 1855, 1867, 1873)* (Treviso, 1874)

Id., *Il distretto di Chioggia. Illustrazioni statistiche amministrative* (Treviso, 1874)

Morini, C., *Corruzione elettorale. Studio teorico pratico* (Milan, 1894)

Mosca, G., *Sulla teorica dei governi e sul governo parlamentare. Studi storici e sociali* (Palermo, 1884), now in: *Scritti politici di Gaetano Mosca*, vol. I, edited by G. Sola (Turin, 1982)

Pasquale, G.A., 'Relazione sullo stato fisico-economico-agrario della prima Calabria ulteriore', *Atti del R. Istituto d'Incoraggiamento alle scienze naturali di Napoli* (1863), tomo XI.

Nasalli Rocca, A., *I prefetti in Italia ... fino a jeri* (Città Di Castello, 1916)

Id., *Memorie di un prefetto*, edited by C. Trionfi (Rome, 1946)

Pasolini, G., *Memorie raccolte da suo figlio*, 2 vols (Rome, 1915)

Pintor-Mameli, G., *Giurisprudenza sulle elezioni amministrative* (Rome, 1875)

Plebano, A., *Storia della finanza italiana dalla costituzione del nuovo Regno alla fine del secolo XIX*, 3 vols (Turin, 1899-1902)

Quarta-Guidotti, L., *Lo scioglimento dei consigli comunali e le attribuzioni del r. commissario straordinario...* (Lecce, 1890)

Regnoli, O., *Dei diritti del comune di Medicina* (Genoa, 1862)

Relazione letta al consiglio comunale di Medicina dal Regio Delegato Straordinario Avv. Aldo Goretti (Medicina, 1886)

Relazione letta dal cav. Pietro Pavan delegato straordinario per l'amministrazione della città di Chioggia all'atto del insediamento del consiglio comunale 18 agosto 1879 (Venice, 1879)

Riberi, L. & F. Locatelli, *Manuale pratico d'amministrazione comunale e provinciale, ossia commentario della nuova legge comunale 20 marzo 1865* (Florence, 1865)

Ricasoli, Bettino. Carteggi di, edited by M. Nobili & S. Camerani (Rome, 1939-)

Ricca Salerno, G., 'Finanze locali', in: *Primo trattato completo di diritto amministrativo italiano*, edited by V.E. Orlando, IX (Milan, 1902), 687-899

Romano, A., *Il sindaco del comune italiano. Guida teorico-prattica preceduta da nozioni generali di pubblica amministrazione* (Naples, 1884)

Romano, S., entry 'Deputazione Provinciale', in: *Digesto Italiano*, IX, parte 2ª (Turin, 1898), 161-184

Rosati, F., *Manuale sull'elettorato amministrativo* (Ancona, 1873)

Sabbatini, P., *Della tutela amministrativa* (Modena, 1885)

Salandra, A., 'Il riordinamento delle finanze comunali', *Nuova Antologia*, 13 (1878), 2nd series, vol. 10, 345-364 and 654-687

Salvemini, G., *Il ministero della mala vita* (1910), now in: *Opere di Gaetano Salvemini*, IV, *Il Mezzogiorno e la democrazia italiana*, vol. 1 (Milan, 1966), 73-141

Santini, A., *Codice dei comuni e delle provincie...* (Rome, 1889)

Scibona, A., *La nuova legge comunale e provinciale del Regno d'Italia...* (Turin, 1865)

Sullo scioglimento delle partecipanze. Memoria del municipio di Medicina ai ministri di Grazia e Giustizia e dell'Interno (Bologna, 1882)

Serpieri, A. & D. Silvagni, *Legge sull'amministrazione comunale e provinciale annotata* (Turin, 1884)

Serra, S., *Le amministrazioni straordinarie dei comuni ed i poteri dei rr. commissarî* (Catania, 1906)

Severino, S., *Del regio commissario straordinario* (Siracuse, 1894)

Shaw, A., *Municipal Government in Continental Europe* (London, 1895)

Sormani Moretti, L., *La provincia di Venezia. Monografia statistica-economica-amministrativa* (Venice, 1880-81)

Id., *La provincia di Verona: monografia statistica-economica-amministrativa* (Verona, 1898)

Spaventa, S., *La politica della Destra*, edited by B. Croce (Bari, 1910)

Sterio, M., *Dello scioglimento dei consigli comunali e della amministrazione dei regi commissari* (Messina, 1904)

Tegas, L., *Interesse generale e interessi locali. Studi* (Brescia, 1871)

Testera, C., *Elettorato amministrativo e liste ed elezioni comunali e provinciali* (Turin, 1894)

Id., *Amministrazione patrimoniale e contabilità dei comuni, delle provincie e delle istituzioni di beneficenza...* (Turin, 1897)

Tocqueville, A. de, 'La centralisation administrative et le système représentatif' (1844), in: Id., *Oeuvres complètes*, III, *Ecrits et discours politiques*, vol. 2 (Paris, 1985), 129-132

Id., 'Rapport fait à l'Académie des Sciences Morales et Politiques (1846) sur le livre de M. Macarel, intitulé: *Cours de droit administratif*', in: Id., *Oeuvres complètes*, XVI, *Mélanges* (Paris, 1989), 185-198

Tommasini, F., 'Osservazioni sull'istituto dello scioglimento dei consigli comunali e provinciali', *Archivio di diritto pubblico*, 5 (1895), 241-320

Torelli, L., *Le condizioni della provincia e della città di Venezia nel 1867. Relazione alla deputazione provinciale* (Venice, 1867)

Id., *L'istmo di Suez e l'Italia* (Milan, 1867)

Id., *Descrizione di Porto Said del canale marittimo e di Suez* (Venice, 1869)

Id., *Statistica della provincia di Venezia* (Venice, 1870)

Id., *Dieci paralleli fra il progresso dei lavori della Galleria del Cenisio e quelli del Canal di Suez a partire dal 31 maggio 1867 al 15 novembre 1869* (Venice, 1870-71)

All'illustrissimo Tribunale Civile di Bologna. Dei diritti del comune di Medicina sul patrimonio medicinese. Esposizione di fatto e di ragione pel comune nella causa contro la partecipanza (Bologna, 1872)

Tuccio, F.P., *Guida per l'elettore amministrativo* (Palermo, 1889)

Turiello, P., *Governo e governati in Italia* (Bologna, 1882)

Vivien, A.F.A., *Etudes administratives*, reprint of the 3rd edition, 2 vols (Paris, 1974)

SECONDARY WORKS

Aimo, P., 'Stato e autonomie locali: il ruolo dei prefetti in età liberale', *Passato e Presente* (1987), n. 14-15, 211-224

Alaimo, A., *L'organizzazione della città. Amministrazione e politica urbana a Bologna dopo l'unità (1859-1889)* (Bologna, 1990)

Aliberti, G., 'Prefetti e società locale nel periodo unitario, in: Id., *Potere e società locale nel Mezzogiorno dell'800* (Rome, 1987), 147-183

Allegretti, U., *Profilo di storia costituzionale italiana. Individualismo e assolutismo nello stato liberale* (Bologna, 1989)

L'amministrazione nella storia moderna, 2 vols (Archivio ISAP, n.s. 3, Milan, 1985)

Anderson, E.N. & P.R. Anderson, *Political Institutions and Social Change in Continental Europe in the Nineteenth Century* (Berkeley and Los Angeles, 1967)

Antonielli, L., *I prefetti dell'Italia napoleonica* (Bologna, 1983)

Aquarone, A., *Alla ricerca dell'Italia liberale* (Naples, 1972)

Gli archivi dei regi commissari nelle province del Veneto e di Mantova 1866, 2 vols (Rome, 1968)

Ballini, P.L., *Le elezioni nella storia d'Italia dall'Unità al fascismo. Profilo storico-statistico* (Bologna, 1988)

Bartoli, D., *L'Italia burocratica* (Milan, 1965)

Bellettini, A., *La popolazione del dipartimento del Reno* (Bologna, 1965)

Beneduce, P., '"Punto di vista amministrativo" e Stato di diritto: aspetti del germanesimo dei giuristi italiani alla fine dell'Ottocento', *Annali dell'Istituto storico italo-germanico in Trento*, 10 (1984), 119-194

Berengo, M., *L'agricoltura veneta dalla caduta della Repubblica all'Unità* (Milan, 1963)

Bergeron, L., *France under Napoleon*, translated by R.R. Palmer (Princeton, 1981)

Borzomati, P., *La Calabria dal 1882 al 1892 nei rapporti dei prefetti* (Reggio Calabria, 1974)

Id., 'Utilità e limiti delle relazioni dei prefetti', in: *Economia e società nella storia dell'Italia contemporanea. Fonti e metodi di ricerca*, edited by A. Lazzarini (Rome, 1983), 109-117

Bourguet, M.-N., *Déchiffrer la France. La statistique départementale à l'époque napoléonienne* (Paris, 1988)

Breuilly, J., 'State-Building, Modernization and Liberalism from the Late Eighteenth Century to Unification; German Peculiarities', *European History Quarterly* 22 (1992), 257-284

Broers, M., 'Italy and the Modern State: the Experience of Napoleonic Rule', in: *The French Revolution and the Creation of Modern Political Culture*, vol. 3, *The Transformation of Political Culture 1789-1848*, edited by F. Furet & M. Ozouf (Oxford, 1989), 489-503

Bologna, edited by R. Zangheri (Bari, 1986)

Broglie, G. de, *Guizot* (Paris, 1990)

Caldora, U., *Calabria napoleonica (1806-1815)* (Naples, 1960)

Caracciolo, A., *Il parlamento nella formazione del Regno d'Italia* (Milan, 1960)

Id., *Stato e società civile. Problemi dell'unificazione italiana*, 2nd ed. (Turin, 1977)

Cardoza, A.L., *Agrarian Elites and Italian Fascism. The Province of Bologna, 1901-1926* (Princeton, 1982)

Carocci, G., *Agostino Depretis e la politica interna italiana dal 1876 al 1887* (Turin, 1956)

Cassese, S., *Questione amministrativa e questione meridionale. Dimensioni e reclutamento della burocrazia dall'unità ad oggi* (Milan, 1977)

Id., 'Il prefetto nella storia amministrativa', *RTDP*, 33 (1983), 1449-1457

Id., 'Centro e periferia in Italia. I grandi tornanti della loro storia', *RTDP*, 36 (1986), 594-612

Id., *Le basi del diritto amministrativo* (Turin, 1989)

Id., & G. Melis,'Lo sviluppo dell'amministrazione italiana', *RTDP* 40 (1990), 333-357

Casula, P., *I prefetti nell'ordinamento italiano. Aspetti storici e tipologici* (Milan, 1972)

'Cento anni di amministrazione italiana', fasc. speciale di *Amministrazione civile*, 5 (1961), n. 47-51

Cingari, G., *Storia della Calabria dall'unità ad oggi* (Bari, 1982)

Id., *Reggio Calabria* (Bari, 1988)

Davis, J.A., *Conflict and Control. Law and Order in Nineteenth-century Italy* (London, 1988)

De Giorgio, D., 'La provincia di Reggio dopo la liberazione del 1860. La missione Cornero', *Historica*, 11 (1958), 163-169

De Rosa, G., 'La società civile veneta dal 1866 all'avvento della Sinistra', in: Id., *Giuseppe Sacchetti e la pietà veneta* (Rome, 1968), 173-232

Fehrenbach, E., 'Verfassungs- und sozialpolitische Reformen und Reformprojekte in Deutschland unter dem Einfluß des napoleonischen Frankreich', in H. Berding & H.-P. Ullmann, *Deutschland zwischen Revolution und Restauration* (Düsseldorf, 1981), 65-90

Finer, H., *The Theory and Practice of Modern Government*, 4th ed. (London, 1965)

Fioravanti, M., 'Costituzione, amministrazione e trasformazioni dello Stato', in: *Stato e cultura giuridica in Italia dall'Unità alla Repubblica*, edited by A. Schiavone (Bari, 1990), 3-87

Fischer, W., 'Staat und Gesellschaft Badens in Vormärz', in: W. Conze (ed.), *Staat und Gesellschaft im deutschen Vormärz 1815-1848*, 2nd ed. (Stuttgart, 1970), 143-171

'Formation und Transformation des Verwaltungswissens in Frankreich und Deutschland (18./19. Jh.)', *Jahrbuch für Europäische Verwaltungsgeschichte*, 1 (1989)

La formazione della diplomazia italiana (1861-1915). Indagine statistica (Rome, 1986)

Franzina, E., *Venezia* (Bari, 1986)

Fried, R.C., *The Italian Prefects. A Study in Administrative Politics* (New Haven, 1963)

Gall, L., *Der Liberalismus als regierende Partei. Das Großherzogtum Baden zwischen Restauration und Reichsgründung* (Wiesbaden, 1968)

Gambi, L., *Calabria* (Turin, 1978)

Id., 'Le "statistiche" di un prefetto del Regno', *Quaderni Storici* 15 (1980), 823-866

George, J., *Histoire des maires, 1789-1939* (Paris, 1989)

Gherardi, R., *Le autonomie locali nel liberismo italiano* (Milan, 1984)

Ghisalberti, C., *Contributi alla storia delle amministrazioni preunitarie* (Milan, 1963)

Id., 'Accentramento e decentramento nell'esperienza italiana', in *Regionalismo e centralizzazione nella storia di Italia e Stati Uniti*, edited by L. De Rosa & E. Di Nolfo (Florence, 1986), 221-249

Giannini, M.S., 'Profili storici della scienza del diritto amministrativo' (1940), now in: *Quaderni Fiorentini per la storia del pensiero giuridico*, 2 (1973), 179-274

Id., 'I comuni', in: *Atti del congresso celebrativo del centenario delle leggi amministrative di unificazione. L'ordinamento comunale e provinciale*, vol. 1, *I comuni*, edited by M.S. Giannini (Vicenza, 1967), 9-47

I giuristi e la crisi dello Stato liberale in Italia fra Otto- e Novecento, edited by A. Mazzacane (Naples, 1986)

Guidi, G., 'Parlamento ed elezioni. Le dinamiche elettorali nel giudizio dei deputati italiani 1870-1882', *Ricerche di Storia Politica*, 4 (1989), 23-75

Guizot, François et la culture politique de son temps, Colloque de la Fondation Guizot-Val Richter, edited by M. Valensise (Paris, 1991)

Gustapane, E., 'I prefetti dell'Unificazione amministrativa nelle biografie di Francesco Crispi', *RTDP*, 34 (1984), 1034-1101

Id., 'L'introduzione nell'ordinamento amministrativo italiano del principio del merito per l'accesso agli impieghi pubblici: il caso del Ministero dell'interno', *RTDP* 37 (1987), 449-466

Hobsbawm, E.J., *Nations and Nationalism since 1780. Programme, Myth, Reality* (Cambridge, 1990)

Istituzioni e borghesie locali nell'Italia liberale, edited by M. Bigaran (Milan, 1986)

Izzo, L., 'Agricoltura e classi rurali in Calabria dall'Unità al Fascismo', *Cahiers Internationaux d'Histoire Economique et Sociale*, 3 (1974).

Jensen, R.B., *Liberty and Order: the Theory and Practice of Italian Public Security, 1848 to the Turn of 1890* (Ann Arbor, Michigan University Microfilm International, 1987)

Knemeyer, F.-L., 'Polizei', *Economy and Society*, 9 (1980), 172-196 (English translation of the entry 'Polizei' in the *Geschichtliche Grundbegriffe. Historisches Lexikon zur politisch-sozialen Sprache in Deutschland*, IV, Stuttgart, 1978, 875-897)

Koselleck, R., *Preußen zwischen Reform und Revolution. Allgemeines Landrecht, Verwaltung und soziale Beweging von 1791 bis 1848* (Stuttgart, 1967, 3rd ed. 1981)

Id., 'Begriffsgeschichte und Sozialgeschichte', in: *Historische Semantik und Begriffsgeschichte*, edited by R. Koselleck (Stuttgart, 1979), 19-36

Kurer, O., 'John Stuart Mill on Government Intervention', *History of Political Thought*, 10 (1989), 457-480

Lee, L.E., *The Politics of Harmony. Civil Service, Liberalism, and Social Reform in Baden, 1800-1850* (Newark, 1980)

MacDonagh, O., 'The Nineteenth-Century Revolution in Government: a Reappraisal', *The Historical Journal*, 1 (1958), 52-67

MacLeod, R., 'Introduction', in: *Government and Expertise. Specialists, Administrators and Professionals, 1860-1919*, edited by R. MacLeod (Cambridge, 1988), 1-24

Marcato, U., *Storia di Chioggia. I fatti e i monumenti più caratteristici. Le prospettive di sviluppo* (Chioggia, 1976)

Marongiu, G., *Alle radici dell'ordinamento tributario italiano* (Padua, 1988)

Martone, L., *Potere e amministrazione prima e dopo l'Unità* (Naples, 1989)

Mascambruno, M.C., *Il prefetto*, I, *Dalle origini all'avvento delle regioni* (Milan, 1988)

Mastropaolo, A., 'Sviluppo politico e parlamento nell'Italia liberale. Un'analisi a partire dai meccanismi della rappresentanza', *Passato e Presente* (1986), n. 12, 29-91

Melis, G., 'La burocrazia e le riviste: per una storia della cultura dell'amministrazione', *Quaderni Fiorentini per la Storia del Pensiero Giuridico Moderno*, 16 (1987), 47-104

Id., 'La partecipazione dell'alta burocrazia italiana al Senato nell'epoca liberale', *Trimestre*, 21 (1988), n. 1-4, 211-236

Id., *Due modelli di amministrazione tra liberalismo e fascismo. Burocrazie tradizionali e nuovi apparati* (Rome, 1988)

Miglio, G., 'Le contraddizioni dello stato unitario', in: *Istituzioni e società nella storia d'Italia. Dagli stati preunitari d'antico regime all'unificazione*, edited by N. Raponi (Bologna, 1981), 555-569

Missori, M., *Governi, alte cariche dello stato e prefetti del Regno d'Italia*, 3rd edition (Rome, 1990)

Monti, A., *Il conte Luigi Torelli* (Milan, 1931)

Mozzarelli, C. & S. Nespor, *Giuristi e scienze sociali nell'Italia liberale* (Venice, 1981)

Nolte, P., *Staatsbildung als Gesellschaftsreform. Politische Reformen in Preußen und den süddeutschen Staaten 1800-1820* (Frankfurt/New York, 1990)

All'origine della 'forma partito' contemporanea. Emilia Romagna 1876-1892: un caso di studio, edited by P. Pombeni (Bologna, 1984), 181-208

Pacifici, V.G., *Angelo Annaratone (1844-1922). La condizione dei prefetti nell'Italia liberale* (Rome, 1990)

Pavone, C., *Amministrazione centrale e amministrazione periferica da Rattazzi a Ricasoli (1859-1866)* (Milan, 1964)

Pedone, A., 'Il bilancio dello Stato', in: *Lo sviluppo economico in Italia. Storia dell'economia italiana negli ultimi cento anni*, edited by G. Fuà, 2nd ed., 3 vols (Milan, 1974-75), II (1974), 203-240

Petracchi, A., *Le origini dell'ordinamento comunale e provinciale italiano*, 3 vols (Venice, 1962)

Polsi, A., 'Le amministrazioni locali post-unitarie fra accentramento e autonomia: il caso del comune di Pisa (1860-1885)', *Società e Storia* (1983), n. 22, 829-867

Pombeni, P., *Introduzione alla storia dei partiti politici* (Bologna, 1985)

Porro, A., *Il prefetto e l'amministrazione periferica in Italia. Dall'intendente subalpino al prefetto italiano (1842-1871)* (Milan, 1972)

Id., 'I problemi dell'amministrazione pubblica in un discorso di Giuseppe Saredo (riflessioni e proposte per una ricerca di storia quantitativa)', *RTDP*, 25 (1975), 872-898

Pototschnig, U., *L'unificazione amministrativa delle province venete* (Vicenza, 1967)

Ragionieri, E., *Politica e amministrazione nella storia dell'Italia unita*, 2nd ed. (Rome, 1979)

Randeraad, N., 'Gli alti funzionari del Ministero dell'Interno durante il periodo 1870-1899', *RTDP*, 39 (1989), 202-265

Id., 'L'amministrazione periferica nell'Italia liberale: una ricerca in corso', *RTDP*, 40 (1990), 1202-1221

Id., 'The State in the Provinces: the Prefecture as a Palace after Unification, in: *The Power of Imagery. Essays on Rome, Italy and Imagination*, edited by P. van Kessel (Rome, 1993), 98-108.

Rebuffa, G., *La formazione del diritto amministrativo in Italia. Profili di amministrativisti preorlandiani* (Bologna, 1981)

Id., 'I lessici e il tempo delle prolusioni di Vittorio Emanuele Orlando', *RTDP*, 39 (1989), 919-936

Richardson, N., *The French Prefectoral Corps 1814-1830* (Cambridge, 1966)

Le riforme crispine, 4 vols (ISAP Archivio, n.s. 6, Milan, 1990)

Romanelli, G., *Venezia Ottocento. L'architettura, l'urbanistica*, 2nd ed., (Venice, 1988)

Romanelli, R., *L'Italia liberale (1861-1900)* (Bologna, 1979)

Id., *Il comando impossibile. Stato e società nell'Italia liberale* (Bologna, 1988)

Id., 'Le regole del gioco. Note sull'impianto del sistema elettorale in Italia, *Quaderni Storici*, 23 (1988), 685-725

Id., *Sulle carte interminate. Un ceto di impiegati tra privato e pubblico: i segretari comunali in Italia, 1860-1915* (Bologna, 1989)

Rosanvallon, P., *Le moment Guizot* (Paris, 1985)

Id., 'Etat et société (du XIXe siècle à nos jours)', in: *L'Etat et les pouvoirs*, edited by J. Le Goff (Paris, 1989), 491-617

Rotelli, E., 'Gli ordinamenti locali preunitari', in: Id, *L'alternativa delle autonomie. Istituzioni locali e tendenze politiche dell'Italia moderna* (Milan, 1978), 96-117

Ruffilli, R., 'La questione del decentramento nell'Italia liberale', in: *L'organizzazione della politica. Cultura, istituzioni, partiti nell'Europa liberale*, edited by N. Matteucci & P. Pombeni (Bologna, 1988), 429-448.

Rugge, F., 'Alla periferia del Rechtsstaat. Autonomia e municipalizzazione nell'Italia di inizio secolo', *Quaderni Sardi di Storia* (1983-84), n. 4, 159-178

Sautel, G., *Histoire des institutions publiques depuis la Révolution française. Administration - justice - finances* (Paris, 1978)

Scaldaferri, R., 'L'organizzazione elettorale di Andrea Costa nel 2° collegio di Bologna nel 1882', *Rivista di Storia Contemporanea*, 12 (1983), 91-107

Scarpa, A.M., 'La situazione economica di Chioggia nel periodo 1859-1873', *Ateneo Veneto*, 7 (1969), 21-38

Scirocco, A., 'Tra stampa amministrativa e stampa di regime: il Giornale d'Intendenza nel Regno di Napoli dell'Ottocento', *Rassegna Storica del Risorgimento*, 76 (1989), 476-490

Siedentop, L., 'Two Liberal Traditions', in A. Ryan (ed.), *The Idea of Freedom. Essays in Honour of Isaiah Berlin* (Oxford, 1979), 153-174

Signorelli, A., 'Partecipazione politica, diritto al voto, affluenza alle urne: contribuenti ed elettori a Catania negli anni Settanta dell'800', *Quaderni Storici* 23 (1988), 873-902

Sofia, F., 'Alla ricerca di un'alternativa al partito: riflessioni su governo e amministrazione nell'Italia liberale', in: *Il partito politico nella Belle Epoque. Il dibattito sulla forma-partito in Italia tra '800 e '900*, edited by G. Quagliariello (Milan, 1990), 229-245

Spagnoletti, A., 'Centri e periferie nello Stato napoletano del primo Ottocento', in: *Il Mezzogiorno preunitario. Economia, società e istituzioni*, edited by A. Massafra (Bari, 1988), 379-391

Storia d'Italia Einaudi. Le regioni dall'Unità a oggi. La Calabria, edited by P. Bevilacqua & A. Placanica (Turin, 1985)

Taradel, A., 'Il modello cavouriano di amministrazione centrale', in: *L'educazione giuridica*, IV, *Il pubblico funzionario: modelli storici e comparativi*, tomo II, *L'età moderna* (Perugia, 1981), 363-437.

Venturi, G., *Episcopato, cattolici e comune a Bologna 1870-1904* (Imola, 1976)

Villani, P., 'Gruppi sociali e classe dirigente all'indomani dell'unità', in: *Storia d'Italia, Annali, I, Dal feudalesimo al capitalismo* (Turin, 1978), 881-978

Vogel, B., 'Beamtenliberalismus in der Napoleonischen Ära', in: D. Langewiesche (ed.), *Liberalismus im 19. Jahrhundert. Deutschland im europäischen Vergleich* (Göttingen, 1988), 45-63

Volpi, F., *Le finanze dei comuni e delle province del Regno d'Italia, 1860-1890* (Torino, 1962)

E. Weis, *Deutschland und Frankreich um 1800: Aufklärung, Revolution, Reform* (Munich, 1990).

Woolf, S.J., 'Towards the History of the Origins of Statistics: France 1789-1815', in: J.-C. Perrot & S.J. Woolf, *State and Statistics in France 1789-1815* (London, 1984), 81-194

Id., 'Les Bases sociales du Consolat. Un mémoire d'Adrien Duquesnoy', *Revue d'Histoire Moderne et Contemporaine*, 31 (1984), 597-618

Id., 'French Civilization and Ethnicity in the Napoleonic Empire', *Past and Present* (1989), n. 124, 96-120

Id., *Napoleon's Integration of Europe* (London, 1991)

Zani, M., 'Le circoscrizioni comunali in età napoleonica. Il riordino dei dipartimenti del Reno e del Panaro tra 1802 e 1814', *Storia Urbana* (1990), n. 51, 44-97

Zanni Rosiello, I., *L'unificazione politica e amministrativa nelle 'provincie dell'Emilia' (1859-60)* (Milan, 1965)

Zeldin, T., *France 1848-1915, I, Ambition, Love and Politics* (Oxford, 1973)

Appendix

The prefects of Venice, Bologna and Reggio Calabria (1861-1895)[1]

AMOUR, ALESSANDRO

Born in Settimo Torinese (Turin), 8 December 1830; died in Bologna, 17 December 1892 – married, four children – graduated in law from the University of Turin, 21 July 1853.
Entered public service as vice judge in 1854 in Turin. Attached to the police of Milan in 1859. Became senior prefectural official in 1876. Appointed prefect of Benevento in 1884. Subsequently prefect of Ferrara, Cuneo, Parma and **Bologna (16 June 1892 - 17 December 1892)**.

ARGENTI, EUGENIO

Born in Genoa, 21 December 1830; date of death unknown – married – graduated in law from the University of Genoa, 7 July 1853.
Entered public service in 1856 as volunteer with the intendance of Mondovì. Nominated prefect of Trapani in 1880. Subsequently prefect of Ascoli, Alessandria, Parma, Cuneo, **Bologna (1 February 1893 - 16 September 1894)**, Mantua and Novara. Retired in 1897.
Publications: *Teoria della misura e della proporzionalità delle grandezze proposta per uno delle scuole liceali* (Padua, 1871); *Lettera ... alla deputazione provinciale sul cimitero di San Martino, borgata di Rosignano. Con note* (Turin, 1885).

BALBONI, CARLO

Born in Ferrara, 2 June 1827; died in Ferrara, 21 November 1873 (his record of service could not be found).

---

1 Sources: Ministero dell'Interno, Matricole del personale; M. Missori, *Governo, alte cariche dello Stato e prefetti del Regno d'Italia*, 3rd edition (Rome, 1990). For some prefects additional information has been drawn from: E. Gustapane, 'I prefetti dell'unificazione amminstrativa nelle biografie dell'archivio di Francesco Crispi', *RTDP*, 34 (1984), 1034-1101; *Dizionario biografico degli Italiani, ad vocem*. The career descriptions have been reduced to a bare minimum; only the prefectural posts are listed in full. The list of publications is no doubt incomplete.

Provisionally in charge of the prefecture of **Bologna (20 March 1865 - 1 June 1865)** maintaining his rank as senior prefectural official (*consigliere delegato*).
Publications: *Un ricordo della memoria di Fil. Pasini ferrarese* (Ferrara, 1854); *Parole ... recitate il 14 luglio 1859 quando la pietà cittadina ai tre martiri ferraresi Malagutti, Parmeggiani, Succi una colonna ... nel luogo dell'atroce supplizio solennemente poneva* (Ferrara, 1859); *I martiri ferraresi immolati dall'Austria nel 1853*, n.d.

BARDESONO, CESARE conte di Rigras

Born in Turin, 27 June 1833; died in Rome, 4 January 1892 – married, five children – income from property 8,000 lire per annum – graduated in law from the University of Turin, July 1854.
Entered public service in 1855 as volunteer with the intendance of Casale. Belonged to the inner circle of Cavour and held high offices in the temporary regional governments during the Unification period of 1859-61. Appointed governor of Capitanata in 1861. Subsequently prefect of Pesaro, Salerno, **Reggio Calabria (1 June 1865 - 8 March 1868)**, Catania, **Bologna (8 October 1868 - 26 August 1873)**, Mantua, Udine, Milan, Florence and Palermo. Retired from active service in 1887. Nominated senator in 1876.

BASILE, ACHILLE

Born in S. Angelo di Brolo (Messina), 28 October 1832; died in Venice, 20 February 1893 – married twice – income from property 4,000 lire per annum – graduated in law from the University of Palermo, 27 December 1861 – practiced as lawyer and taught aestethics and philosophy.
Entered public service in 1861 as intendant of Nicosia. Appointed prefect of Agrigento in 1866. Subsequently prefect of Siracusa, Ravenna, Salerno, Massa e Carrara, Arezzo, **Reggio Calabria (5 March 1876 - 8 September 1876)**, Parma, Catania, Milan, Naples and **Venice (1 July 1892 - 20 February 1893)**. Nominated senator in 1890.
Publications: *Discorso letto dal prefetto della provincia A.B. il 6 settembre 1869 per l'apertura del consiglio provinciale di Girgenti* (Agrigento, 1869).

BIANCHI, BERNARDINO

Born in Valle Lomellina (Pavia), 15 August 1832; died in Bologna, 6 May 1892 – married, three children – graduated in law from the University of Pavia, 8 August 1855 – practiced as lawyer before entrance into office
Entered public service in 1859 as special commissioner of Garibaldi in Lombardy. Thereafter attached to the provincial administration in Lombardy. Was secretary to

the prime minister in 1863-64. Appointed prefect of Udine in 1876. Subsequently prefect of Grosseto, Lucca, Ferrara, Vicenza, Padua, Perugia and **Bologna (1 November 1891 - 6 May 1892)**.
Publications: *Memorie ed affetti: versi* (Milan, 1854); *Pompeo Litta: schizzo contemporaneo* (Milan, 1856); *L'isola benedetta: racconto indiano*, translation of W. Dixon Hepworth (Rome, 1876); *Discorso pronunciato alla solenne inaugurazione della Esposizione Provinciale artistica industriale nel giorno 8 settembre 1877* (Lucca, 1877); *Discorso pronunciato nell'occasione della distribuzione dei premi della Esposizione Provinciale artistica industriale il giorno 30 settembre 1877* (Lucca, 1877).

BOTTI, ULDERIGO

Born in Montelupo Fiorentino (Florence), 4 June 1822; died in Reggio Calabria, 25 June 1906 – unmarried – graduated in law from the University of Pisa.
Entered public service in 1845 as apprentice with the police of Florence. Transferred to the provincial administration in 1849. Provisionally in charge of the prefecture of **Reggio Calabria (1 October 1884 - 16 December 1884)**. Retired in 1887.
Publications: he was a major geologist, paleontologist and archeologist. For a list of his publications in these fields, see *Dizionario Biografico degli Italiani*, XIII, 450-52.

BRESCIA MORRA, barone FRANCESCO

Born in Avellino, 22 April 1832; died in Rome, 28 December 1910 – married.
Elected parliamentary deputy from 1870 to 1876. Entered public service in 1876 as prefect of Chieti. Subsequently, though several times temporarily relieved of his duties, prefect of Cagliari, Lecce, Pisa, Messina, **Venice (16 December 1887 - 16 July 1890)**, Catania and Parma.

CAPITELLI, conte GUGLIELMO

Born in Naples, 6 November 1840; died in Nervi (Genoa), 6 May 1907 – married twice, one child – graduated in law and humanities from the University of Naples in 1860 – mayor of Naples from 1868 to 1870.
Entered public service as prefect of **Bologna (6 November 1873 - 30 March 1876)** but resigned in consequence of the fall of the *Destra*. After trying in vain to be elected as paliamentary deputy, appointed prefect of Aquila in 1885. Subsequently, at short intervals, prefect of Messina, Florence, Genoa, Livorno, Catania, Lucca and again Messina. Retired in 1907.
Publications: *Prose* (Capolago, 1862); *Pochi versi* (Naples, 1863); *Parole dette al municipio di Firenze in onore di Carlo Poerio*, (n.p. 1867); *Della vita e degli studi di Domenico*

Capitelli, presidente del Parlamento napoletano nel 1848 (Naples, 1871); *Risposte alla relazione della Giunta Municipale di Napoli sulle passate amministrazioni* (Naples, 1871); *Pagine sparse* (Naples, 1877); *Studi biografici* (Naples, 1881); *Discorso detto il 12 marzo 1882 ad'un adunanza di elettori napoletani nel Circo Nazionale raccolto stenograficamente dal cav. Ruggiero* (Naples, 1882); *Memorie e lacrime: versi e prose*, 4th enlarged ed. (Lanciano, 1886); *Patria ed arte: conferenze e studi* (Lanciano, 1887); *Riposo ed obblio: versi*, 2nd revised ed. (Lanciano, 1891); *Cuore ed intelletto: versi e prose* (Lanciano, 1891); *Senza cuore: versi* (Messina, 1891); *Excelsior* (Lanciano, 1891);*Rime varie* (Lanciano, 1893); *Excelsior: prose* (Lanciano, 1893); *Rovito, Teodoro, Tempo perso: versi con lettera* (Naples, 1894); *Erato - humana: versi*, new ed. (Florence, 1899); *Un libro sul papa futuro: impressioni e ricordi* (Lucca, 1903); *Per Manina Capitelli: versi* (Messina, 1905); *Prose* (Florence, 1906).

CARACCIOLO DI SARNO, EMILIO

Born in Naples, 23 December 1835; died in Naples, 15 December 1914 – married, one child – income from property 3,000 lire per annum – graduated in law from the University of Naples, 1857.
Entered public service in 1858 in the intendance of Campobasso. Section head of the Ministry of the Interior in 1867. Returned to the provincial administration in 1870. Appointed prefect of Campobasso in 1880. Subsequently prefect of Avellino, Cremona, Bari, Catania, **Venice (16 March 1893 - 1 September 1898)**, Florence, again Bari, and Naples. Retired in 1907. Nominated senator in 1902.
Publications: *Sul riordinamento dell'amministrazione dello Stato* (Florence, 1868); *Note e riforme alla legge comunale e provinciale e riflessioni sul progetto di modificazioni presentato dal Ministro dell'Interno alla Camera dei Deputati nel dicembre 1876* (Padua, 1877); *Relazione al Consiglio Provinciale nella sessione settembre 1881* (Campobasso, 1881); *L'ospedale dei bambini Umberto I in Venezia* (Venice, 1911).

CAROSIO, GIOVANNI BATTISTA

Born in Rocca Grimalda (Alessandria), 5 June 1834; died in Turin, 13 April 1905 (his record of service could not be found).
Provisionally in charge of the prefecture of **Bologna (1 March 1887 - 16 May 1887)**.

CASSITO, RAFFAELE

Born in Lucera (Foggia), 14 September 1803; died in Naples, 4 December 1873 – married, three children – graduated in law – income from property 3,400 lire per annum – practiced as lawyer before entrance into office.

Entered public service in 1846 with the intendance of Foggia. Appointed governor of **Reggio Calabria (28 February 1861 - 1 April 1862)**. Subsequently prefect of Siracusa, Pesaro e Urbino, Grosseto, Massa e Carrara and Benevento. Retired in 1872. Nominated senator in that year without being able to participate in parliamentary sessions.

COLMAYER, VINCENZO

Born in Naples, 12 January 1843; died in Naples, 10 September 1908 – married, three children – income from property 3,050 lire per annum.
Entered public service in 1863 as officer with the *Procura* of Naples. Attached to the central police station of Naples in 1870. Transferred to the provincial administration in 1874. Provisionally in charge of the prefecture of **Venice between December 1881 and September 1882**. Appointed prefect of Belluno in 1884. Subsequently prefect of Lecce, Catanzaro, Catania, **Venice (10 September 1890 - 1 July 1892)**, Palermo, Bari, Livorno and Rome. Retired in 1908.

CORDERO DI MONTEZEMOLO, marchese MASSIMO

Born in Mondovì (Cuneo), 14 April 1807; died in Rome, 5 April 1879 – married, one child – graduated in law – landowner – income from property 10,000 lire per annum.
Entered public service in 1831 as volunteer in the office of the *procuratore generale* in Turin. *Luogotenente* in Sicily in 1860. Prefect of **Bologna (7 September 1862 - 20 March 1865)**. Subsequently, after an interval of two years prefect of Naples and Florence. Retired in 1876. Parliamentary deputy for Garessio in 1848-49. Nominated senator in 1850.

CORNERO, GIUSEPPE

Born in Alessandria, 24 April 1812; died in Rocca d'Arazzo (Asti), 15 December 1895 – married, three children – graduated in law.
Elected parliamentary deputy for Alessandria II and Mombercelli from 1848 to 1860. Appointed prefect of **Reggio Calabria (1 April 1862 - 30 August 1863)**. Subsequently prefect of Ravenna, **Bologna (1 June 1865 - 8 October 1868)**, Siena, Pisa, Livorno and Piacenza. Retired in 1889. Nominated senator in 1868.

DANIELE VASTA, GIOVANNI

Born in Catania, 25 December 1833; died in Turin, May 1909 – married twice, three children – studied law at the University of Catania.

Entered public service in 1860 as subprefect of Nicosia. Appointed prefect of Arezzo in 1877. Subsequently prefect of Belluno, Rovigo, Trapani, Vicenza, Siracusa, Siena, Lecce, **Reggio Calabria (1 September 1890 - 1 July 1891)**, and (after being relieved of his duties for three years) Padua. Retired in 1896.

DE FEO, FRANCESCO

Born in Mirabello Sannitico (Campobasso), 13 November 1828; died in Campobasso, 9 November 1879 (his record of service could not be found).
Appointed prefect of **Reggio Calabria (7 December 1873 - 5 March 1876)**. Subsequently prefect of Chieti, Porto Maurizio, Forlì. Retired in 1877.
Publications: *Discorso per l'apertura della sessione ordinaria 1874 del consiglio provinciale di Calabria Ulteriore Prima* (Reggio Calabria, 1874).

FARALDO, CARLO

Born in Mentone (Nice), 14 May 1818; died in Turin, 30 June 1897 – married – graduated in law from the University of Turin – income from property 6,000 lire per annum.
Entered public service in 1847 as substitute judge in Mentone. Secretary general of the Ministry of the Interior in Palermo in 1861-62. Appointed prefect of Ravenna in 1863. Temporarily relieved of his duties from 1863 to 1865. Subsequently prefect of Siracusa, Messina, Cuneo, Cremona, Verona, Foggia, **Reggio Calabria (28 September 1877 - 10 October 1877, without actually taking up his office there)**, Macerata, **Bologna (29 July 1878 - 5 December 1880)**. Retired in 1880.
Publications: *Discorso pronunciato all'apertura della sessione ordinaria del consiglio provinciale di Verona* (Verona, 1874).

FRUMENTO, FRANCESCO

Born in Savona, 16 August 1834; died in Savona, 19 February 1924 – married, four children – graduated in law – income from property 5,500 lire per annum.
Entered public service in 1861 as volunteer with the provincial administration of Savona. Appointed provisionally prefect of **Reggio Calabria (1 April 1895 - 16 April 1896)**. Subsequently prefect of Teramo, Porto Maurizio and Siena. Retired in 1901.
Publications: *Perchè siamo andati a Tripoli: conferenza letta per invito della sezione giovanile nazionalisti, il 7 dicembre 1911* (Savona, 1912).

GENTILI, ALFONSO

Born in Paola (Cosenza), 6 May 1829; died in Catanzaro, August 1906 – married, eight children – studied law – income from property 4,000 lire per annum.
Entered public service in 1860 as sub-governor of Paola. Appointed prefect of Agrigento in 1878. Subsequently prefect of Reggio Emilia, **Reggio Calabria (16 December 1884 - 1 August 1887)** and Catanzaro. Retired in 1890.
Publications: *Osservazioni sull'opuscolo saggio di provvedimenti finanziari del Deputato Minghetti e nuova proposta sull'Asse Ecclesiastico* (Ferrara, 1866); *Le imposte ed il circondario di Melfi, o semplificazione del sistema tributario e pareggio del bilancio dello stato* (Naples, 1868); *Brevi considerazioni sulle condizioni finanziarie del Regno d'Italia* (Livorno, 1871).

GIACOMELLI, nob. ANGELO

Born in Trivignano Udinese (Udine), 19 April 1816; died in Treviso, 16 September 1907 – married, one child – studied at the Polytechnic Institute of Vienna – descendant of impoverished nobility.
Elected parliamentary deputy for Treviso (1876-82). Appointed prefect of Cremona in 1882. Subsequently prefect of Siena, **Reggio Calabria (16 December 1888 - 1 September 1890)** and Piacenza. Retired in 1891.
Publications: *La coltivazione delle camelie* (Padua, 1847); C. Schneitler & J. Andrée, *Le più recenti ed utili macchine e strumenti rurali; loro teoria, costruzione, ecc.: manuale compilato da A.G.* (Venice, 1863); *Agli elettori del collegio di Treviso* (Treviso, 1880); *Reminiscenze della mia vita politica negli anni 1848-53* (Florence, 1893).

GILARDONI, ANTONIO

Born in Salerno, 22 June 1822; died in Lacco Ameno (Naples), 21 August 1891 – married, four children – studied literature and law
Entered public service in 1840 as apprentice with the prefecture of police in Naples. Pursued his career in the Ministry of the Interior in Naples. Transferred to Turin in 1862. Appointed prefect of Treviso in 1876. Subsequently prefect of Potenza, Cremona, **Reggio Calabria (3 April 1881 - 1 September 1882)** and Pesaro e Urbino. Retired in 1889
Publications: *Relazione sull'amministrazione della provincia di Treviso, letta dal prefetto in occasione dell'apertura della sessione ordinaria del consiglio provinciale, anno 1877* (Treviso, 1877); *Per l'inaugurazione della sessione ordinaria 1879 del consiglio provinciale di Cremona. Parole* (Cremona, 1879).

GIURA (DI), GIOVANNI

Born in Chiaromonte (Potenza), 16 April 1831; died in Chiaromonte, June 1908 – married, nine children – graduated in law – income from property 7,000 lire per annum – practiced as lawyer before entrance into office.
Entered public service in 1861 as intendant of the district of Avezzano. Appointed prefect of Ravenna in 1877. Subsequently prefect of Foggia, Salerno, Lucca, Caserta, Livorno, Lecce, **Bologna (16 September 1894 - 1 September 1897)**. Retired in 1897.

GRAVINA, marchese LUIGI

Born in Catania, 30 April 1830; died in Giarre (Catania), 19 October 1910 – married – lived in exile for some time after the Sicilian revolution of 1848 – was one of Garibaldi's *Mille di Marsala*.
Entered public service in 1860 in the provincial administration of Catania. Elected parliamentary deputy for Regalbuto and Giarre from 1861 to 1876. Appointed prefect of **Bologna (19 April 1876 - 30 October 1877)**. Subsequently prefect of Naples, Rome, Milan and again Rome. Nominated senator in 1876.
Publications: *Elogio funebre del sac. Rosario Di Blasi* (Piazza Armerina, 1884).

LAMPONI, marchese FILIPPO

Born in S. Vittoria in Matenamo (Ascoli Piceno), 4 June 1827; died in Reggio Calabria, 29 March 1881 – married, two children – graduated in law – practiced as lawyer in Aquila di Macerata before entrance into office.
Entered public service in 1860 in the provincial administration of Macerata. Appointed prefect of Potenza in 1876. Transferred to **Reggio Calabria (10 October 1877 - 29 March 1881)**, where he died.
Publications: Sallustio, *Sull'ordinamento della repubblica: ragionamenti dalla latina lingua nella volgare recati per F.L.* (Camerino, 1847).

LONGANA, ANTONIO

Born in Serravalle, now Vittorio Veneto (Treviso), 28 November 1831; died in Milan (?), 2 March 1883 – married – graduated in law from the University of Padua, 3 April 1852 – income from property 1,000 lire per annum – practiced briefly as lawyer before entrance into office.
Entered public service in 1852 as apprentice of the intendance of finance in Padua. Transferred to the provincial administration of Siena in 1862. Provisionally in charge of the prefecture of **Bologna (26 August 1873 - 6 November 1873)**.

MAGENTA, PIETRO

Born in Gambolò (Pavia), 5 January 1807; died in Andermatt (Switzerland), 18 July 1862 (his record of service could not be found)
Appointed prefect of **Bologna (17 November 1861 - 18 July 1862)**.
Publications: *Ricerche su le pie fondazioni e su l'ufficio loro a sollievo dei poveri con un'appendice sui pubblici stabilimenti di beneficenza della città di Pavia* (Pavia, 1838).

MANFRIN, conte PIETRO

Born in Castelo di Godego (Treviso), 18 November 1827; died in Castione (Treviso), 3 September 1909 – married, three children – graduated in law from the University of Pisa.
Entered public service in 1860 as apprentice with the Ministry of Education. Attached to the Ministry of the Interior in 1861. Resigned in 1866. Elected parliamentary deputy for Oderzo and Pieve di Cadore from 1865 to 1880. Appointed prefect of **Venice (5 November 1880 - 1 December 1881)**. Resigned in 1881. Nominated senator in 1879.
Publications: *Il sistema municipale inglese e la legge comunale italiana: studi comparati*, 2nd ed. (Padua, 1872); *Del neo-guelfismo in Italia* (Florence, 1873); *L'ordinamento delle società in Italia secondo il codice di commercio* (Padua, 1875); *L'avvenire di Venezia. Studio* (Treviso, 1877); *Il comune e l'individuo in Italia. Studio* (Rome, 1879); *Chi deve essere ministro per la Marineria: studio* (Rome, 1880); *I Veneti salvatori di Roma* (Rome, 1884); *Memoria diretta agli on.[i] deputati e senatori intorno al nuovo disegno di legge comunale e provinciale* (Padua, 1888); *Gli ebrei sotto la dominazione romana*, 4 vols (Rome, 1888-1897); 'Pelasgi e Veneti primi', *Miscellanea di storia veneta edita per cura della r. dep. veneta di storia patria* (Venice, 1891); *La cavalleria dei Parthi nelle guerre contro i Romani. Con annotazioni di un ex-ufficiale intorno la cavalleria italiana* (Rome, 1893); *Dell'arbitrio amministrativo in Italia: memoria* (Rome, 1894); *Risposta ai contradittori dell'opuscolo 'Dell'arbitrio amministrativo in Italia'* (Rome, 1894); *L'abolizione delle decime* (Padua, 1895); *Tirannia burocratica* (Rome, 1900); *Le origini di Venezia, per conoscere a chi appartenga la laguna veneta (da antiche cronache e manoscritti)* (Rome, 1901); *Un problema della vita italiana* (Castelfranco Veneto, 1904); *La dominazione romana nella Gran Bretagna*, vol. I, 2 tomi (Rome, 1904-1906); *A proposito della nuova legge per una tasse sugli automobili* (Rome, 1906).

MAYR, CARLO

Born in Ferrara, 3 October 1810; died in Ferrara, 24 July 1882 – married, four children – graduated in law and philosophy from the University of Ferrara, 3 October 1831 – income from property 12,000 lire per annum – practiced as lawyer before entrance into office.

Entered public service in 1849 as prefect of Ferrara and minister of the Interior of the revolutionary Roman Republic. Appointed intendant of Forlì in 1859. General intendant of **Bologna (until 16 July 1861)**. Prefect of Caserta, Alessandria, Genoa, **Venice (28 July 1872 - 19 April 1876)** and Naples. Attached to the Council of State in 1877 as section president. Elected parliamentary deputy for Ferrara I from 1861 to 1863. Nominated senator in 1868.

Publications: *Rapporto della commissione nominata dagli uffici per l'esame e le modificazioni alla proposta dell'8 settembre relativa al conferimento de' poteri governativi e per riferire in proposito* (Bologna, 1859).

MEZZOPRETI GOMEZ, EMIDIO

Born in Montepagano (Teramo), 14 October 1826; date of death unknown – married, one child – income from property 12,000 lire per annum – studied literature and law in Naples – apprentice with a lawyer's office in Teramo before entrance into office. Entered public service in 1860 with the provincial administration of Teramo. Provisionally in charge of the prefecture of **Reggio Calabria from 7 October 1871, later prefect until 13 October 1873**. Subsequently prefect of Grosseto. Retired in 1874.

Publications: *La donna avanti e dopo il cristianesimo* (Naples, 1859); *Discorso pronunciato all'apertura della sessione del 1864 del consiglio provinciale di Alessandria* (Alessandria, 1864); *Per la inaugurazione del comizio agrario circondariale di Urbino. Discorso* (Urbino, 1867); *Per l'apertura della sessione 1870 del consiglio provinciale di Sassari. Discorso* (Sassari, 1871); *Per l'inaugurazione della Società dei segretari e impiegati comunali della provincia di Sassari. Parole* (Sassari, 1871); *Parole per l'apertura della sessione 1872 del consiglio provinciale della Prima Calabria Ulteriore* (Reggio Calabria, 1872); *Elogio funebre di S.M. Vittorio Emanuele II re d'Italia* (Florence, 1878)

MUSSI, GIOVANNI

Born in Pontoglio (Brescia), 13 February 1835; died in Rovato (Brescia), 15 November 1887 – married – graduated in law.

Elected parliamentary deputy for Chiari in 1876-78. Appointed prefect of Udine in 1879. Subsequently prefect of **Bologna (5 December 1880 - 1 September 1882)** and **Venice (1 September 1882 - 15 November 1887)**.

OLDOFREDI TADINI, conte ERCOLE

Born in Brescia, 6 September 1810; died in Calcio (Bergamo), 24 September 1877 (his record of service could not be found).

Appointed prefect of **Bologna (16 July 1861 - 17 November 1861)**. Elected parliamentary deputy for Romano and Martinengo in 1860. Nominated senator in November 1861.

PASOLINI, conte GIUSEPPE

Born in Ravenna, 8 February 1815; died in Ravenna, 4 December 1876 (his record of service could not be found)
Appointed prefect of Milan in 1861. Subsequently prefect of Turin, with an interruption in 1862-63 during which he was minister of Foreign Affairs. Appointed royal commissioner of **Venice, 13 October 1866, subsequently prefect until 4 April 1867**. Nominated senator in 1860. Briefly president of the Senate in 1876.

PATERNOSTRO, FRANCESCO

Born in Corleone (Palermo), 18 March 1840; died in Rome, 5 December 1913 – married – graduated in law.
Elected parliamentary deputy for Corleone from 1870 to 1882. Nominated senator in 1882. Appointed prefect of Agrigento in 1886. Subsequently prefect of **Reggio Calabria (1 August 1887 - 16 December 1888)**, Lucca and Ferrara. Retired in 1890.
Publications: *Agli elettori del collegio di Corleone* (Rome, 1878).

PERRINO, FERDINANDO

Born in Naples, 27 August 1837; died in Naples, July 1902 – unmarried (his record of service could not be found).
Entered public service in 1860 as councillor with the provincial administration of Caserta. Appointed prefect of Ascoli Piceno in 1886. Subsequently prefect of Caltanissetta, Avellino, Arezzo, **Reggio Calabria (1 July 1892 - 16 March 1892)**, Salerno, Trapani and Sondrio. Retired in 1896.

PETRA, NICOLA, duca di Vastogirardi, marchese di Caccavone

Born in Naples, 28 March 1835; died in Naples, 29 August 1883 (his record of service could not be found).
Appointed prefect of Catanzaro in 1868. Subsequently prefect of Trapani, Lecce, **Bologna (30 October 1877 - 29 July 1878)**, Messina and Bari. Retired in 1881.

RAMBELLI, VIRGINIO

Born in Alfonsine (Ravenna), 1 December 1830; died in Potenza, 19 December 1900 – unmarried.
Entered public service in 1849 as clerk with the administration of justice in Faenza. Transferred to the provincial administration of Cesena in 1859. Provisionally in charge of the prefecture of **Reggio Calabria (16 March 1893), later prefect until 1 April 1895**, Grosseto and Potenza, where he died.
Publications: *Diario storico cesenate nel quale per ogni giorno dell'anno si racconta un fatto tolto dalle storie e cronache di Cesena, o si accennano le notizie biografiche di un uomo illustre Cesenate* (Cesena, 1867).

SALARIS, EFISIO

Born in Cagliari, 13 March 1826; died in Florence, 7 March 1888 – married, one child – graduated – income from property 5,000 lire per annum.
Entered public service in 1848 as volunteer with the intendance of Cagliari. Appointed prefect of Porto Maurizio in 1867. Subsequently prefect of Campobasso, Arezzo, Massa e Carrara, Brescia, Bari, Novara, Parma, **Bologna (1 September 1882 - 1 March 1887)**. Retired in 1887.

SALVONI, conte VINCENZO

Born in Jesi (Ancona), 3 August 1821; died in Rimini (Forlì), 3 September 1896 – married, three children – income from property 15,000 lire per annum.
Entered public service in 1860 as provincial commissioner of Fermo. Elected parliamentary deputy for Rimini and Jesi from 1860 to 1863, and from 1867 to 1873. Appointed prefect of Bari in 1874. Subsequently prefect of Trapani, **Reggio Calabria (8 September 1876 - 28 September 1877)**, Foggia, Macerata, Campobasso and Lucca. Retired in 1887.

SCELSI, GIACINTO

Born in Collesano (Palermo), 31 July 1825; died in Rome, 6 May 1902 – married twice, five children – income from property 8,000 lire per annum – graduated in law – practiced as lawyer before entrance into office.
Entered public service in 1848 with the provincial administration of Cefalù. Lived in exile until the liberation of Sicily. Appointed governor of Cefalù in 1860. Appointed prefect of Agrigento in 1861. Subsequently prefect of Ascoli Piceno, Sondrio, Foggia, Como, Reggio Emilia, Messina, Ferrara, Mantua, Brescia, Pesaro e Urbino, Livorno,

Modena, **Bologna (16 May 1887 - 16 September 1891)** and Florence. Retired in 1896. Publications: *Condizioni economiche, morali e politiche della provincia di Ascoli Piceno* (Ascoli Piceno, 1864); *Statistica generale della provincia di Sondrio* (Milan, 1864); *Statistica generale della provincia di Capitanata* (Milan, 1868); *Condizioni economiche e morali della provincia di Como* (Como, 1869); *Statistica generale della provincia di Reggio nell'Emilia* (Milan, 1870); *Statistica della provincia di Ferrara* (Ferrara, 1875); *Statistica della provincia di Pesaro e Urbino* (Pesaro, 1883).

SERPIERI, ACHILLE

Born in Rimini (Forlì), 8 September 1828; died in Messina, 19 September 1887 – married, two children – income from property 3,000 lire per annum – graduated in law from the University of Bologna, 18 July 1851 – practiced as lawyer before entrance into office.
Deputy of the Assembly of the Romagne in 1859. Entered public service in 1859 in the provincial administration of Cesena. Appointed prefect of Caltanissetta in 1876. Subsequently prefect of **Reggio Calabria (12 March 1868 - 7 October 1871)**, Sassari, Foggia, Massa e Carrara, Cremona and Caltanissetta. Retired in 1878. Re-appointed prefect of Messina in 1887, where he died in the cholera epidemic of that year.
Publications: *Provincia di Reggio di Calabria. Relazione sulle condizioni e bisogni della viabilità* (Reggio Calabria, 1869); *Primi saggi statistici sulle condizioni amministrative economiche e morali della provincia di Reggio Calabria* (Reggio Calabria, 1870); *Discorso inaugurale ... al consiglio provinciale di Sassari per la sessione ordinaria dopo le rielezioni del 20 ottobre 1872* (Sassari, 1872); *Discorsi pronunziati in occasione dell'apertura della 2ª Esposizione sarda in Sassari 17 agosto 1873* (Sassari, 1873); *Della necessità e dei modi di migliorare i bilanci comunali. Discorso letto al consiglio provinciale di Massa e Carrara inaugurando la sua sessione ordinaria il 14 agosto 1876* (Massa, 1876); *Discorso per l'inaugurazione della sessione ordinaria 1877 del consiglio provinciale di Cremona* (Cremona, 1877); *La giurisprudenza della Corte dei Conti del Regno d'Italia... Raccolta di decisioni con annotazioni e massimario a cura dell'avv. A.S.*, 2 vols (Rome, 1880-83); (with D. Silvagni) *Legge sull'amministrazione comunale e provinciale annotata* (Turin, 1884).

SIGISMONDI, DECOROSO

Born in Bomba (Chieti), 15 April 1817; died 18 October 1870 (his record of service could not be found).
Governor of Teramo. Subsequently prefect of Catanzaro, Benevento, **Reggio Calabria (20 September 1863 - 1 June 1865)**, Salerno, Sondrio, Lucca. Retired in 1868.

SORAGNI, AGOSTINO

Born in Modena, 26 November 1829; died in Milan, 29 January 1898 – married – graduated in law from the University of Modena, 24 July 1852 – practiced as lawyer before entrance into office.
Entered public service in 1859 as secretary with the provisional government of Modena. Appointed prefect of Grosseto. Subsequently prefect of Caserta, Brescia, **Reggio Calabria (16 August 1891 - 1 July 1892)**, Novara, Alessandria. Retired in 1895.

SORMANI MORETTI, conte LUIGI

Born in Reggio Emilia, 3 December 1834; died in Correggio (Reggio Emilia), 9 January 1908 – married, two children – graduated in law from the University of Pavia, 16 February 1858.
Entered public service in 1859 as secretary at the Minstry of War. Attached to the Foreign Office in 1860. Elected parliamentary deputy for Correggio from 1865 to 1876. Provincial councillor of Reggio Emilia from 1868 to 1876. Appointed prefect of **Venice (30 April 1876 - 5 November 1880)**. Again elected deputy for Correggio from 1882 to 1886. Subsequently, appointed prefect of Verona, Perugia and Treviso. Retired in 1906. Nominated senator in 1886.
Publications: *Pensieri sulla educazione* (Verona, 1855); *Della industria agricola manifattu-riera e commerciale nel Ducato di Modena in ordine ad un istituto di credito. Studi e proposte* (Milan, 1858; republished Bologna, 1985); *Convenzioni colle società ferroviarie. Discorso pronunziato alla Camera* (Florence, 1870); *Le condizioni economiche ed amministra-tive della provincia di Venezia, esposte al consiglio provinciale nella prima seduta della sua sessione ordinaria del 1877* (Venice, 1877); *Le condizioni economiche ed amministrative della provincia di Venezia, esposte il 12 agosto 1878 al consiglio provinciale nella prima seduta della sua sessione ordinaria del 1878* (Venice, 1878); *Agli enti morali interessati e contri-buenti all'esecuzione dei lavori di risanamento della zona del litorale di Malamocco che dal forte di S. Nicolò di Lido s'estende al forte di Quattro Fontane. Relazione* (Venice, 1879); *Sulle condizioni agrarie della provincia di Venezia: considerazioni esposte ... nella riunione tenuta il 24 agosto 1879 all'Ateneo per promuovere il riordinamento dei vari Comizi Agrari della provincia e la loro associazione in consorzio* (Venice, 1879); *Le condizioni economiche ed amministrative della provincia di Venezia esposte l'11 agosto 1879 al consiglio provinciale nella prima seduta della sua sessione ordinaria 1879* (Venice, 1879); *Nell'inaugurazione del monumento a Tiziano Vecellio in Pietro di Cadore il giorno 5 settembre 1880* (Venice, 1880); *La provincia di Venezia. Monografia statistica - economica - amministrativa* (Venice, 1880-81); *Relazione sui lavori e sugli studi del consorzio agrario provinciale e del consorzio agrario e di pescicoltura di Venezia per gli anni 1881-81, letta ... il 26 marzo 1883* (Venice, 1883); *L'orto sperimentale istituito nel marzo 1885. Discorso inaugurale del presidente ... e notizie* (Venice, 1885); *La pesca, la pescicoltura e la caccia nella provincia di Venezia: memoria* (Venice, 1887); *L'esposizione coloniale e indiana: lettere da Londra al giornale*

milanese Il Caffè, gazzetta nazionale, nel settembre 1886 (Rome, 1887); *La provincia di Verona: monografia statistica - economica - amministrativa* (Verona, 1898); *Discorso inaugurale tenuto il 3 settembre 1899 nella sede del congresso interregionale per la pesca ai Giardini in Venezia* (Venice, 1899); *Per la navigazione interna specialmente nella valle del Po: memoria, appunti, documenti a completamento d'anteriori pubblicazioni* (Treviso, 1905); *Per l'inaugurazione della nuova sede sulla nave Scilla della scuola veneta di pesca in Venezia, coll'annesso asilo pei figli derelitti dei marinai-pescatori dell'Adriatico* (Vicenza, 1906).

TAMAJO, GIORGIO

Born in Naples, 17 January 1817; died in Siracusa, 15 October 1897 – married, four children.
Entered public service in 1860 as secretary of state for public security in Sicily. Elected parliamentary deputy for Messina from 1861 to 1880. Nominated senator in 1879. Appointed prefect of Agrigento in 1880. Subsequently prefect of Arezzo, **Reggio Calabria (16 September 1882 - 1 October 1884)**, Siracusa and Siena. Retired in 1890.

TORELLI, LUIGI

Born in Villa di Tiramo (Sondrio), 10 February 1810; died in Villa di Tiramo, 14 November 1887 – married, three children – studied law at the Academy *detta de' Cavalieri Teresiani* in Vienna – income from property at least 15,000 lire per annum. Entered public service in 1833 with the Austrian administration (until 1836). Elected parliamentary deputy for Arona and Intra (1849-1858). Nominated senator in 1860. Appointed governor of Sondrio in 1859. Subsequently prefect of Bergamo, Palermo and Pisa. Minister of Agriculture, Industry and Commerce (1864-65). Again prefect of Palermo. Appointed **prefect of Venice (5 May 1867 - 28 July 1872)**. Retired in 1872. Publications: an exhaustive bibliography can be found in A. Monti, *Il conte Luigi Torelli* (Milan, 1931), 491-503 (who copied the impressive list from F. Lampertico). A selection of Torelli's publications relevant to his work as prefect has been included here: *Pensieri sull'Italia di un anonimo lombardo* (Parigi, 1846); *Pensieri sull'Italia scritti nel 1845 e commentati dall'autore nel 1853* (Turin, 1853); *Dell'avvenire del commercio europeo ed in modo speciale quello degli stati italiani. Ricerche*, 3 vols (Florence, 1858); *Statistica della provincia di Sondrio* (Turin, 1860) *Lettere intorno al riordinamento dei debiti dei comuni ...al barone Bettino Ricasoli ...* (Pisa, 1862); *Statistica della provincia di Pisa* (Pisa, 1863); *Della necessità di congiungere la rete delle strade ferrate italiane colla rete Elvetico-Germanica. Lettere* (Milan, 1863); *Relazione intorno alle condizioni della provincia di Palermo e proposte fatte al consiglio provinciale* (Palermo, 1866); *Rapporto al ministero dell'interno relativo agli avvenimenti di Palermo (16-22 settembre 1866) dell'ex-prefetto della provincia, seguito dalla esposizione del medesimo fatta al consiglio provinciale di quella provincia il 3 settembre 1866 intorno alla pubblica sicurezza* (Florence, 1866); *Le condizioni* *della provincia e della città di Venezia nel 1867. Relazione alla deputazione provinciale* (Venice, 1867); *Relazione presentata dal prefetto di Venezia il 7 settembre 1868 al consiglio provinciale intorno all'esecuzione data ai provvedimenti presi dal consiglio stesso nelle tornate del 1867* (Venice, 1868); *La questione del potere temporale del Papa considerata nel 1845, nel 1853 e nel 1870* (Venice, 1870); *Statistica della provincia di Venezia* (Venice, 1870); *Manuale topografico archeologico dell'Italia compilato a cura di diversi corpi scientifici e preceduto da un discorso intorno allo scopo del medesimo per opera di L.T.* (Venice, 1872); *Degli scavi da fare in Italia. Dissertazione e proposte* (Venice, 1872); *Ricordi intorno alle Cinque Giornate di Milano (18-22 marzo 1848)*, 2nd ed. (Milan, 1883).

Index